DARI
Dari–English
English–Dari
Dictionary
&
Phrasebook

Nicholas Awde
with
Asmatullah Sarwan
and
Saeid Davatolhagh & Sami Aziz

D0111811

HIPPOCRENE BOOKS INC
New York

**Historical and cultural background by Fred J. Hill.
Additional thanks to Ian Carnochan, Thea
Khitarishvili, Nicholas Williams, and Caroline Gates
for their help in compiling this volume.**

Typeset and designed by Desert Hearts.

For information, address:
HIPPOCRENE BOOKS, INC.
171 Madison Avenue
New York, NY 10016
www.hippocrenebooks.com

Library of Congress Cataloging-in-Publication Data

Awde, Nicholas.
  Dari : Dari-English, English Dari dictionary &
phrasebook / Nicholas Awde ; with Asmatullah
Sarwan and Saeid Davatolhagh & Sami Aziz.
    p. cm.
  English and Dari (Dari in roman).
  ISBN-10: 0-7818-0971-1
  ISBN-13: 978-0-7818-0971-9
    1. Dari language--Dictionaries--English. 2. English
language--Dictionaries--Dari. 3. Dari language--
Conversation and phrase books--English. I. Title.

PK6876.A95 2003
49'.56321--dc21

                                        2003040644

Printed in the United States of America.

CONTENTS

- An Afghan person is an **Afghân**.
- The adjective for Afghan is **Afghâni**.
- Afghans call themselves **Afghânyân**.
- Afghanistan is **Afghânestân**.
- The Dari language is **Dari**.

INTRODUCTION

Afghanistan first entered recorded history when the region was incorporated into the great Persian Achaemenid Empire, founded by Cyrus the Great in the middle of the 6th century BC. The dynasty was toppled by the great push eastwards of Alexander the Great. En route to India, the young Greek commander marched his army into the Achaemenid province of Bactria, an extensive region which covered parts of modern-day Afghanistan, Uzbekistan, and Tajikistan, where he met with fierce resistance. It was in Bactria that he married Princess Roxana, the daughter of the local ruler.

After Alexander's death, his empire was divided amongst his generals, and Bactria was incorporated into the kingdom of Seleucus I Nicator. Under the Seleucid dynasty he founded, Greek influences gradually began to filter into the region of Afghanistan. Meanwhile, the lands to the south of the great Hindu Kush mountain range came under the influence of the northern Indian Maurya dynasty.

In the middle of the 3rd century BC, under the rule of the Seleucid governor Diodotus, Bactria broke loose and became an independent kingdom. Its Indo-Greek rulers soon transformed into a major regional power, extending their power over the rest of Afghanistan and neighboring regions that lie in present-day Pakistan and ex-Soviet Central Asia.

In the latter part of the 2nd century AD, the Yüechi, a group of Central Asian tribes, conquered Bactria, establishing their own ruling dynasty, the Kushans. They proved to be extremely able empire builders, pushing the limits of their realm into north-west India, and ranked as one of the great powers of the time. The Kushans played an important part in introducing Buddhism into Central Asia and China and the religion greatly influenced their own art.

Nevertheless, they had a reputation for tolerance, allowing Afghanistan to become a veritable melting pot of thriving and productive cultures, amongst them Roman, Hellenistic, Hindu and Persian. Cultural exchange rode on the back of a flourishing trade network that reached as far as Rome. Bactria itself formed a vital link in the legendary Silk Road that extended from China to the Middle East and Europe.

By the 3rd century BC the Kushans had gone into decline. In Bactria, the Hepthalites, a tribe related to the Yüechi, gained power, only to be ousted by Turkic tribes in the 6th century. Other parts of Afghanistan were incorporated into the powerful Sassanian Empire, which had sprung up in neighboring Persia.

The Arabs and Islam

The overthrow of the Zoroastrian Sassanians by the driving force of Arabs and their new religion Islam, in the middle of the 7th century, permanently changed the balance of power of the whole region. Within the space of a few decades, the Arabs had carved themselves a huge Islamic empire that stretched from Spain and Morocco in the west to China in the east. The newcomers had entered Afghanistan at an early stage in their expansion, but at once realized that the region was extremely rebellious and difficult to control.

Eventually, however, a succession of local Muslim dynasties emerged in the region. The greatest of these were the Ghaznavids, founded by a former Turkish slave named Sebüktigin. His son, Mahmud of Ghazna, built up an empire whose territories reached into Iran and India. Its capital at Ghazna (modern-day Ghazni) became a great cultural center with a splendid artistic and architectural tradition. Mahmud also did much to facilitate the spread of Islam in the region, which until now had been slow to dislodge local beliefs and practices. His descendants, the Ghaznavids, managed to hold on to power until the middle of the 12th century before being toppled by local rivals.

Invaders from Mongolia

In 1219, the infamous Mongol leader Genghis Khan violently stormed into Afghanistan and incorporated the region into his vast realm. Yet after his death, his empire fragmented and the region's local rulers vied with each other to reassert their power.

The late 14th century saw the spectacular rise of Timur, a leader of Mongol and Turkish descent, who established a new dynasty based in Samarkand. Timur brought a significant part of Afghanistan into the realm of his Muslim empire. Under his rule and that of his successors, Herat, in western Afghanistan, became a flourishing cultural and scientific center.

The founder of the great Moghul dynasty, Babur, made Kabul his capital after seizing it in 1504. A descendant of Genghis Khan and Timur, Babur had spent his early career unsuccessfully attempting to conquer Samarkand, Timur's old capital in what is now Uzbekistan. He threw in the towel and instead turned his attention towards the Punjab and Indian sub-continent. Using Kandahar as a base he embarked on a wave of raids on the Punjab and by 1526 had seized Delhi and Agra.

Over the next two centuries, Afghanistan was split between the two empires of the Moghuls and the Persian Safavids. By the mid-18th century, rival ethnic Afghan groups put aside their differences and joined forces under the leadership of Ahmad Shah Durrani, managing to seize control over the region.

Yet mutual antagonisms resurfaced, eventually leading Afghanistan headlong into a civil war, which raged from 1819 to 1826. One of the chiefs, by the name of Dost Muhammad Khan, emerged the victor and was proclaimed emir—or princely ruler—of the country.

Caught in the Great Game

However, Afghanistan was not to be allowed to choose its own destiny — British and Russian imperial rivalry would see to that. To the north, Russia had gradually been increasing its influence in the region, chasing dreams of gaining access to the Indian Ocean and the immense trade its ports would bring. Yet its imperial rival Great Britain had no wish to see Russia extend its influence all the way to the borders of India, the "jewel in the crown" of its own empire.

In April 1839, in order to pre-empt the Russians, the British hatched a plot to install an Afghan ruler of their choice. This fateful move heralded the first of three Anglo-Afghan wars. In April 1839, a British force of 5,000 along with 12,000 camp followers marched into Afghanistan, taking Kandahar and then Kabul, encountering little resistance on the way. Yet, as the Duke of Wellington had warned the British government at the time, the problem was not getting into Afghanistan — it was getting out. History proved him right.

Initially, the plan was a success, Dost Muhammad was deposed and Shah Suja, an unpopular choice with many Afghans, was proclaimed emir. Yet Kabul proved to be unruly and rebellion broke out. In a hopeless situation, the British were eventually left with little choice but to cut their losses and abandon the city. In January 1842, a lone rider reached a British post on the road to the Khyber Pass, and broke news of the terrible massacre that had taken place as they retreated. Those who had not perished at the hands of the Afghans had been finished off by the bitter cold of the Afghan winter.

In the aftermath, Dost Muhammad was restored to power and ruled until his death in 1863. Then, during the reign of his son Shir Ali, the British once again invaded Afghanistan, angry at having been snubbed by the emir in favor of the Russians. A second Anglo-Afghan war erupted, which lasted from 1878 until 1880. Afghanistan emerged from this latest encounter with a new leader, Abd ar-Rahman, a cousin of Shir Ali. Although Britain agreed to withdraw from the country, it forced Afghanistan to accept its authority on matters relating to foreign affairs.

Together with Russia, Britain subsequently set about formally establishing the boundaries of what was to become modern Afghanistan. But not only was Abd ar-Rahman's reign undermined by British interference, he had also had to contend with a host of independent-minded local rulers who were ill-disposed to taking orders from the central government. Nevertheless, Abd ar-Rahman's ultimate success in keeping the country together and his attempts to modernize the country have earned his right to be called the founder of modern Afghanistan.

Creating a new kingdom

Abd ar-Rahman was succeeded by his son Habibullah in 1901. The new emir continued much as his father had done. During the First World War, he was careful to steer the country along a neutral path. In 1919, Habibullah was assassinated and succeeded by his son Amanullah Khan.

The new emir proved to be independently minded and immediately demanded an end to British meddling in Afghan affairs. That same year he ordered an attack on the British, and for the third time an Anglo-Afghan War broke out, this time lasting barely a month. The conflict proved to be a turning point for Afghanistan. In the peace that followed, Afghanistan came away with full control over its foreign affairs.

Amanullah Khan, who discarded the title of emir in favor of king, introduced the country's first constitution in 1923. He had great ambitions to introduce extensive reforms to modernize Afghan society, plans which included the emancipation of women. Yet, he soon courted the displeasure of the more traditional leaders and clerics who rejected his vision for the country. Discontent gave way to a resurgence of inter-ethnic factionalism leading to revolution and Amanullah Khan's downfall in 1928.

After several years of political strife, the reign of Mohammed Zahir Shah, a distant relative of Amanullah, brought a degree of stability to Afghanistan between the 1930s and 1960s. It was a period that saw positive attempts made at modernization, although the government had to proceed far more cautiously when it came to social reforms.

Republic and conflict

In 1964, Afghanistan took the major step of introducing a new constitution that provided for a constitutional monarchy. The following year, the country held its first elections to its newly created upper and lower houses of parliament. Yet, despite further elections in 1969, restrictions governing the democratic process and bitter disputes as to how the country ought to have been governed led the country into crisis.

A power struggle ensued, leading to the overthrow of Zahir Shah in 1973. A new republic was declared, headed by a military regime under the leadership of Dawud Khan, a former prime minister as well as a relative and brother-in-law of the deposed king. The new republic further intensified political divisions, eventually leading to a full leftist rebellion in 1978, which led to the downfall of the government and the establishment of a new Soviet-backed regime. In 1979, the Soviet Union entered Afghanistan to support to the new government in its fight against a rebel movement.

After a decade of fighting, the Soviet troops finally withdrew from Afghanistan having achieved little success — worse, it had proved to be their Vietnam. The 1990s saw a continuation of the civil war, which culminated in the rise to power of the Taliban, who set about imposing a form of government, based on their own strict interpretation of Islam, over the parts of the country they controlled. They fared little better than their Mojahedin predecessors and were deposed in 2001, once again with the deployment of forces from the West, this time headed by the United States.

After the traumatic events of the recent past, the new millennium brought with it a real chance for the Afghan people to open a new and peaceful chapter in their history, and the opportunity rebuild their country into a flourishing and vital player in the Central Asian and wider international community.

The Darí language

Dari has always been used for business and government transactions — along with Pashto, it therefore constitutes one of the official languages of Afghanistan and as such is taught in schools and used everywhere around the country as a first, second or even third language. Dari is also a significant language of broadcasting and the press.

Dari shares a long history of literature both classical and modern with the Persian (Farsi) of Iran and the Tajik of Tajikistan. These three languages have a common grammar and vocabulary but have been split by politics and geography. Today Dari is closer to Tajik than Persian, although most Afghan dialects are closer to literary Persian than many dialects of Iran are to literary Persian.

Between the languages you'll find a slight difference in pronunciation as well as minor aspects of grammar — though far less than you'd find between closely related languages like Italian and Spanish. In fact, the relationship between Dari and the Persian of Iran and Tajik of Tajikistan has always been a continuous one, and so the situation perhaps is more like that of the English of Britain, America and Australia, or the French of France, Belgium and Quebec. The most noticeable distinction however is in vocabulary and usage, which differ perceptibly from Persian and are closer to Tajik.

Poets of the Golden Age

Historically known also as Persian, Dari derives its name from the word **darbar** which means "royal court." It had long been the language used by the rulers of Afghanistan and their administration, and therefore it became known as the "courtly language". Many powerful kingdoms of the past such as those of the Moghuls in India also used Dari in their own courts.

The literature of Dari is immensely rich — in fact, some of the world's greatest poems have been written in Dari, and the list is endless of acclaimed poets who have made their contribution to the treasury of world literature. Their work continues to be translated from their original Dari versions to numerous other languages, and are widely read in the West.

After the Arab conquest of Khorasan (as Afghanistan was then known) during the 7th century, Islam replaced the previous state religion of Zoroastrianism, with Arabic becoming the language of law, religion and culture. However with the rise of Samanids and political revival of Khorasan, Dari emerged as a literary medium and its use swiftly became widely established. The earliest examples date back to 752 in letter form, while poetry was already starting to take shape on the page during the 9th century.

By the following century, a tremendous amount of literature was now written and translated into Dari. The earliest main genres are the epic, qasida (ode), masnavi (narrative), and ghazal (lyric). Writing in the 10th century, the poet Rudaki produced a remarkable corpus of work, and he soon became regarded as the father of Dari poetry. After Rudaki's death the epic tradition, with its sources in Avesta and Middle Dari texts, began. The first epic poet was Marvazi Samarqandi who composed a

Shahnameh ('The Book of Kings') in 910. Daqiqi Balkhi, another poet of the 10th century, wrote a better known *Shahnameh* in 975. However, Firdawsi Tusi composed another *Shahnameh* (1010) which soon became the best known epic.

Qasida, another form of poetry, was also first written by Rudaki in Dari. Of many the panegyrists in the history of the language's literature, Anvari Balkhi is regarded as the foremost while in philosophical qasidas Naser-e Khosrow is held in high esteem. The great Omar Khayyam was another poet of this era who still today is considered to be of astonishing originality.

During the Samanid era, the foundation of Dari prose was also laid, concentrating on a series of brilliant works on religion, philosophy, medicine and grammar, which had the effect of bringing to an end the domination of Arabic language over religious literature.

The 13th and 14th centuries heralded the Golden Age of Dari poetry. During this period lived and wrote the geniuses Jalaluddin Rumi (or Mawlana Balkhi), Sadi and Hafiz, who all excelled in weaving the themes of love and mysticism in the ghazal.

The first mystic masnavi is believed to be written by Hakim Sana'i of Ghazna and is known as *Hadiqat al-Haqiqa* ('The Enclosed Garden of Truth'). He was followed by Attar and Rumi. Rumi's *Masnavi-ye Manavi* consists of six books that contains 30,000 couplets, considered to be the most profound and greatest work of Dari literature, and perhaps of all Islamic secular literature, while Nezami's love story *Khosrow o Shirin* ('Khosrow and Shirin') is the best known of the romantic masnavis. Many of these works are available in translation in the world's major languages, including English, often in bestselling editions. ■

For further background information, see the Introduction to Hippocrene's 'Pashto Dictionary & Phrasebook', and 'The Afghans' (Bennett and Bloom, 2003).

A VERY BASIC GRAMMAR

Dari belongs to the Iranian branch of the Indo-European family of languages. Its closest relatives are Persian (Farsi) and Tajik, and speakers of the three not only readily understand each other but share a long history of common literature. Other members of this family include Pashto, Urdu/Hindi, and, more distantly, English, German, French, Italian and Spanish. Dari is written in the Persian form of the Arabic script (see page 24) — this book uses an easy-to-understand transliteration throughout.

—Structure

Like English, the linguistic structure of Dari is refreshingly simple. In word order, the verb is usually put at the end of the sentence, e.g.

Shomâ telefun dârêd?
"Do you have a telephone?"
(literally: "You telephone have?")

—Nouns

Dari has no words for "the," "a" or "an" in the same way as English does — instead the meaning is generally undestood from the context, e.g. **dâktar** can mean "the doctor," "a doctor" or just simply "doctor."*

Nouns form their plural by simply adding **-ân** or **-hâ/-â**, e.g. **zan** "woman" → **zanân** "women," **akhbâr** "news-

---

* If you want to specifically emphasise "a" or "an" then you can use the word **yak/yag** "a/an" or add **-ê/-yê**, e.g. **yak dâktar/dâktar-ê** "a doctor," **zanâ-yê** "(some) women".

paper" → **akhbârhâ** "newspapers". Although **-ân** is theoretically used for human plurals and **-hâ/-â** for things, in everyday conversation they are more or less interchangeable.

There are some irregular plurals — analogous to occurrences in English like "man/men" or "child/children", e.g. **majles** "meeting" → **majâles** "meetings", **khat** "line" → **khotut** "lines", **salâh** "weapon" → **aslehâ** "weapons".

The genitive is formed using **-e/-ye**,* e.g. **môtar-e mard** "the car of the man" or "the man's car," **shâr-e Kâbol** "the city of Kabul", **têl-e petrôl** "gasoline" (literally: "oil of petrol"). For more on genitive constructions, see the sections on adjectives and possessives.

—Adjectives

These generally come after the noun and use the genitive **-e/-ye** as a connector,* e.g.

| "new" **naw** | — | **môtar-e naw** "new car" |
| "old" **kôhna** | — | **môtar-e kôhna** "old car" |

Some other basic adjectives are:

open **bâz**	quick **zud**
shut **basta**	slow **âhesta**
cheap **arzân**	big **kalân**
expensive **qêmat**	small **khord; chucha**
hot **garm**	old *person* **pir**
cold **yakh**	young **jawân**
near **nazdik**	good **khub**
far **dur**	bad **bad**

Adding **bê-** to an existing noun gives the meaning of "without" or "-less", e.g. **gonâ** "crime" → **bêgonâ** "innocent'(= "without crime"), **hush** "mind" → **bêhush** "unconscious" (= "without mind"), etc.

---

* This **e/ye** is called the **ezâfat**. Also used to form adjectives, it is not always pronounced fully, particularly after words ending in vowels, e.g. **bâzu-y** (= **bâzâ-ye**) **zan** "the arm of the woman", or not at all, e.g. **lâri** (= **lâri-ye**) **âdam** "the truck of the man".

—Adverbs

Most adverbs have a single form that does not change. Some examples:

here	**injâ**	up	**bâlâ**
there	**ânjâ/onja**	down	**pâyin**
well	**khub**	now	**hâlâ**
badly	**bad**	tomorrow	**fardâ; sabâh**

Some have more than one form without change in meaning, e.g. **kam/kamtar** "less", **zyât/zyâtar** "very".

—Prepositions

Examples:

to	**ba/be; tâ**	with	**bâ**
for	**barây-e; bare**	on	**bâlâ-ye**
in	**dar; da**	after	**pas-e**
from	**az**	in front of	**pêsh-e ruye**

e.g. **da Afghânestân** "in Afghanistan," **az Inglestân** "from England".

—Pronouns

Basic forms are as follows:

SINGULAR	PLURAL
I **ma***	we **mâ**
you *singular* **tu**	you *plural* **shomâ**
he/she/it **ô**	they **wâ****

For "he/she/it" you will also find in formal or written Dari the forms **in** ("this person") and **ân** ("that person"), while the conversational language uses **i** and **u** respectively. Likewise for "they", where the alternatives are **inhâ**, **ânân** and **êshân**, the preference in everyday conversational speech is **wâ** or **yâ**. There is no essential change in meaning. Use **shomâ** for anyone you don't know well or who is older or more senior.

* The common written form is **man**.
** The common written form is **ânhâ**.

Possessive pronouns are:

SINGULAR	PLURAL
my **-em***	our **-emâ**
your **-et***	your **-etân**
his/her/its **-esh***	their **-eshân**

e.g. **akhbârem** my newspaper
akhbâresh his/her/its newspaper
akhbâremâ our newspaper

Simple demonstratives in formal or written Dari are:

this **in**	these **inân****
that **ân**	those **ânân****

More conversational forms are reduced to the following:

this **i**	these **yâ**
that **ô**	those **wâ**

When these are used to modify a noun, you simply use the singular forms whether the noun is singular or plural, e.g. **i mard** "this man", **i mardâ** "these men", **ô zan** "that woman", **ô zanâ** "those women".

—Verbs

Verbs are very easy to form, adding a number of prefixes and suffixes to the basic verb form. In fact the concept underlying the structure of Dari verbs is so similar to those of the majority of European languages that its system of regularities and irregularities will soon appear quite familiar.

Every Dari verb has a basic form that carries a basic meaning. To the end of this are added smaller words or single vowels that add further information to tell you who's doing what and how and when, e.g.

kharidan "to buy"
kharidom "I bought"
bokharom "I may buy"

---

* The written forms are **-am**, **-at**, **-ash**.
** The written forms are **inhâ**, **ânhâ**.

mêkharom "I am buying/will buy"
mêkharidom "I was buying"

Adding a form of the verb "to be" creates compound tenses, e.g. **kharida budom** "I had bought.'

Some verbs, as in European languages, have different stems for different tenses, e.g. **didan** "to see" → **didom** "I saw", **mêbinom** "I see"; **goftan** "to speak" → **goftom** "I spoke", **mêgôyom** "I am speaking"; **âmadan** "to go" → **âmadom** "I went", but **myâyom** "I am going".

We saw the personal pronouns above, but these are only used for emphasis. Like French or Spanish, the verb already gives this information:

SINGULAR	PLURAL
I **-am/-om**	we **-ên**
you *singular* **-i**	you *plural* **-êd**
he/she/it **(-ad/-a)**	they **-an(d)**

e.g.

mêkharom I buy	**mêkharêm** we buy
mêkhari you buy	**mêkharêd** you buy
mêkhara he/she/it buys	**mêkharan** they buy
kharidom I bought	**kharidêm** we bought
kharidi you bought	**kharidêd** you bought
kharid he/she/it bought	**kharidan** they bought

You'll see that these are similar in form to the possessive pronouns on page 17.

"Not" is **na/ne**, e.g. **na-mêkharom** "I don't buy" — **na-kharidom** "I did not buy", **estâd shaw!** "stop!" — **estâd na-shaw!** "don't stop!"

—Essential verbs

The verb "to be" is expressed in a variety of ways. The most common form you will find is the simple series of present endings:

SINGULAR	PLURAL
(h)astom I am	**(h)astêm** we are
(h)asti you are	**(h)astêd** you are
(h)as(t) he/she/it is	**(h)astan** they are

e.g. **Man dâktar astom.** "I am a doctor".

Although used slightly differently, the present tense of "to be" is contracted in a similar way to English (e.g. "I'm" for "I am", "she's" for "she is"):

SINGULAR	PLURAL
-am/-m I am	**-êm** we are
-i you are	**-êd** you are
-as(t)/-s he/she/it is	**-an(d)** they are

e.g. **man âmada-m** "I am ready" (literally: "I ready am"), **ô chi-st?** "what is it?"

The negative forms are:

SINGULAR	PLURAL
nêstom I am	**nêstêm** we are
nêsti you are	**nêstêd** you are
nês(t) he/she/it is	**nêstan** they are

Budan is another form of "to be". Its present form is:

SINGULAR	PLURAL
mêbâshom I am	**mêbâshêm** we are
mêbâshi you are	**mêbâshêd** you are
mêbâsha he/she/it is	**mêbâshan** they are

Past tense:

budom I was	**budêm** we were
budi you were	**budêd** you were
bud he/she/it was	**budan** they were

This has the meaning of "being in a place/a position", e.g. **khâna mêbâshan** "they are in the house", **chand mâh da Afghânestân mêbâshêd?** "how many months have you been in Afghanistan?" It is also used to form verb tenses, e.g. in the example given in the Verb section above, **kharida budom** "I had bought."

The verb "to have" is:

SINGULAR	PLURAL
dârom I have	**dârêm** we have
dâri you have	**dârêd** you have
dâra he/she/it has	**dâran** they have

Examples:

Môtar dârom. "I have a car."
Môtar nadârom. "I don't have a car."
Nân dârêd? "Do you have (any) bread?"
Chi kâr dârêd? "What job do you do?"

Paralleling French, Italian and Spanish, this verb can be also used in the third person to express the sense of "there is/there are", e.g. **Nân dâra?** "Is there (any) bread?", **Khatar na-dâra!** "There is no danger!'

"To want" is expressed using the verb **khâstan**, which has an irregular present form **khâh-**, e.g.

Man yak tiket ba Kâbol mêkhâhom.
I want a ticket to Kabul.
(lierally: "I one ticket to Kabul want.")

"To like" is expressed in a similar way to French ("il me plaît") or Spanish ("me gusta"), using **dôst dâshtan** "to please" (note **dâshtan** has an irregular present form **dâr-**), e.g.

Man futbâl dôst dârom. I like football.
Man futbâl dôst nadârom. I don't like football. ■

PRONUNCIATION GUIDE

Dari letter	Dari example	Approximate English equivalent
a	**akhbâr** "newspaper"	*a*pple
â	**âw** "water"	f*a*ther, as in South British English
b	**balê** "yes"	*b*ox
ch	**chây** "tea"	*ch*urch
d	**dôkân** "shop"	*d*og
e	**brenj** "rice"	p*e*t
ê	**mêz** "table"	like the *a* in p*ai*d
f	**futbâl** "soccer"	*f*at
g	**gâz** "gas"	*g*ot
gh	**gharb** "west"	—
h	**hazâr** "thousand"	*h*at
i	**injâ** "here"	h*ea*t
j	**jahân** "world"	*j*et
k	**kocha** "street"	*k*ick
kh	**khân** "chief"	lo*ch*, as in Scottish English
l	**lâri** "truck"	*l*et
m	**mêhmân** "guest"	*m*at
n	**nân** "bread"	*n*et
o	**omêd** "hope"	c*o*t, as in British English
ô	**môtar** "car"	c*oa*t
p	**pôlis** "police"	*p*et
q	**qahwa** "coffee"	—
r	**râdyô** "radio"	*r*at, but "rolled" as in Scottish English
s	**sênamâ** "cinema"	*s*it
sh	**shâr** "town"	*sh*ut
t	**taksi** "taxi"	*t*en
u	**hoquq** "rights"	sh*oo*t

w	**waqt** "time"	*w*orld
y	**yakh** "ice"	*y*es
z	**zelzela** "earthquake"	*z*ebra
zh	**rezhim** "regime"	era*z*ure
'	**ma'nâ** "meaning"	—

Nothing beats listening to a native speaker, but the following notes should help give you some idea of how to pronounce the following letters.

Like English, the spoken language has a range of variations in pronunciation that are not reflected in the written language. Most of the language in this book, however, is deliberately close to the written language thus enabling you to be understood clearly wherever you may be.

—Vowels
1) The combination **ay** is pronounced as the "y" in English "why", e.g. **paysa** "money".
2) The combination **aw** is pronounced as the "ow" in English "how", e.g. **chawki** "chair".
3) There is widespread alternation of vowels, particularly **a** with **e**, **i** with **ê**, and **u** with **ô**. This does not affect meaning or your ability to be understood.

—Consonants
gh is pronounced like a sort of growl in the back of your throat — like when you're gargling. Frequently transcribed into English for other languages that have this sound as "gh", the German or Parisian "r" is the easy European equivalent. [= غ]

kh is the rasping "ch" in Sottish "loch" and German "ach", frequently transcribed in English as "kh". It is also pronounced like the Spanish/Castillian "jota". [= خ]

q is pronounced like a **k**, but right back in your mouth at the throat end. Imagine you have a marble in the back of your throat and that you're bouncing it using only your glottis, and make a **k** sound at the same time. [= ق]

r varies between two forms: from the rolled Scottish variant to a lightly breathed tap of the tongue that sometimes sounds similar to **zh**. This is the same **r** found in Persian and Turkish.

ʼ represents the same pronunciation of two underlying sounds: the "glottal stop" — a simple stop of the breath instead of a consonant — or a representation of the pharyngal consonant *ʻain* found in words of Arabic origin (it also occurs in classical Hebrew). In Dari, when it comes before a consonant, it prolongs the preceding vowel, sometimes with a slight "creak" of breath separating the two, e.g. **maʼnâ** "meaning" is pronounced "**maʼanâ**" or simply "**mânâ**", **sheʼr** "poem" as "**sheʼer**". When it comes after a consonant, it is usually pronounced as a sort of stop or catch in the flow of breath before articulating the following vowel, e.g. **sanʼat** "industry" is pronounced in two distinct segments as "**san-at**". [= Turkish **ʼ**/Persian ء or ع]

—Spelling notes

1) Like English, there are variants in the pronunciation of spoken language that are not reflected in the spelling, e.g. **âb** "water" is frequently pronounced "**âw**," **yak** "one" is "**yag**" when modifying other words. Like English, however, these rarely confuse meaning, and are easily picked up once you have found your "Dari ear." Also as in English, speakers tend to drop certain consonants, particularly at the ends of words, e.g. you will hear "**astan**" for **hastand** "they are".

2) In the rare cases where the letters **sh** represent the two separate sounds **s** and **h** in sequence, they are divided by an apostrophe, e.g. **Es-hâq** "Isaac". Likewise for **z** and **h** to distinguish the sequence from the single sound **zh**, e.g. **maz-hab** "sect" or "religion".

3) Remember that **h**, as a separate letter, is always pronounced in combinations like **mashhur** ("**mash-hur**") "famous", **solh** ("**sol-h**") "peace." Note that many speakers (like many speakers of British English) will drop it, particularly at the beginning of words, e.g. **ast** "is" instead of "**hast**".

4) The Dari alphabet frequently marks doubled letters (e.g. **jarrâh** for the spoken **jarâh** "surgeon"). For the most part these doubled letters simply reflect established spelling conventions and have no effect on pronunciation. For this reason they have not been marked in this dictionary/phrasebook. ∎

The Darí alphabet

Dari letter	Roman equivalent	Name of letter	Dari letter	Roman Equivalent	Name of letter
ا، آ	a, â	alef	ض	z	zâd
ب	b	bê	ط	t	toy
پ	p	pê	ظ	z	zoy
ت	t	tê	ع	'	'ayn
ث	s	sê	غ	gh	ghayn
ج	j	jim	ف	f	fê
چ	ch	chin	ق	q	qâf
ح	h	hê halwa	ک	k	kâf
خ	kh	khê	گ	g	gâf
د	d	dâl	ل	l	lâm
ذ	z	zâl	م	m	mim
ر	r	rê	ن	n	nun
ز	z	zê	و	w, u, ô	wâw
ژ	zh	zhê	ه	h	hê gerdak
س	s	sin	ي، ی	y, i, ê	yâ
ش	sh	shin	ء	'	hamza
ص	s	sâd			

1. Note that the short vowels **a**, **e**, and **o** are not normally written.
2. **'Ayn** and **hamza** are not normally written in the transliteration used in this book, and they are rarely pronounced in conversational Dari.
3. **Hê halwa** is more technically called **hê hoti**, **hê gerdak** is also called **hê hawaz**.

Numbers

·	١	٢	٣	٤\٣	٥	٦	٧	٨	٩	١٠
0	**1**	**2**	**3**	**4***	**5**	**6**	**7**	**8**	**9**	**10**

* The two forms for 4
are interchangeable.

DARI
Dictionary

DARI—ENGLISH
DARI—INGLISI

A/Â

âb water; **âb-e garm** hot water; **âb-e jôsh** boiling water; **âb-e sard** cold water; **âb-e mêwa** fruit juice; **âb-e jôsh dâdagi** gruel; **âb-e mâdani** mineral water; **âb-e nushidani** drinking water; **Âb-e nushidani hast?** Is there drinking water?; **Âb qat'a shodast.** The water has been cut off.; **âb shâr** waterfall; **âb-dân** reservoir

abda seventeen

âbi blue

abr cloud

abrêshom silk

abzâr forôshi hardware store

âchâr pickles

âdâb etiquette

adabiyât literature

adad number

adâlat justice

âdam man; person; someone

adâptar adapter *electric*

âdat-e mâhâna period *menstrual*

âdi common; normal; ordinary

âdras address

âdras-e elektroniki e-mail address

adweya medication

afat-e tabiyi natural disaster

afgâr slightly wounded/injured

Afghân Afghan

Afghânestân Afghanistan

Afghâni Afghani

afghâni afghani *currency*

afsâna legend

afsar officer

âftâb; âftaw sun; **âftâb gir** sunblock; **âftâb zadagi** sunburn

âftâbi sunny; **Hawâ âftâbi ast.** It is sunny.

aftâdan; aftidan to fall

Âqâ Mr.; Sir

aga(r) if; **agar nê** otherwise; **agar chi** although; **agar momken bâshad** if possible

âgâhi knowledge

agarchi although

Âgest August

aghaz beginning

âghâz kardan to begin

aghlab often

ahamiyat importance

âhan iron

âhesta slow(ly); gently

ahmaq fool; stupid

âhu deer

âhwâl news

ajala hurry; **Man ajala dârom.** I'm in a hurry.

ajib strange

akâdemi academy

akâs photographer

akhbâr forôshi newsstall

akhbâr news; newspaper; journal; **akhbâr-e Inglisi** newspaper in English

âkher final; last; **âkher-e hafta** weekend

âkheri final *noun*

âkherin recent; last

aknun now

akâsi photography

aks photo; picture; **aks bardâri**

aksariyat

photography; **aks gereftan** to photograph

aksariyat majority

âksêjan oxygen

Aktobar October

alâyem symptom

alaf grass

alahida separately

alâmat sign; symptom; **alâmat-e tarâfiki** road sign

alâqa interest

alâqa dâshtan to interest

alâsha jaw

alâwa bar ân in addition to

alâyda separately

âle now

âli excellent; perfect

alkôl alcohol

Âlmân German; Germany

Âlmâni German

almâri cupboard; **almâri-e mêz** drawer

âlu plum

âlubâlu cherry

âluda kardan to pollute

âm same; also; even

ama but

âmâda ready

âmadan to come

âmâdagi gereftan to prepare

amali kardan to do; to carry out

amal-e ertejâyi reaction; reactionary

amaliyât operation *surgical*

ambulâns ambulance

amiq deep

amneyat security

âmokhta shodan use to: to get used to

amrâye with

hamrâhi with

Amrikâ America

Amrikâyi American

âmukhtan to learn

ân that; **ân che-st?** what's that?; **ân taraf** way: that way

ânân they; those

an'anawi traditonal

anbâr store; depot; cellar; **makhzan-e sukht** fuel dump

andâkhtan to throw

andâza limit

andâza size; measurement; **andâza-ye sor'at** rate; **andâza gereftan** to measure

angôsht finger

angôshtar ring

angur grape(s)

ânhâ they; those; **ânhâ-râ** them

ânjâ there

anjir fig(s)

anjoman assembly; society; association

ankabut spider

antibayâtik antibiotic

anwâ variety

anwâri cupboard

apârtment; apârtomân apartment

aprêtar operator

April April

Âqâ Mr.

aqab behind

aqaliyat minority

aqâreb relatives

aqida idea

Aqrab Scorpio *month/sign*

Arab Arab

Arabi Arabic

ârâm calm

mosâken tranquilizer

ârenj elbow

ara saw; **ara kardan** to saw

araq sweat; **araq kardan** to sweat

ârâyishgâh beauty salon

arâzi-ye mayn farsh shoda minefield

ârd flour

ârezu dâshtan to wish

arghawâni purple

arshad senior

arzân cheap; **arzântar** cheaper

arzan millet
arzesh worth
asâb nerve(s)
Asad Leo *month/sign*
asâker troops
asal honey
âsân easy
âsar monument
asb horse; asb-e nar stallion; asb dawâni horse racing; asb swâri horseback riding; asb swâri kardan to ride a horse
âs-e âb watermill
âsh stew
ashaye-ye eks X-rays
âshak dumplings
ashk tear *of eyes*
âshpaz cook
âshpaz khâna kitchen
âshub riot
âsib trauma
asir prisoner; asir-e jangi prisoner-of-war
askar soldier
asl origin
aslehâ arms; weapon
asli main; original
âsmâm sky
asnâd-e mótar car papers/registration
asp *see* asb
âyspiren aspirin
asri modern
âstâ slow(ly); gently
Âstarâliyâ Australia
Âstarâliyâyi Australian
astmâ asthma
Âsyâ Asia
âsyâ watermill; mill
atanemeli national dance *of Afghanistan*
âtash *see* âtesh
âtashak syphilis
ater; atr perfume; deodorant
âtesh fire; âtesh bas ceasefire; âtesh rushan kardan to light a fire; âtesh bas truce

atfâl children
atrâf suburb
atrâf-e shâr about town
âw *see* âb
âwardan bring
âwâz song
awbâz diver
awgâr slightly wounded/injured
âwêzân kardan to hang
awlâd child
âwordan to bring
awal first
awalan first(ly)
âyâ...? do/does...?
Aydz AIDS
âyenda future; next
âyesta slow
âyin iron
âyina mirror
âynak (eye)glasses
âynak-e âftâbi sunglasses
Âyrish Irishman; Irishwoman
Âyrishi Irish
Âyrlaynd Ireland
Âyrlaynd-e Shamâli Northern Ireland
âys-krim ice-cream
az by; from; of; since; az i bâd/pas from now on; az i pêsh so far; az i/u khâter consequently; az khâter-e because of; az kojâ? where from?; az bayni through; az pêsh owing to; az râh-e by way of; az ruy-e according to; az sar-e since; ever since
âzâd free
âzâdi freedom
azân call to prayer
azhâb (political) parties
azimat departures
aziz dear *loved*
azmâyesh trial *test*
azmâyesh kardan to test; to try
azorda sad

B

ba at; by; in; to; **ba har hâl** however; **ba wasila-ye** by means of; **ba wasila-ye sarwês** by bus; **ba wasila-ye pôst** by post; **ba yak qesm** somehow; **ba suy-e** onto; **ba shart-e ke** on condition that; **ba khater-e** because (of)

bâ with; **bâ ham** together; **bâ wojud-e** despite

bâbâ old man; elder *noun*

bacha boy; son

bad bad; evil; **bad bakht** unfortunate; **bad bakhtâna** unfortunately

ba'd; bâd after; then; **bâd az nâne shaw** after supper; **bâd az zohr** afternoon; p.m.; **bâd az (ân ke)** after

bâd wind

bâdâm almond

badan body

ba'dan; bâdan afterwards

bâdenjân aubergine; eggplant; **bâdenjân-e rumi** tomato

bad-hazmi indigestion

bâdrang cucumber

badtar worse; **Hâlem badtar ast.** I feel worse.

bâgh garden; orchard; yard

bahâna excuse

bahâr spring *season*

bahera sea

bahs discussion; **bahs kardan** to discuss

baja time

bakhsh district; section

bakhshesh forgiveness; pardon; gift; tip; **bakhshesh bâsad!** excuse me!

bakhshidan to forgive; to pardon; to offer

bakht luck

baks bag; suitcase; briefcase; baggage; *freight* container; **baks desti** handbag

ba-koli completely

bâkteri bacteria

bâl wing

bâlâ top; up; **bâlâ khâna** balcony

bâlâpôsh coat; overcoat

bâlâ-ye above; **bâlâ-ye ruy-e** on

bâlâ-ye tabiyi natural disaster

balê yes

bâlesh; bâlesht pillow; cushion

bal'idan to swallow

bâlkôni balcony

balun-e gâz gas bottle/canister

bam bomb; **bam-e monfajer nashoda** unexploded bomb

bâm roof

bâmân-e khodâ! goodbye!; *to which the response is* **khodâ hâfez!**

bamb *see* bam

bâmbak swelling

bambârân bombardment

bâmper bumper/fender

bânat bonnet/hood *of car*

band bond; link; dam; **band-e dest** wrist; **band-e ostokhân** joint

bandar port

bandâzh Band-Aid; plaster; bandage

bandi prisoner; **bandi-khâna** prison

bânjân aubergine; **bânjân-e rumi** tomato

bânk bank; **bânk-dâr** banker

bânknôt bank note

banyân vest; waistcoat

baqa frog

bâqimânda rest; remainder

bâqi mândan to stay; to remain

bar: bar tebq-e according to; **bar gashtan** to return

bâr load; cargo; time *unit*; spring *season*

bara lamb

barâbar-e equal to

barâmadagi swelling; sprain *medical*

barâmadan to come out; to go out

barân rain; **bârân mêbârad** rain: it is raining

barây-e; barê for; **barây-e chi** why

barây khodâ alms

bâr-dâr pregnant

barf snow; **Barf mêbârad.** It is snowing.; **barf kuch** avalanche

barg leaf; **barg rezan** autumn/fall

bâridan to rain

bârik thin

bâr-kash truck; van

barkenâr kardan to sack

barma kardan to drill

barnâma timetable; **barnâma-ye parwâz-ha/ mosâferat** travel timetable

barq electricity; signal; **Barq qat'a shodast.** The electricity has been cut off.; **barq-e sari** flash

barqi electric; electrician

bara lamb

bas bus; enough; sufficient; **bas! enough!; bas ast!** that's enough!; **bas kardan** to be enough; to stop

bashar human being

bâsketbâl basketball

basta package; parcel; closed; **basta kardan** to close; **basta budan** to be closed

bastan to shut; to tie

bastar-e do nafara double bed

batan womb

batar; battar worse

bâtlâq marsh; swamp

bâwar confidence; **bâwar dâshtan** to believe; **bâwar kardan** to trust

bâyad must; have to

baynolmelali international

bâysekel bicycle

bâz again; falcon; open; **bâz kardan** to open; **bâz âmadan** to come back; to return; **bâz rasi kardan** to control

bâzâr market; **bâzâr-e syâh** black market

bazgasht return

bâzi game; **bâzi kardan** to play

ba'zi some

bazjoy inquiry

bâzu arm

be *see* ba

bê without; **bê bôra** without sugar; **bê az u** anyway

bê-âbân desert

ba-âhestagi slowly

bêchâra poor

bêd willow tree

bêdâr awake; **bêdâr budan** to be awake; **bêdâr kardan** to wake

bedun-e without; except; **bedun-e mâliyât** tax-free

bêgâna foreign; alien; strange

bêgham calm

bêgonâh innocent

bêhamtâ unique

behesht heaven

behi quince

bêhtar better; best; **Bêhtar astom.** I feel better.; **bêhtar kardan** to improve

bêhtarin best

bêkâr unemployed; idle

bêkâri unemployment

bêkhâna homeless

bêkhatar safe

bêkhawi insomnia

bêkhi absolutely

bel bill/check

bêl shovel

bêlak-e shâna shoulder blade

beland high; large

belandi height
belkol completely
bêma insurance; bêma shoda insured; bêma-ye tebi medical insurance; Dârâyi-ye man bêma shodast. My possessions are insured.
bêmâr ill; bêmâr budan to be ill
bêmâri illness; disease; bêmâri-ye ertefa' altitude sickness; bêmâri-ye qalbi heart condition; bêmâri-ye shakar diabetes
bêmaza tasteless
bênehâyat therefore
berâdar brother
bêrang colorless
bêral barrel
bêrân destroyed; ruined
bêru(n) out; outside; bêrun raftan to go out
bêshqâb plate
bêshtar more
bestar bed; bestar budan to be confined to bed
bestari invalid; bedridden
bêshtarin most
besyâr very; much; many; a lot; often; besyâr kam too little; seldom; besyâr mohem grave; serious; besyâr sard freezing; besyâr zyâd too many/much
bêtar better; best
bêtri battery
beyâbân desert
bi- see bê-
binâyi eyesight
bini nose
biyogrâfi biography
bir beer
bira gum
birôbar crowd(s); congestion
bist twenty
bobakhshêd! excuse me!
bôdana quail
bofarmâyêd! please do!

bohrân crisis
bojolak ankle
bokhâr steam
bokhâri stove for heating
boji sack; bag
boland tall; high; loud; boland kardan to lift; boland shodan to take off something; boland shodan to rise
bonyâd foundation organization
bôra sugar
bôrdan to take
boridan to cut
borj tower
boro! go!
bors; boros brush; boros-e moy hairbrush; bors-e dandân toothbrush
boshqâb plate
bosidan to kiss
bôtal bottle; bôtal-e âw a bottle of water; water bottle
boz goat
boz-del afraid
bozorg big; great; bozorg shodan to grow up
bozorgtar bigger; greater; elder
bozorgtarin biggest; greatest; eldest
brandi brandy
brek brake(s)
brenj rice raw
Britânyâ Britain
Britânyâyi Briton; British
budan to be
budeja budget
bum owl
burut mustache
but shoe(s); boot(s); but-hâ shoes; boots
but-dôz cobbler
buy smell; odor
buynâk fragrant
byâ! come on!; byâ borawêm! let's go!
byâbân desert
byâdar brother

C/CH

châdar veil; scarf

châdari veil *for whole body*

châgh fat; obese

châh well; **châh-e têl** oil well; **châh kandan** to drill a well

chakak leak

chakidan to leak

châklêt chocolate

chakosh hammer

châl manoeuvre

châlân kardan to start up

chalaw rice *plain cooked*

chaman grass

châna chin

chand how much; **chand dâna?** how many?; **Chand sâl dârêd?** How old are you?

chandin several

chang claw

changak hook *noun*

chap left; **chap gerâ** left-wing

châp publication; **châp-khâna** printer's; **châp kardan** to print

chapa reversed

chaparkat bed

chapli sandal(s)

châq fat; obese

châqu knife; **châqu-ye jêbi** penknife

châr four; **châr taraf** environs

charbi fat *noun*

chârda fourteen

charkh wheel

charkhidan to spin

charm leather

châr-mâghz walnut

chârom fourth

châr-pây quadruped

châr-râhi crossroads; round-about

chars hashish

Chârshambê Wednesday

chasbândan to stick

chashm eye; **chashmân** eyes

châsht midday; noon

chaspidan to stick

chat ceiling

chatal dirty

chatri umbrella

chawki chair

chawki seat; **chawki-ye charkhi barâye mayub** wheelchair

chây-sob(h) breakfast

chây tea; **chây bâ lêmu** tea with lemon; **sher-chây** tea with milk

chây-jôsh kettle

chây-khâna tea-house

châynak teapot

che? what?; **che naw'?** what kind?; **che qesm?** what kind?; **che waqt?** when?

chechak smallpox; chickenpox

chek check; **chek-e mosâferati** traveler's checks

chel forty

chelam; chelem hookah

chenâr plane tree

chenin such

cheqadar?; cheqa? how much?; **cheqadar ast?** how much is it? ; **cheqadar râh ast?** how far is it?

cherâ why; **cherâ ke** because; since; **cherâ nê?** why not?

cherâgh lamp; flashlight; lightbulb; **cherâgh-e têli** oil-lamp

cherk dirty

cheshma spring *of water*

chetô; chetôr; chotô; chetawr how

chi? what?; **chi-waqt** when

chi-khasâ(-ye) especially as

Chin China

chini chinaware

Chinâyi Chinese

chiz thing; **chiz-hâ** things

chize something

chize-kam almost; nearly

chob wood
chôpân shepherd
choqor deep
chora hernia *inguinal*
chôshak feeding bottle
chub wood; **chub desti** walking stick
chubi wooden
chucha little; small
chun when; since; **chun ke** because; like
chuna lime *mineral*
chuti mat

D

da ten; in; **da(r) wakht-ê ke** while; **da(r) lab-e** on the side of; **da(r) i nazdikiyâ** recently; **da(r) khâna-ye** at; **da(r) qadim/sâbeq** in the past
dâdan to give
dafa *unit of* time
dafatan suddenly
dafan kardan to bury
daftar office; **daftar-e etelâyât** information office; **daftar-e forosh-e tiket** ticket office; **daftar-e mosâferati** travel agency
dagarman adjutant
dagar-wâl colonel
dâgh hot; **dâgh-e zarm** scar
dah ten
daha decade
dahan; dahân mouth
dahlêz corridor; passage
dahom tenth
dâkhel interior; internal **dâkhel shawêd!** come in!; **dâkhel shodan mana' ast** no entry
dâktar doctor; **dâktar-e dandân** dentist; **dâktar-e**

atfâl pediatrician; **dâktar-e zanân** gynecologist
dâl lentils
dalâk barber
dâlar dollar
dalil cause; proof; **dalil-e mosâferat** reason for travel
dalqhak clown
Dalw Aquarius *month/sign*
dâm trap
dam: dam kardan to simmer; **dam gereftan** to pause; to take a break
dâmâd; dâmât son-in-law
damâgh nose
dâman skirt; lap
damidan to blow
dân mouth
dâna grain; seed; item; thing; unity
dânâyi wisdom
danda stick
dandân tooth; **dandân dard** toothache; **dandân-hâ** teeth
dâneshmand scientist
dânestan to know
Denmârki Dane; Danish
daqa minute
daqiq exact
daqiqa minute *noun*
dar in; **dar bayn-e** among; **dar in keshwar** in this country; **dar muqâbel-e** in front of; **dar surat-ê ke...** in case (of)...; **dar ewazi** instead of; **dar râs** headman; **dar zadan** to knock; **dar dâdan** to light *a fire*
dara valley
dârâ owner
daraja-ye tab temperature
darakht tree; **darakht-hâ** trees
darâmadan to enter
darâmad-hâ earrings
darândan to tear

daraw harvest; **daraw kardan** reaping

darây shoghol businessman/woman

darâz long; **darâz kashedan** to lie down; **darâz kardan** to lengthen

darâzi length

dard pain; **dard kardan** to hurt; **Kojây shomâ dard mêkonad?** Where does it hurt?

dardmand; dardnâk painful

darwâza-ye worudi check-in counter

Dari Dari

daridan to be torn

darjan dozen

dark: dark-e ebtedâyi common sense; **dark kardan** to realize

dara valley

dars lesson

dars dâdan to teach

daru(n) inside; **darun-e** inside; into

darwâza gate; door

daryâ river

daryâft kardan to receive

daryaftan to find out

dâs scythe

dâsh oven

dasht plain *noun*

dâshtan to have

dast *see* dest

dâstan story

dastarkhân tablecloth

dast-gâh-e si-di/musik CD player

dastger kardan to arrest

dastur grammar

dawâ pill; drug; medicine; **dawâ-khâna** dispensary; pharmacy; **dawâ-ye bêhushi** anesthetic; **dawâ-ye khâb** sleeping pill(s); **dawâ-ye zed-e ofôni** antiseptic

da'wâ trial *legal*

dâwat invitation; **dâwat kardan** to invite

dawidan to run

dawlat state *nation*

dawr zadan to turn

dawra reign

dawrân era

dâyel kardan to dial

dâyera circle

daynamo dynamo

dê village

defâ kardan defend

dêg pot; **dêg-e bokhâr** pressure cooker

dega; degar another; other; **dega jây** elsewhere

dêh village

dêhqân farmer

dekishnari dictionary

del heart; **del-badi** nausea

delak-e pây calf *of body*

delâwar brave

demokrâsi democracy

dên religion

deq sad

dêr late; **dêr kardan** to be late; to delay

dereshi; derishi *western* suit *of clothes*

dêrôz yesterday

dest hand; **dest-kesh** gloves; **dest-e chap** (on the) left; **dest-e râst** (on the) right; **dest rasidan** to reach; **dest zadan** to touch; **dest-o pâ** limbs

desta handle

destband bracelet

dest-e dôwom secondhand

desti immediately

destkawl handbag

dest-râsti dar syâsat right-wing

destmâl napkin; **destmâl-e bini** handkerchief; **dest-pâk** hand-towel

dêwâl wall

dêwâna insane

dêwâr wall

dêzal diesel

didan to look; to see

digar other; another; late afternoon; **digar jâ** elsewhere

dina-rôz yesterday

diplomât diplomat

Disambar December

dishab; dishaw last night

disko nightclub; disco

dizal diesel

do two; **do bâr** twice; **do chand/barâbar** double; **dogânagi** twins; **do hafta** fortnight

do'â kardan pray

dobâra again

dôgh whey

dôkân shop; **dokân-e sâmân âlât barqi** electrical goods store

dôkândâr shopkeeper

dôkhtan to sew

dokhtar daughter; girl; Miss

dokma button

dôl drum

dom; domb queue

dombal boil *medical*

dombâl kardan to track; **dombâl gashtan** to look for

donyâ world

dôrbin binoculars

dorôgh-gôy liar

dorokhshidan to shine

dorost right; correct; precise; just

doshak mattress

Doshambê Monday

doshman enemy; hostile

doshmani feud

doshnâm insult

dashwâr difficult

dosiya file; dossier; case

dôst friend; **dôst-e bacha; dôst-e pesar** boyfriend;

dôst-e dokhtar girlfriend; **dôst dâshtan** to like; to love

dowâzda twelve

dôwom second *adjective*

dozakh hell

dozd thief; mugger; pirate

dozdi robbery; mugging; theft; **dozdi kardan** to rob; to mug

dozdidan to rob

dozi *see* dozdi

drêwar driver

du *see* do

dud smoke; smoked; **dud kardan** to smoke *food*

dudraw chimney

dukhtan to sew

dur far

durbin binoculars

dust *see* dôst

dusya file; dossier; case

dwâzda twelve

E/Ê

ebtedâ beginning

edâma dâdan to continue

êd *see* id

eftâr breaking of one's fast

eghteshâsh riot

ehsias: ehsâs kardan to feel; **ehsâs-e sharmindagi kardan** to feel ashamed

ehtemâlan probably

ehtemal dâshtan to be likely

ehtyât attention

ejâza permission; **bedun-e ejâza** without authorization; **ejâza dâdan** to allow

ejrâ performance; **ejrâ kardan** to perform; to undertake

ejtemâyi social

ekhrâj deportation; **ekhrâj kardan** to deport; to expel

ekhtelâs corruption

ekhterâ invention

ekserê X-ray(s)

elâj treatment; cure; **elâj kardan** to cure

êlâl crescent

elat cause

elmi scientific

emâm imam

emârat building; structure

emkan dârad it is probable

emruz today; **emruz sobh** this morning

emshab; emshaw tonight; this evening

emtehân; emtyân exam; test; **emtehân kardan** to try

emzâ signature; **emzâ kardan** to sign

êna here is/are

enfejâr explosion

enjinyar engineer

Enjil Bible

enjin engine

enqelâb revolution

ensân human; man; person

ensâni humanitarian

ensedad-e râh roadblock

entekhâb kardan to choose; to elect

entekhâbât election

enteqâl dâdan to transport; **enteqâl-e khun** blood transfusion

entarnet internet

enteshâr dâdan to publish; to spread

entezâr: entezâr dâshtan to expect; **entezâr kashedan** to wait

Epril April

eqlêm climate

eqtesâd economics; economy; **eqtesâd dân** economist

eqtesâdi economic

êr-kândishan air conditioner; air conditioning

eror mistake

ersâl kardan to send

ertebât connection; ertebâtât communications

esfanj sponge

es-hâl diarrhea

êshân they

eshâra sign; signal; **eshâra-ye tarâfiki** traffic lights; **eshâra-ye môtar** indicator light

eshghâl-e yak keshwar occupation of a country

eshkam stomach

eshpesh louse

eshq love

eshtebâh mistake; **eshtebâh kardan** to make a mistake

eshtehâ appetite

eshtireng steering wheel

eshtôp stove

Eskâtlaynd Scotland

Eskâtlayndi Scot

eskelêt skeleton

Eslâm Islam

Eslâmi Islamic

esm name; **esm-e fâmil** family name; surname

Esrâyil Israel

Esrâyili Israeli

estâd kardan to stop

estâdgâh station; **estâdgâh-e bas/ sarwês** bus stop/station; **estâdgâh-e rêl** railway station; **estâdgâh-e qatâr** train station

estefrâq vomiting; **estefrâq kardan** to vomit

estekhrâj-e têl oil production

estelâh term; **estelâh-e âmiyâna** idiom; slang

estêmâl kardan to use

esteqlâl independence

esterâhat rest; break; **esterâhat kardan** to rest; to relax

estêshan station; **estêshan-e râdyô** radio station

e'tebâr credit; trust

etefâq oftâdan to happen

etehâd; etehâdiya union; **etehâdiya-ye tejârati** trade union

etehâdiya federation

Etehâdiya-ye Orupâyi European Union

etelâ dadan to confirm

etelâyât information

e'tesâb kardan to strike *from work*

eto(r) like this

êwaz(-e) instead of

eyâlat state *federal*

Eyâlât-e Motaheda-ye Amrikâ United States of America

ezâfa excess

ezâfi extra

ezdewâj marriage

F

fâbrika factory

fahmândan to explain

fahmidan to understand

fâkolta faculty

faks fax

falaj kardan to paralyze

fâluda ice-cream

fâmel family

fan art; technique

fanar spring *metal*

fanni technical

farâmush kardan to forget

Farânsawi French

farâr kardan to escape

fardâ tomorrow; **pas-fardâ** the day after tomorrow

farhang dictionary; culture

farmâyesh dâdan to order *someone*

farnechar furniture

farq difference; **farq dâshtan** to be different; **farq kardan** to make a difference

farsh carpet; rug

Fârsi Farsi; Persian *language*

faryâd kardan to cry; **faryâd zadan** to shout

farz kardan to suppose

fasâd corruption

fâsed corrupt

fâsela interval

faskha kardan to cancel

fasl chapter; season

fawq above; up

fawq-ol-âda extraordinary

fawran immediately

fawri immediate; urgent

fawt shodan to be deceased

fâyda; fâyeda profit; **fâyeda kardan** profit: to make a profit

fâyedamand beneficial

fâyr kardan to shoot

faysala kardan to decide

fazâ space

fêl; fe'l verb

Febriwari February

feker thought; **feker kardan** to think

felân (kas) such (a)

fêlan for the moment

felez metal

ferestâdan to send; to transmit

ferestinda sender; transmitter

ferqa garrison

fesâd corruption

feshâr pressure; **feshâr-e khun** blood pressure; **feshâr-e khun-e bâlâ** high blood pressure; **feshâr-e khun-e pâyin** low blood pressure

festiwal festival

fil elephant

film film; **film-sâz** filmmaker; **film-e ranga** color film; **film-giri** shooting *film*

filmorgh turkey

firni cream

fita cassette; tape

fizik physics

fizyotrâpi physiotherapy

fôlâd steel

forma form

forôkhtan to sell

forôsh sale; selling; **forôsh gâh-e lebâs** clothes shop

forôshenda sales assistant; seller; salesperson

foto photo

fotokâpi photocopy; **fotokâpi kardan** to photocopy

fut foot *measurement*

futbâl football; soccer

G/GH

gâdi cart

gâhe sometimes

gahgahe sometimes

gala flock; herd; **gala-ye gâw** cattle

ganda rotten

gandana leek(s); chives

gandida rotten; septic

gandom wheat

ganks dizzy

gap conversation; **gap shodan** to happen; **gap zadan** to speak

garâzh garage

garchi although

gârd guard; **gârd-e sarhadi** border guard; **gârd-e reyâsate-ye jamhuri** presidential guard

gardan neck; **gardan band** necklace

gardana mountain pass

gardanenda operator

gardesh kardan to hike

gardidan to turn

garg scabies

garm hot; warm; **Garm ast.** It's hot.; **Garm astom.** I'm hot.; **garm kardan** to heat

garmi heat; **garmi-ye shadid** severe heat

gârnizun garrison

gârson waiter; waitress

garzandôy tourist

gashniz coriander

gasht time *unit*

gashtan to turn

gâw cow; **gâw-e nar** bull

gawak snail

gây sometimes

gaz yard *distance*

gâz gas; **Gâz qat'a shodast.** The gas has been cut off.; **gâz-e lêtar** lighter fluid

gazhdom scorpion

gazidan to bite; to sting

gazmê shab nightguard; nightwatchman

geyâ plant

gel mud; clay

gelam; gelim carpet *woven*

gêlan gallon

gelâs glass

gel-gir fender *of car*

ganrâl general *noun*

gêr gear

gerâm gram

gerân expensive

gerang heavy

gerd round

gerê; gereh knot; **gerê khordan khun dar rag** thrombosis

gereftan to get; to take; to catch

geristan to weep

gerôgân hostage

gerya kardan to weep

ghalat mistake; wrong

ghâleban usually

ghâl-ma-ghâl argument; uproar

ghaltidan to fall down

gham sadness

ghamgin sad

ghamnâk distressing

ghâr cave

gharb west *noun*

gharbi west(ern)

gharib poor
gharq shodan to sink; to drown
ghawasi diving
ghaw-ghaw kardan to bark
ghawâs diver
ghâyeb absent
ghayrâzir absent
ghayrat honor; duty
ghayr-e except (for); moreover; **ghayr-e momken** impossible; **ghayr-e qânuni** illegal
gherâmat compensation
ghezâ food; **ghezâ khori** feeding station; **ghezâ dâdan** to feed; **ghezâ sefâresh dâdan** to order a meal
ghobâr fog; mist; **ghobâr âlud** foggy
ghodud gland
gogerd match(es)
ghorfa kiosk; booth; **ghorfa-ye mahâseb** cashier's booth
ghorub sunset
ghorur pride
ghul foolish
ghuri dish
gilâs see **gelâs**
giyâh plant; plant
giyar gear
golu(n) dardi sore throat
godi doll
godi-parân (paper) kite
goftan to say; to tell
goftugôy discussion; **goftugôy kardan** to discuss
gol flower; goal; **gol-e golâb** rose; **gol dân** vase; **gol forôsh** florist; **gol kardan** to extinguish
gôla projectile; bullet; joint
golâb rose
golâbi pink
golf golf
goli pill; tablet
golôla see **gôla**
golu; golun throat
gom kardan to lose
gomrok customs border

gonâ mistake; sin
gonâgar sinner
gonjeshk sparrow
gôr grave noun
gorda kidney
gorêkhtan to flee
goresnagi famine
gorg wolf
goresna hungry; **Goresna hastom.** I'm hungry.
goresnagi hunger
goruh group
goruh-e koras choir
gorup group; bulb; **gorup-e khuni** blood group
gôsâla calf
gosfand sheep
gôsh ear; **gôsh-dardi** ear infection; **gôsh-e dâktar** stethoscope; **gôsh kardan** to listen
goshna hungry; **goshna budan** to be hungry
gôsht meat; **gôsht-e gâw** beef; **gôsht-e gospand** mutton; **gôsht-e morgh** chicken meat
gospan; gospand sheep
gostâkh rude
gostâresh dâdan to extend
gozar ford; passage
gozâresh dâdan to report
gozargâh crossing
gozashta past adjective/noun
gozashtan to pass; to cross
gozâshtan to put
grip influenza
grup lightbulb
gurda kidney
gusha corner
gyâ plant

H

hâ yes
had limit
hadaf goal; aim

hadaf-e mosâferat reason for travel

hâdesa accident

hadya gift

hafda seventeen

hâfeza memory

hafr zadan to talk

haft seven

hafta week **hafta-ye gozashta** last week; **hafta-ye âyenda** next week

haftâd seventy

haftawâr weekly

hajda eighteen

hâji pilgrim

hakam referee

hâkem ruler; **hâkem-e motlaq** dictator

hakim doctor *traditional*

hal: hal kardan to solve

hâl state; situation; **hâl-e hâzer** present *time*; **Hâl-e shomâ chetôr ast?** How are you?

hâlâ now

halâl permitted; halal

Hâlandi Dutch *language*

Hâlandi Dutch *thing*

hâlat state; situation; **hâlat-e ezterâri/khas** emergency

halazun snail

hâle now

halq larynx

halqa ring

ham all; also; even; every

hama: hama bâ ham all together; **hama chiz** everything

hamagi everybody; everyone

Hamal Aries *month/sign*

hamâm bath(s); **hamâm-e âftâb** sunbathing; **hamâm kardan** to bathe; to shower

hambargar hamburger

hamchonin; hamchenin also; equally; in this way; as well

hâmela pregnant; **Man hâmela hastom.** I'm pregnant.

hamêsha always

hamin lahza right now

hamkâr colleague

ham-kâri cooperation

haml kardan to carry

hamla attack; raid; **hamla-ye qalbi** heart attack; **hamla kardan** to attack

hamrâh companion; **hamrâh-e** with

hamsâya neighbor

hamshêra nurse

hamwâr level *adjective*

hangâm-e during

hanôz still; yet; **hanôz na** not yet

haq right

haqiqat truth; fact

haq-o-zahma wage(s); commission

har each; every; **har yek** each; **har yeki** any; **har do** both; **har do... wa** both... and; **har kas** anyone; **har ke** whoever; **har kodâm** whoever; **har kojâ** anywhere; **har chand ke** despite; **har wakht ke** as soon as

harakat kardan to move

harâm forbidden; haram

harârat temperature; **hararat sanj** thermometer; **Harârat bâlâ ast.** The temperature is high.; **Harârat pâyin ast.** The temperature is low.

harb war

harbi pôhantun military university

hardo... wa both... and

harf letter *of alphabet*; talk; word(s); **harf zadan** to talk

hargez never

harkat kardan to move

hâsel harvest; **hâsel khêz** fertile

hashara insect; **hasharât** insects; **hashara kosh** insecticide
hasht eight
hashtâd eighty
hasâs allergic
hatman (most) probably
hawâ weather; air; atmosphere; climate
hawda seventeen
hawz pool; **hawz-e awbâzi** swimming pool
haywân animal
hâzer present *time*
hazâr thousand
hazhda eighteen
hazm digestion
hêch no; nothing; **hêch chiz** nothing; **hêch jây** nowhere; **hêch kas** nobody; **hêch kodâm** none; neither; **hêch wakht** never; **hêch yak** no; none; not any
hefzolseha hygiene
helâl crescent
helikôptar helicopter
hemâyat kardan to back
Hend India
Hendi Indian; Hindi
Hendu Hindu; **dên-e Hendu** Hinduism
Hendustân India
herfa profession
herfawi professional *person*
hesâb account; **hesâb-dâr** cashier
hesâbat-e mâli finance
hesâr fence; fort
hezâr thousand
hezb party *political*
hich *see* **hêch**
hizom firewood
hodudan about; approximately; **hodudan penjâ mêl** about 50 miles
hojra bed and breakfast
hojum raid
hokômat; hokumat government; **hokômat-e motlaqa** dictatorship; **hokômat-e mardom** democracy
honar art
honarmand artist
hoquq rights; **hoquq-e bashar** human rights; **hoquq-e madani** civil rights
hôtal hotel
huma suburb
hushyâr intelligent
Hut Pisces *month/sign*

I

i this; these; they
id feast; holiday *religious*
ijâ here
imêl e-mail
imeni safety
in this; he; she; it; **in hafta** this week; **in taraf** this way
inân; inhâ these; they
Inglestân England
Inglis English *person*
Inglisi English *language*
inja; injâ here
inqadr so much/many
Irân Iran
Irâni Persian; Iranian
Isawi Christian
Isawiyat Christianity
istâd: istâd shaw! stop!; **istâd nashaw!** don't stop!
istâdan to stop; to stand
istgâh *see* **estâdgâh**
isu hereabouts
Itâlyâ Italy
Itâlawi Italian

J

jabazâr marsh
jabha front
jabira compensation
Jadi Capricorn *month/sign*
jadid new; modern

jadidan recently
jadwal list
jagra kardan to bargain
jahân world
jahâni universal
jahanom hell
jahel lake
jâkat sweater
jak-e môtar jack *of car*
jalâ dâdan to varnish
jâleb interesting
jalsa session
jali net
jama kardan to arrange; to add
jâma clothes
jâme'a community; society
jam'iyat population; **jam'iyat-e parâganda** diaspora
jân dear; loved
jan pâk towel; sanitary towels
jâneshin kardan to replace
jang war; fight; battle; contest; **jang-e dâkheli** civil war; **jang kardan** to fight; to wage war
jangal wood; forest; **jangal-e anbuh** thick forest
jang-ju fighter
jantari calendar
jânwar animal
Jenwari January
Jâpân Japan
Jâpâni Japanese
jarâh surgeon
jarâhi surgery *operation*
jaraqa zadan sparkle
jarêda journal; newspaper
jarsaqil derrick
jarima fine *of money*
Jarmani German
jâru kardan to sweep
jasad corpse
jashn gala; celebration
jashnwâra festival; **jashn-wâra-ye film** film festival; **jashnwâra-ye museqi** music festival
jâsus spy
jâsusi espionage

jaw barley
jawâb answer; **jawâb dâdan** to answer
jawân young
jawâni youth
jawâri corn; maize
jawhar ink
jawidan chew
Jawzâ Gemini *month/sign*
jây place
jâyeza prize
jâz jazz
jazâ dâdan to punish
jebha forehead
jeddi serious
jegar liver
jehâd jihad
jehat directions
jenâyat crime
jenâyat-kâr criminal
jenâza burial; funeral
jens sex *gender*
jens-e sâderâti export *noun*
jenub south *noun*
jenubi south(ern)
jerâb sock(s)
Jarmani German; Germany
jêb pocket
jodâ kardan to sort; to split
joftgiri sex *act*
jôk leech
Jom'a Friday
jamhuri republic
jomla sentence
jonub south *noun*
jonubi south(ern)
jôr kardan to repair
jôra couple; pair
jorâb sock(s); **jorâb-e zanânâ** pantyhose
jôrâyi recovery *medical*
jôshanda herbal tea
jôshidan to boil
jostoju exploration; **jostoju kardan** search
jostojo kardan seek
jowâb-e chây urine
jôy stream; gutter

joz except
Julây July
Jun June
jurâb *see* jorâb
juri health; wellbeing
jushidan to boil
jwân *see* jawân
jwâni *see* jawâni
jwâri corn; maize

K/KH

kabâb kebab
kâbena cabinet *political*
kabk partridge
kâbus mare
kabutar pigeon
kachâlu potato
kadan to do; to make
kaddu pumpkin
kaf-e zamin floor *ground*
kâfi restaurant; café, teahouse; enough; sufficient; **kâfi budan** to be enough; **Kâfi-st, tashakor!** That's enough, thanks!
kafsh shoe; **kafsh-hâ** shoes
kaftâr hyena
kaftar pigeon
kâghaz paper; **destmâl-e kâghazi** tissues; **kâghaz-e sigâret** cigarette papers; **kâghaz-e tashnâb** toilet paper; **kâghaz-parân** (paper) kite; **kâghaz parâni** bureaucracy
kâh hay; straw
kâhel lazy
kâhu lettuce
kaj sideways; crooked; twisted
kajdom scorpion
kâkâ uncle *paternal*
kâkh palace
kal bald
kala head
kâlâ clothes; **kâlâ-shôyi** laundry; washing
kalân large
kâlej college
kalema word
kalisâ church
kam little; less; **kam-o-bêsh** more or less
kamân-e rostam rainbow
kamar waist; back; **kamar dard** backache
kamarband belt
kambud shortage
kamê; kame a little
kamp camp; **kamp-e panâhendagan**, **kamp-e mohâjerin** refugee camp
kampal blanket
kâmpyutar computer; **kâmpyutar-e syâr** laptop *computer*
kâmra camera
kamtar less; **kamtar az** under
kâmyâb lucky; winner
kana tick *insect*
Kânâdâ Canada
Kânâdâyi Canadian
kânâl channel; canal; **kânâl-e teliwizyun** TV channel
kandan to dig
kândom condom
kânfarâns conference
kanfarm kardan to confirm; **Mêkhâhom parwâzam râ kanfarm konom.** I want to confirm my flight.
kansarf kardan to conserve
kânsart concert
kensel kardan to cancel
kânser cancer
kâpi copy; **kâpi kardan** to copy
kapsul-e gâz butane canister
kar deaf
kâr work; job; business; **kâr-e desti** handicraft; **kâr-e emdâdi/eyâna** charity; **kâr-e mohem** enterprise; **kâr kardan** to work; **kâr budan**

to be necessary; **kâr dâshtan** to need

karam cabbage

kârwân caravan

kârd knife; machete

kardan to do; to make

kârêz canal

kârgar worker; **kârgar estekhrâj-e têl** oil worker

kârkhâna factory

kârmand worker; **kârmand daftar** office worker; **karmand-e baynolmelali** international operator

kârmandân staff

kârt card; **kredet-kârt/kârt-e e'tebâri** credit card; **kârt-e sawâr shodan dar tayâra** boarding pass; **kârt-hoyat** I.D. card

kârta quarter *town*

kârton carton

kas person

kâsa bowl

kasâfat rubbish

kase; kasê someone

kaset cassette; **kaset-e wêdyô** video cassette

kashak elastic

kashf kardan to discover

kashedan to pull; to extract

kashish priest

kâshtan to plant; to grow; to sow

keshti ship; boat

keshtirâni kardan to sail

kata rôda large intestine

katara fence

kati with

Kâtolik Catholic

kawbây jeans

kawk partridge

kâwu lettuce

kay when

kâyel lazy

kayk flea

ke that; who

kêbal cable

kechap ketchup

kêk cake

kalach clutch *of car*

kelid; keli key

kalisâ cathedral

kelk finger

kelkak little finger

kelken window

kenâr beside *preposition*

kenâr-âb outside toilet(s)

kenâr daryâ river bank

kanesht synagogue

kerâya fare; **kerâya kardan** to hire

kerim *see* **krim**

kerm worm; **kerm-e darakht** caterpillar

kesb; kesp occupation; job; trade; profession

kashidan to pull; to extract

keshmesh raisin(s)

keshta plum

kesht farm

keshti ship; boat

keshtirâni kardan to sail

keshwar country; **keshwar-e mostaqel** independent state; **keshwar-hâ-ye moshtarak-ol-manafê** commonwealth

ketâb book; **ketâb-foroshi** bookshop; **ketâb-khâna** library; **ketâb-e râhnâma** manual; guidebook; **ketâb-e dâstân** novel; **ketâb dâstân-e Inglisi** novels in English; **ketâb-e loghât** dictionary; **ketâb-e râhnamâ** directory

ketâbcha notebook

khâyen; khâyenana treacherous

khâb dream *noun*; **khâb âlud** sleepy; **Man khâb âlud astom.** I am sleepy.

khabar; khabarâ information; news; **khabar kardan** to inform; **khabar dâshtan** to be informed.; **Polis râ khabar kon!** Call the police!

khâbidan to sleep; to go to bed

khafa angry; annoyed; **Khafa mêshawad.** She/He is choking!

kârikâtor cartoon

khâhar sister

khâk dust; land; mud

khâkandâz rubbish; dump; toilet(s) *outside*

khâkjâro rubbish; garbage

khalâs kardan to finish; to release

khâli empty; **khâli kardan** to empty; to drain

khalifa craftsman

khalta sack; bag

kham: kham shodan to bend

khâm raw

khâmôsh silent; **khâmôsh kardan** to switch off

khâmôshi silence

khân leader; chief

khâna house; building; accommodation

khanda laugh; laughter; **khanda dâr/mozhik** funny; **khanda kardan** to laugh

khândan to read; to study; reading

khânawâda family

khanjar dagger

Khânom Mrs.; Madame; wife

khar donkey

khâr thorn

kharâb bad; ruined; damaged; broken-down; evil; **kharâb kardan** to damage; **kharâb shodan** to be damaged; **Môtar-e mâ kharâb shodast.** Our car has broken down.

kharâba ruins; rubble

kharâbi destruction

kharbôza melon

kharch expenditure; costs; **kharch kardan** to spend; **Che meqdâr kharch dârad?**

charge: What is the charge?

khârej abroad; **khârej az shâr/dêh** countryside

khâreji foreign; foreigner

khâresh itch

khar-gôsh rabbit

kharidan to buy

khâridan to itch

kharidâri kardan to buy

kharid-kardan shopping

kharita sack; bag; **kharita-ye khâb** sleeping bag

kharj *see* kharch

kherman harvest

khashan rude

khashamgin angry

khasta bodan to tire

khasta tired; nut; stone *of fruit*

khastagi tiredness

khastagi-âwar tiring

khâstan to want; to wish

khat line; letter; writing; **khat kash** ruler *measure*; **khat-e rêl** railway; **Khat mashghul ast.** The line is busy.

khatar danger; **khatar kardan** to risk

khatarnâk dangerous

khatna circumcision

khaw sleep; **khaw didan** to dream

khay so; then

khayma tent

khayr good; well; so; then

khayriya charity; **mo'asesa-ye khayriya** charity *organization*

khayât tailor; dressmaker

khazân autumn/fall

khazâna treasury

khazâna-dâr treasurer

khedmat service; **khedamat-e otâq** room service

khêl clan

khelâl-dandân toothpick

khers bear

khêshâ relationship; alliance

khêshâwand relative

khesht brick *noun*

kheshti brick *adjective*
khêstan to get up; to rise
khêstândan to wake up
khêz zadan to leap
khiyâbân street
khô; khob *see* khub
khô; khôy perspiration
khod own *adjective*
Khodâ God; Khodâ hâfez! good-bye!
khodam myself
khodesh himself; herself; itself
khodat yourself
khodâwand lord
khodeshân themselves
khodetân yourselves
khod-kâr; khod-rang pen; biro
khonok cool; cold
khonsâ kardan to undo; khonsâ-kardan-e bam bomb disposal
khorâk meal; snack; khorâk-hâ meals
khorâs rooster
khorâsak whooping-cough
khord little; small; khord kardan to chop; to grind
khôrdan to eat; to swallow
khordtar smaller
khoruj exit; departures; khoruj-e ezterâri emergency exit
khorus rooster
khosh happy; nice; khosh hâl happy; khosh kardan to prefer; khosh âmadêd! welcome!; khosh dâshtan to like
khoshi happiness
khoshk dry; barren; khoshk kardan to dry
khoshunat violence
khosusan especially
khub good; well
khuk pig; boar
khun blood; khun dadan blood transfusion

khun-rêzi bleeding; hemorrhage
khwâb sleep
khwâr; khwâhar sister
khyâl opinion
khyânat kardan to betray
ki who?
kilô; kilôgerâm kilogram
kilômeter kilometer
kêno orange
klâb club
klenik clinic
kô mountain
kôch kardan to move home
kocha street
kochak little; small
kochaktar smaller
kochalak uvula
kôd code; kôd-e baynolmelali international code; kôd-e telifuni-ye Kâbol dialing code for Kabul
kodak child
kodakân children
kodâm? which?; kodâmâ which *plural*; kodâm jây anywhere; somewhere; where
kôft ache
kôfta ground meat; mince
kôh mountain
kôhna old; stale
kojâ? where?; kojâ-st? where is?
kok khordan to stitch *surgical*
kolâh hat; kolâh-e pik cup
kolang pickax
kolcha cake
kolarâ cholera
kolâ hat *fur*
kol-e all; every
koltur culture
komak aid; help; komak, komak! help!; komak kardan to help; komak-e awaliya first aid; komak-e ensâni humanitarian aid
kambâyn combine harvester
konj corner
kontenar container *freight*

kantrol control; **kantrol kardan** to control; **kantrol-e nufus** birth control
konyak cognac
kôr blind
korâb-e zanânâ tights; pantyhose
korsi chair; heel; (political) seat
korti coat
kôshesh kardan to try
koshtan to kill
kôt coat; **kôt-band** clothes hanger
kôta cabin; hut
kotâch low
kôtal mountain pass
kotekh tampon
kôza jug; jar
krên crane *machine*
Kresmes Christmas
krim cream; **krim-e rish** shaving cream; **krim-dandân** toothpaste
ku where
kubidan ram
kuchi nomad
kud fertilizer
kudatâ coup d'etat
kuh *see* **kôh**
kulâk blizzard
kur blind
kushesh kardan struggle
kutâ; kutâh short
kolâli pottery

L

lab lip; **lab serin** lipstick
laba edge
labaniyât dairy
laborâtwâr laboratory
lagâm bridle
lagâmak chaps *medical*
lagan basin; **lagan-e khâsera** pelvis
lâghar thin
laghzesh-e zamin landslide
laghzidan to slip
lahja dialect
lahza moment
lâjward lapislazuli
lâken but
lampa lamp
lang lame
langar-gah dock
lâri lorry; truck
larza; larzesh shiver
lashem smooth
lashkar army
lâya têl oil spill
lâyeq able; capable; worthy
layla hostel
lâysens driver's license
lâzem necessary; **lâzem ast** it's necessary
lebâs clothes; **lebâs pushidan** to put on clothes; **lebâs shôyi** laundry; **lebâs-e awbâzi** swimsuit
left lift; elevator
lehâf blanket; duvet; sheet
lehâz consideration
lekchar lecture
lêmu lime; lemon
lenz lens; **lenz chashm** contact lenses
lesân-e alâmat sign language
lêtar liter; lighter; **Segrêt-lêtar dârêd?** Do you have a light?
lezat pleasure
list list
loch naked
lochak swindler
loghat word
loj-e saltanati podium
lokomotiv locomotive
lola hose
longi turban
lotfan! please!
lubyâ bean(s)
lula pipe; tube
lyâz consideration

mawâd-e sukht fuel

mawj wave; **mawj-e garmi** heatwave

mawjud existing

mawlawi religious scholar

mawzu subject

May May

mâyân ourselves

mayda kardan to get change *money*; to powder

maydân field; ground; square; **maydan-e futbâl** football pitch; **maydân-e hawâyi** airport; **maydân-e têl** oil-field; **maydân-e mayn** minefield

mayhan homeland

mâyl mile

mayn mine *explosive*

mayub disabled

maza flavor; taste; snack; **maza kardan** to taste

mazadâr tasty

mazâq joke

mazaqi humorous

maz-hab sect; religion

mazreya farm

mêbakhshêd! excuse me!

mêda stomach; outbreak *skin*

meqnâtisi magnetic

meh fog; mist; **meh âlud** foggy

mêhmân guest; visitor; **mêhmân khâna** guesthouse

mêhmâni party

mêhrabân kind

mêhrabâni kindness; **mêhrabâni kardan** to be kind

mêhtar-e asb (horse) groom; syce

mêkhânik mechanic

mêkh nail *metal*

mêkhak corn *medical*

mêl mile

mêla kardan camping

melal nations

melat nation *people*

meli national

meliyat nationality

melyun million

me'mâr architect

mênyu menu

meqdâr amount; **meqdâr-e kam** a little bit

mergi epilepsy

Mêrman Mrs.; Madame

mes copper

mesâl example

mesl-e like; **mesl-e (az) i** like this; **mesl-e (az) u** like that

mestari garage-owner; mechanic

meswâk toothpick

mêtar meter

mêwa fruit; **mêwa hay haray** citrus; **mêwa-ye khoshk** nut

mêz table; desk; **mêz-e pazirâyi** reception desk; **mêz-o-chawki** furniture

mêzân level; **mêzân-ol-harâra** thermometer

Mêzân Libra *month/sign*

mêzbân host

mikrob-hâ germs

milyun million

mitar meter

miyân middle

mo hair; **mo khoshkun** hairdryer

mo'adab polite

mo'alef composer; compiler

mo'alem teacher

mo'âmela business; enterprise

mo'arefi kardan introduce

mo'âser contemporary

mo'âsh pay

mo'asesa institute

mo'âwen-e ra'is jamhur vice-president

mo'âyena kardan to examine

mo'azerat mêkhahom! sorry!

mobârak blessed

mobâyl mobile phone

moch wrist

mod fashion

modern modern

modir administrator; manager

mofid useful

moft free *of charge*

mohâfezat protection; mohâfezat kardan to protect

mohâjer migrant; refugee

mohâjerat migration; flight

mohâjerin migrants; refugees

mohandes architect; engineer

mohawata campus

mohem important; mohem nêst! It doesn't matter!

mohr stamp *official*

mohreqa typhoid

mohtamal probable; mohtamal ast it is probable

Mojâhed Mojahed

Mojâhedin Mojahedin

mojala magazine

mojarad single

mojasema statue

mojâwerat nearby

mo'jeza miracle

mokâlema conversation

mokhâberât telecommunications

mokhâlefat opposition; protest; mokhâlefat kardan to protest; to oppose

mokhtalef different

mokhtarê inventor

molâ mullah

molâqât meeting; molâqât kardan to meet; to visit

molki civilian

moli radish

momken maybe; perhaps; possible

monâfeq hypocrite

monâr minaret

monâseb suitable; acceptable

monfajer shodan to explode

moqâbel(-e) opposite

moqâyesa: dar moqâyesa bâ than; moqâyesa kardan to compare

morâqeb budan to watch

morâqebat care; morâqebat sehi healthcare

morch pepper

morda dead

mordâb swamp; marsh

môrdan to die

mordâri rubbish

môreqa typhus

morgh chicken

morghâbi duck

mortajê reactionary

morwârid pearl

moryâna-khorda rust

mosâbeqa match; mosâbeqa-ye futbâl soccer match; mosâbeqa-ye zehni quiz

mosâbeqât = *plural of* mosâbeqa

mosâfer passenger; traveler

mosâferat travel *noun*

mosâheba interview

mosâken painkiller; mosâken-hâ painkillers

Mosalmân Muslim

moshâheda survey; moshâheda kardan to survey

moshâhedagar surveyor

moshâwer consultant

moshkel difficult; problem; trouble; moshkel nêst! no problem!

mosibat disaster

Mosolmân Muslim

mostaqel independent

mostaqim direct; straight

mostaqiman directly

mota'alem student

mota'asefam! I'm sorry!

motâbeq-e according to

mo'tâd drug addict

motaham kardan to accuse

motahed kardan to unify

motaleya kardan to study

môtar car; motor; môtar-e ghezâ khori dining car; môtar-e khâb sleeping car

motâreka truce
môtarsaykel motorbike
môtarwân driver; chauffeur
motâsefâna unfortunately
motakhases specialist; motakhases-e zerâyat agronomist
motawaset average *adjective*
motlaqan absolutely
motmayen sure *adjective*
motmayenan sure *adverb*
motmayin certain
mowâfeq okay; in agreement
mowâfeqa kardan to agree
mowâzeb careful; mowâzeb bâsh! careful!
mowâzebat care
moy hair
moza boots
mozâhera demonstration *political*
mozakar male
mozâkera konenda negotiator
mozâkerât-e solh peace talks
mezâyl missile
mozik music
mozd pay; wage
mozdur laborer; mercenary
mozer harmful
mozhik funny
mrastun orphanage
mu'alef composer; compiler
mu'azebat kardan to maintain
muqâbel front *noun*
muriyâna termite
museqi music; museqi-ye klâsik classical music; museqi-ye mahali folk music
mush mouse; rat; mush khormâ ferret
musht fist
muy hair
mozyam museum
mwalem teacher
myâna-ye; myânê between

N

na not; na khayr! no!
nâ-binâ blind
nâbud kardan to destroy
nâ-chandân hardly
nâdân fool *noun*
nâdâr poor
nâ-drost false
nâf navel
nafar individual; person
nafas breath
nafas-tangi asthma
nâf-raftagi hernia *umbilical*
nâgahân suddenly
nehâdan to lay
nâheya district
nahr stream
nahwa syntax
najâr carpenter
nâ-jôr unwell
nâ-juri ill health; nâ-juri mâhâna menstruation; period
nâk pear
nâkâmi failure; weakness
nakh thread
nâkhon; nâkhun nail *of body*; nâkhon gir nail clippers
nakhot; nakhod chickpea(s)
nal pipe; tap/faucet
nâldawân plumber
na'l-e asb horse show
nâlesh moan; nâlesh kardan to groan
nâm name; noun; nâm-e fâmeli; nâm-e khânawâdagi surname; Nâm-e shomâ chist? What is your name?; Nâm-e man Fered hast. name: My name is Fred.
namak salt
namakin salty
namâyenda representative
namâyendagi representation; namâyendagi kardan to represent
namâyesh play; performance;

show; **namâyesh dâdan** to exhibit

namâyeshgâh exhibition

namâz prayer

nâm-bây baker

nâ-momken impossible

namudan to show; to do

namuna model; example

nân bread; food; meal; **nân-e chasht** lunch; **nân-shaw** dinner; supper; **nân-e sorkh karda/bereshta** toast *bread*

nânwây; nânbay baker

nânwâyi bakery

nâ-pâk dirty

naqâsh er

naqâshi ing

naqsha map; plan; **naqsha-ye râh** road map; **naqsha-ye shâr** city map; **naqsha-ye Kâbol** map of Kabul

nârâhat uncomfortable; **Kojây shoma nârâhat ast?** Where does it hurt?

nâ-râzi unhappy

nârenj orange

narenji orange *color*

narm soft

nars nurse

nasaza goftan to swear; to curse

nashrât-e râdyôyi radio broadcast

nâ-shenâs unknown

nâsher publisher

nasihat advice

naswâr snuff

naswâri brown

nasyât advice

nâ-tawân disabled

nâ-tawâni failure

natija result; **Natija-ye mosabeqa chi-st?** What's the score?

naw new

nawad ninety

nâ-wakht late

nawâkhtan to play *a musical instrument*

nawâsa grandchild

nâwel novel

naweshta writing; inscription; **naweshta kardan** to write

naweshtan to write; **In râ chetor mênawisêd?** How do you spell it?

nawisenda writer

Nawrôz New Year's Day

nay reed; flute; **nay shakar** sugar cane

nazar sight; view; idea

nazariya theory

nâ-zây sterile; barren

nazd-e close to; with; **Kitâbam nazd-e Ahmad ast.** Ahmad has my book.

nazdik close; **nazdik-e** close to

nazdiki nearby

nâzer observer

nazm order *noun*

nâzok thin; delicate

nê no; not

nafrat dâshtan to hate

negâ dâshtan to keep; to hold

negâ kardan to keep; to watch; to supervise

negahbân guard; **negahbân-e sarhadi** border guard; **negahban-e asb** horse groom

negahbâni kardan to guard

nêgarân worried; **nêgarân budan** to be worried

negres sciatica

nejât dâdan to save; to rescue

nekâh marriage

nektây (neck) tie

narkh cost; price

nêru force; **qowâ-ye hawâyi** air force; **sepâh-e hâfez-e solh** peace-keeping troops; **nêru-hâ-ye eshghâl gar** occupying forces

nês injection

nesbat be than

nesf half; **nesf kardan** to halve
nesf-e shab midnight
nêsh sting *noun*
neshân mark; symbol; **neshân dâdan** to show
neshâni address
neshastan to sit; to land *an airplane*
nêshtar lancet
nezâ contest; dispute
nezâmi military *adjective*
nim half
niru *see* **nêru**
nish zadan to sting; to bite
niyâz dâshtan to need
noh nine
nôkar servant
nokhost first
nokhs inconvenient; harmful; **nokhs kardan** to be harmful
nokhsan inconvenient; harmful; toxic
nôl beak
nomâyesh show *noun*
nomra number
noqra silver
noqs inconvenient
nôsh kardan to drink
noskha copy; receipt; recipe; formula; prescription *medical*
Nowambar November
nozda nineteen
nufus population
nur light; **nur sanj** light meter
nushidan to drink
nushidani drink

O/Ô

o and
ô he/she/it; him/her/it
oftâdan to fall
ofunat infection
ojâq stove
olum science
oloswâli district

orband ceasefire; truce
ordu army
omêd hope
omor age
omuman generally
omumi general; public
ôna there is/are
onja there
operâ opera
oqâb eagle
ordu military
ordugâh camp; campsite
Ôrôpâ; Ôrupâ Europe
Ôrôpâyi; Ôrupâyi European
ostâd; ostâz teacher
ostoghân; ostokhân bone; **ostokhân-e rân** femur
otâq room; **otâq-e amaliyât/ jarâhi** operating theater; **otâq-e khaw** bedroom; **otâq-e mashwerat** conference room; **otâq-e nân** dining room; **otâq-e yak nafara** single room; **otâq-e do nafara** double room
oto(r) like that
ozor forgiveness; **ozor khâstan** to beg pardon
ozw member; **ozw-e tanasol** genitals

P

pâ leg; foot
pâyin down; below; **pâyin raftan** to sink
padar father; **padar kalân** grandfather; **padar-mâdar** parents
pahlawâni wrestling
pahlu(-ye) beside; along
pahn wide; **pahn kardan** to spread
pâk clean; pure; **pâk kardan** to clean; to clear up
paka fan

pâkat; pâkat-e khat envelope
Pâkestân Pakistan
Pâkestâni Pakistani
pakhsh kardan to publish
pakhta cotton
pâki hygiene; razor (blade)
pakôl hat *Nuristani*
palag plug *electric*
pâlak spinach
palaster plaster; Band-Aid
palâstik plastic
palaw pilaf/pilau rice
pâlidan to look for
palpot camouflage
pal-rish razor
pâlu-ba-pâlu side by side
pâlu-ye *see* pahlu
pamp pump; **pamp kardan** to pump
panâ bordan to flee
panâhenda refugee; **panâhendagân** refugees
panâh-gâh shelter; harbor
panchar puncture; flat tire
panêr cheese
panj five
panja fork; **panja-ye pâ** toe
panjâ fifty
panjara window
Panjshambê Thursday
pânzda fifteen
par feather
pâra kardan to tear
parâganda kardan to scatter
parenda bird
parâshot parachute
parastâr nurse
parcha-ye qondaq diaper
parda curtain
pardâkht payment
pardâkhtan to pay
pare-rôz the day before yesterday
parêzâna diet
pârk park; **pârk kardan** to park

pârking-e môtar car park
pârlemân parliament
pâr-sâl last year
pârsal parcel
partâb kardan to throw
pârtizân guerrilla
partâftan to throw
pâru shovel
parwâ worry; **parwâ nadâra!** it doesn't matter!
parwâna butterfly
parwâz flight; **parwâz-e baynolmelali** international flight; **parwâz-e enteqâli** flight transfer; **Parwâz kensel shodast.** The plane is cancelled.; **parwâz kardan** to fly
pas behind; again; **pas-e** after; **pas az (ân ke)** after; **pas dâdan** to restore; **pas kardan** to clear; to remove; **pas raftan** to withdraw; **pas âmadan** to return;
pas(ân) then; **pasân (tar)...** after which...
pasandâz kardan save *money*
pasântar later
pas-fardâ the day after tomorrow
pasha mosquito
pashakhâna mosquito net
pashm wool
pashmi woolen
Pashtô Pashto *language*
Pashtun Pashtoon *person*
pâsport passport
patlun trousers
patu men's scarf
pawder *see* podar
pawnd pound
pây foot; leg
pâyân down; end; **pâyân dâdan** to end
pêch-kash; pêch-taw screwdriver
paydâ kardan to find
pâyetakht capital *city*

pây-gâh base
payghâm message
payghâmbar prophet
pâyidan to stay
pâyin down; **pâyin kardan** to lower; **pâyin shodan** to descend
paykâr battle; combat
paynj five
Paynjshambê Thursday
pâyp pipe *smoking*
paysa money; currency
pâytakht capital city
pêch screw
pêchkâri syringe
pêch-kash; pêch-taw screwdriver
Pêghla Miss
pelâg; palâk plug *electric*
pêlat pilot
peng pin
penhân shodan to hide
penjâ fifty
pensel pencil
pensilin penicillin
per; pêr *see* pir
pêrâhân shirt; **pêrâhân-o tombân** traditional dress
pêrôz winner
pêrôzi success; victory
pesar son; boy
pêsh front; forward(s); **pêsh-e** by; at **pêsh az** before; **pêsh-e ruy-e** in front of; **pêsh az (ân ke)...** before...; **yek sâl pêsh** a year ago
pêsha occupation; profession
peshak cat
pêshâni forehead
pêshqâb plate
pêshtar early; previously
pesta pistachio
peyâda raw footpath
pilul pill
pir old; old man; elder; spiritual leader
pirâhan shirt
pitsa pizza

piyâno piano
podar powder; **podar-e kâla-shôyi** washing powder
pôhând professor
pôhanzay faculty
pôhantun university
pokhta cooked; mature; ripe; **pokhta kardan** to cook
pokhtan to cook
pol bridge
poli sodium bicarbonate
pôlis police; policeman; **pôlis-e makhfi** secret police; **pôlis-e tarâfik** traffic police
pomba cotton
pondidagi swelling *medical*
por full; **por kardan** to fill
porsân kardan to ask for
porsidan to question
porza forôshi spare parts store
pôshândan to dress
pôshidan to get dressed
posht back; **posht-e** behind; after
poshti pillow
post mail; post; seat *political*; **post-e hawâyi** air mail; **post-e râjistar** registered mail
pôst skin
posta (postage) stamp
pôsta-khâna post office
post-baks postbox; mailbox
postkârd postcard
pot hidden; **pot shodan** to hide
prêktes practise; **prêktes kardan** to practice
profaysar professor
progrâm program; **progrâm-e râdyôyi** radio program; **progrâm-e kâmpyutari** computer program
projektor projector
pul money; **pul-e syâh** change; coins
puldâr rich
pura complete; exactly; accurately

pushândan to wrap
pushidan: jâma/lebâs pushidan to get dressed; to wear
peyâla; pyâla cup
pyâz onion

Q

qâbel competent; Âyâ in sarak qâbel-e gozar kardan ast? Is the road passable?
qâbela nurse; midwife
qâbel-e worthy of
qablan previously
qaborgha rib
qaber grave; tomb
qabrestân cemetery
qabul kardan to accept
qabz constipation
qâchâq-bar smuggler
qad size
qadifa towel
qadim(i) ancient; antique
qafas cage
qâghaz paper
qâhr shodan to get angry
qahrumân hero
qahwa coffee
qal'a; qalâ fort
qalam pen
qalamro territory
qalb heart
qâlen carpet *knotted*
qâm qortak larynx
qamar masnoye satellite
qamari lunar
qand sugar lump
qânun law; qânun-e asâsi constitution
qânuni legal
qarâr-dâd contract; agreement
qarârgâh headquarters
qarn century
qarya village
qarz debt; qarz dâdan to lend

qarz gereftan to borrow
qasam khordan to swear *oath*
qasar castle; palace
qasd dâshtan to intend
qashang beautiful
qâshoq; qâshog spoon; qâshoq-e chây khori tea-spoon
qasâb butcher
qat'a shodan to be cut off
qatâr train; queue; row; line
qâtel killer
qâter mule
qatl murder; qatl-e âm genocide; qatl kardan to kill
qatra-chakân dropper
qâwa *see* qahwa
qawi strong
qawm clan
qawmi (blood) relationship
Qaws Sagittarius *month/sign*
qaychi scissors
qâyeq boat
qaymâq cream
qâz goose
qâzi judge
qemâr khâna casino
qêmat cost
qertâsya forôshi stationer's
qesem; qesm kind; sort; type
qesmat part; section
qêmat price; expensive; Qêmat-e in cheqadar ast? cost: How much does this cost?
qeyâm *see* qyâm
qodrat power
qodrat strength
qofl lock; padlock; qofl-e darwâza door lock; qofl kardan to lock
qola summit
qolâb hook *noun*
qolba kardan to plow
qolf *see* qofl
qola peak
qomândân commander

qondâq nappy; diaper

qonsulgari consulate

Qorân Koran

qorbâni victim; **qorbâniyân** victims

qorma stew

qorut hard cheese

qotb namâ compass

quti can; canister; **quti-ye têl** oilcan

qyâm kardan to rise

R

râbar rubber

râbeta relationship

rabudan to kidnap; to hijack; kidnapping; hijacking

ra'd thunder; **ra'd-o barq** lightning

rad kardan to veto

râdâr radar

radif row; line

râdyô radio

râdyôgrâfi radiography

rafiq companion; friend

raftan to go

rag vein

râgbi rugby

râh road; street; way; path; route; **râh-dâri** road-block

rehâ kardan to release

râhat: râhat budan to be comfortable; **Korsi râhat ast.** The seat is comfortable.

râhbar guide; leader

râhbari kardan to lead

râhnâma guidebook; **râhnâ-mayi kardan** to guide

ra'is chief; head; boss; **ra'is-e dawlat** head of state; **ra'is-e jamhur** president

râjê-ba about; regarding

râkêt missile

Ramazân Ramadan

rân thigh

rânanda driver

rândan to drive

rang color; ink; paint; **rang parida** pale; **rang kardan** to paint

rangin kamân rainbow

rangmâl painter; decorator

rangmâli painting; decorating

râpôrchi spy

raqâbat competition

raqam kind; sort; type

raqs; raqsidan dance; dancing; **raqs-e mahali** folk dancing

ras exact; precise

rasândan to send; to supply

rasid receipt

rasida ripe

rasidan to arrive; to reach

rasâmi painter

rasm custom; tradition; painting; drawing; **rasm kardan** to draw

rasm-e baynolmelali international code

rasmi official *adjective*

rasm-o rawâj customs; habits

râst right; true; correct; direct; straight

râsta right way up

râsti? really?

rasturân restaurant

rasul prophet

rawâ permitted

rawâbet-e diplomâtik diplomatic ties

rawâj tradition

rawâsh rhubarb

ra'y vote; **ra'y dâdan** to vote

râyegân free *of charge*

râz secret *noun*

râzi satisfied

rêg sand; gravel

rêgistan desert

reham womb

rêkhtan to pour; to spill

rench spanner; wrench

rezarf reservation *ticket*

reshta range
rêsmân; rêspân rope; thread; **rêsmân-e yadak keshi** tow rope
restôran restaurant
rêwars reverse
rezâyat bakhsh satisfactory
rêzesh cold *medical*
rezhim regime; **rezhim gereftan** to diet
rimal mascara
rish beard; wound; **rish safêd** elder; **rish safêdân** elders
riyâzyât mathematics
rôbâ fox
robâyenda kidnapper; hijacker
rôd river
rôda intestine(s)
rôghan cooking oil; fat; ghee; **rôghan-e nabâti** vegetable oil
rôghan-dân saucepan
rojây sheets
rokhsat(i) holiday; vacation
româtizom rheumatism
rôshan light; bright; **rôshan kardan** to switch on; to light up; **rôshan sâkhtan** lighting
rôshan-feker intellectual
rôshani light; brightness
roshd development; **roshd kardan** to grow; to develop
rosum-e mahali folklore; local customs
royâ dream *noun*
rôypâk napkin; serviette; towel
rôz day; **rôz-o-shaw** day and night; **rôz-e tawalod** birthday
rôza fast; fasting; **rôza gereftan** to fast
rôzâna daily
rôz-nâma newspaper; journal
ru *see* ruy
ru-ba-ru straight on
ruh soul
ru-mêzi tablecloth
Rus Russia; Russian *person*

Rusi Russian
Rusiya Russia
rustâ village
ruy face; **ruy gereftan** to put on a veil
ruypâk napkin; serviette; towel
ruz *see* rôz

S/SH

sâ'at hour; watch; clock; **Sâ'at shesh ast.** It is six o'clock.
sabad basket
sabâh tomorrow
saber; sabr patience; **saber kardan** to wait
sâbet kardan to prove
sabt kardan to record; to score
sâbun soap
sabz green
sabza grass
sabzi cooking vegetables; greens; spinach; **sabzi forôshi** greengrocer's shop; **sabzi khôr** vegetarian
sabzijât vegetables
sad hundred; dam
sadâ noise; sound; voice; **sadâ kardan** to call
sâda plain; simple
sadaf shell *snail/sea*
sâder kardan to export
sadr-e a'zam prime minister; premier
sâf clear; light; pure
safa page
safar kardan to travel; **safar ba khayr!** bon voyage!
safêd white
sâfi rag
safir ambassador
sag dog; **sag-e gala** sheepdog; **bêmâri-ye sag-e dêwâna** rabies
sâheb owner

Sâheb Mr.

sâhel shore; coast

sahib fair; just

sahih correct; exact; **sahih kardan** to correct

sahm share

sahrâ desert

sajda prostration

sâjeq chewing gum

sâken shodan to dwell

sâket silent; *electric* socket

sakhra rock; cliff

sakht hard

sâkhtagi counterfeit

sâkhtan to make; to build; to manufacture

sâkht-e... made in...

sâkhtomân building; structure

sâl year; **sâl-e kabisa** leap year

salâd salad

salâh weapon

salâm alêkom hello!; *to which the response is* **wâlêkom asalâm**

salâm! hello!

salâmat health; security

salâmati health; **salâmati!** cheers!

sâlâna annual

salâta salad

sâlem healthy

salib-e sorkh Red Cross

salmâni barber; hairdresser; beauty salon

sâlon-e museqi concert hall

saltanat reign *noun*

saltanati royal

sâmân supply

samâroq mushroom

samâwâr; samâwât samovar

Sambola Virgo *month/sign*

sanad document

san'at industry; craft

sandali brazier

sandewich sandwich

sanduq chest; box; boot/trunk *of car*

sâneha accident

sang stone; stone

sangchel pebble

sangi (of) stone

sangin heavy

sânti centimeter

sânya second *of time*

saqaw water carrier

saqf roof

sar head; **sar dard** headache; **sar push** hood/bonnet *of car*; **sar az** from; **sar az i/u ham** however

sar' epilepsy

sarak road; street; route; **sarak-e yak tarafa** one-way street

sarâshêbi slope

Saratân Cancer *month/sign*

sarây warehouse

sarâyat contagion

sar-bâz kon corkscrew; bottle-opener; can-opener

sarchapa reverse

sar-charkhak dizziness

sard cold

sardardi bâd az sharâb noshi hangover

sarf kardan to spend

sarf-o nahw grammar

sar-gozasht biography

sarhad border; frontier

sâri contagious

sari' rapid; express

sari'an rapidly

sarmâ khordagi cold *noun*

sarmâ gazidagi frostbite

sarmâya capital *financial*

sarosadâ noise

sarshenâs well-known

sarwês bus; coach; service

sâsej sausage

sash six

sât hour; time; watch; clock

satel bucket

sath-e hamwar plane; **sath-e zamin** floor *ground*

satilâyt satellite

satl bucket

sât-têri amusement; entertainment

sawâl question; **sawâl kardan** to ask

sawâr shodan to ride *a horse*

sawdâ kharidan to go shopping

Sawr Taurus *month/sign*

say kardan to look

sâya shade

sayl/sayr kardan to admire

sâynsdân scientist

Sâzmân-e Melal-e Motahed United Nations

sâzmân-e khayriya charity *organization*

sê three; **sê bâr** three times; **sê paw** three-quarters

sêb apple

sebqat kardan to overtake

sefârat embassy

sefâresh dâdan to order *verb, someone*

sefer zero

saqel indigestible

segrêt cigarette(s); **segrêt kashedan** smoking; **segrêt kashedan mana' ast** no smoking

sehât health

seka-hâ coins

sel tuberculosis; **sel-e ostokhân** tuberculosis of the bones

sêl mountain stream; flood

selâh weapon

selsela range; series

sen age

senf class

senjâq pin

senjed wild olive

sepâh troops

Septâmbar September

seql indigestible

ser secret

sêr garlic; **sêr budan** to be full up; **Man sêr astom!** I am full up!

serka vinegar

seri secret *adjective*

serwatmand rich

seryâl series

Sêshambê Tuesday

setâra star

sêwom third

sêzda thirteen

shâyer poet

shab evening; night; **shab ba khayr!** good night!

shabâna night: at night

shabânarôz night and day

shabê like; similar; **shabê budan** to be similar

shâdi monkey

shadid intense; severe

shafâ dâdan to heal

shafâ-khâna hospital; clinic

shaftâlu peach

shâgerd pupil; student

Shâghâlay Mr.

shâh king

shâhed witness

shahid martyr

shâh-parak butterfly

shahr *see* **shâr**

shahrâh motorway; highway

shâh-rag artery; jugular vein

shârwand citizen

shak doubt

shâk shock; **shâk-e barqi** electric shock

shakar sugar

shakhm kardan/zadan to plow

shakhs character; person

Shakhs-e Âwâra Displaced Person

shakhsi civilian; personal

shakl form; shape

shâl shawl

shalgham turnip

shâm evening

sham'a candle; **sham'a dân** candlestick; **sham'a-hâ** candles

shamâl north *noun*

shamâli north(ern) *adjective*

Shambê Saturday

shâmel element; **shâmel shoda** included; **shâmel budan** to contain

shampâyn champagne

shâmpu shampoo

shamsi solar

shâna comb; shoulder

shândan to fix

shânzda sixteen

shâr town; city; **shârwâli** town/city hall

sharâb wine

sharbat syrup

sharik shodan to share

sharm shame

sharmida ashamed

sharq east *noun*

Sharq-e Myâna the Middle East

sharqi east(ern) *adjective*

shart condition; term

shârwâl mayor

shârwâli municipality

shash six

shâsha urine

shashom sixth

shast sixty; thumb

shatranj chess

shaw night; evening

shawaki; shawâna in the evening; at night

shawhar husband

shay material

shâyad perhaps

shayâr kardan to plow

shaykh spiritual leader

shaytân devil

shekam stomach; **shekam dard** stomachache

shekam-dâr pregnant

shekanja torture; **shekanja kardan** to torture

shekârchi-ye ghayr-e qânuni poacher

shekâr-e ghayr-e qânuni poaching *animals/game*

shekast defeat

shekastan to break; to fracture

shekâyat complaint; **shekâyat kardan** complain

shekastagi fracture

shekastan; shekastândan to break

shenâ kardan to swim

shenâkhta: **shenâkhta nashoda** unknown; **shenâkhta shoda** well-known

shenâkhtan to recognize

shenâsâyi identification

shenâwar diver; **shenâwar budan** to float

shenidan to hear

shepesh lice

shêr lion

she'r poem; poetry

shêrkat: **shêrkat-e hawâyi** airline; **shêrkat kardan** participate

sheshtan to live (in); to dwell; to sit

shêb slope

sênamâ cinema

shêrdân tap/faucet

shir milk

shir-brenj rice pudding

shir-dâr breast-feeding woman

shirin sweet

shirini candy; sweets; **shirini-e bâd az nân** dessert

shir-yakh sorbet; ice-cream

shisha glass *substance*

shodan to become

shoghol business

shohadâ martyrs

shojâ brave

shôkh humorous

shokhi joke

shokor guzâr grateful; **Shokor guzârom.** I am grateful.

sho'la; shôla flame

shomâ you *polite/plural*

shomâra number; **shomâra-ye otâq** room number; **shomâra-ye pâsport** passport number

shomordan to count

shonidan to hear; to listen

shôr salty; saline

shôrâ assembly

shorbâ soup

shorô kardan to begin

shorwâ soup

shosh lung

shostan to wash

shotor camel

shotorwân camel driver

shôrâ council

shoy husband

shoy-dâr married *said by a woman*

shukhi humor

shurâ council

shurawi soviet

si thirty

sim wire; cable; string

sambôl symbol

sim-e khârdâr barbed wire

sina chest; breast(s)

sina-o-baghal pneumonia

sistam system

siyâh black

siyâsat politics; **siyâsat madâr** politician

siyâsi political

sizda thirteen

ski zadan to ski

sôb; sobh morning; a.m.; **sobh-dam** dawn; **sobh ba khayr!** good morning!

sôbaki in the morning

sôbat conversation

sobok light *not heavy*

sobut proof

sohbat conversation

sokhanrân-e dawat shoda guest speaker

sokhansara speaker

sôkhtan; sôkhtândan to burn

solh peace; truce

soltân sultan

somb hoof

sonat circumcision

son-e toward(s)

soqut kardan to crash

sor'at speed

sorfa cough; **sorfa kardan** to cough

sorkh red

sorkhakân measles

sorudan to sing

sost weak

sotun-e foqarât spine; spinal column

sôy-e; son-e in the direction of

sôzan needle

sôzesh burn *noun*

stêk steak

stun-e foqarât spine; spinal column

su direction

su'-e hâzema indigestion

sud interest *financial*

sup soup

suparmârkêt supermarket; department store

surâkh hole

surat face; **surat hesâb** bill/check; **dar surati** in case

surma mascara

susmâr lizard

suzan needle

suzândan burn

swâr shodan to ride *a horse*

swich switch *electric*

syâ sorfa diphtheria

syâh black

T

tâ at; to; bottom; thing; unity; **tâ ba; tâ jây-ê ke; tâ inka** until

ta'ahod obligation; **ta'ahod kardan** to undertake

tab fever

tâb khordan swing

tab'a citizen

tabaqa floor; story

tabar ax

tabâshir chalk

tabdil change; **tabdil kardan** to exchange

tâbe'iyat citizenship

tâbestân summer

tabiyat nature; nationality

tabiyi normal

tabl drum

tâblêt tablet

tâblo picture

tabsera review *newspaper*

tafakor thought

tahâjom invasion

tahe bottom

tahqiq investigation; research; inquiry; **tahqiq kardan** to investigate; to research

tahsilât education

tahwil dâdan to hand over

tahwil-dâr warehouseman

tahwil-khâna store; warehouse

tajâwoz kardan rape

tâjer businessman/woman

tak single

tâk vine

takân shock *medical*; **takân dâdan** to shake

takhasosi technical

ta'khir delay

takhmin konenda surveyor

takhnik technique

takht: **takht-e khâb** bed; **takht-e shâhi** throne

takhta plank; board; blackboard; splint

teks tax *noun*

taksi taxi

takya kardan to lean

talab kardan seek

talafoz pronunciation; **talafoz kardan** to pronounce

talak trap; **talak-e enfejâri** booby trap

talâq divorce

talkh bitter; spicy

talkhân dried mulberries

tamâm whole; **tamâm-e** all; every; **tamâm kardan** to finish; to run out

tamâman completely

tamâs gereftan to contact; **Man mêkhâhom bâ sefârat-am tamâs bogirom.** I want to contact my embassy.

tambâku tobacco

tâmir building

tamjid kardan to praise

tamrin kardan to exercise

tan body; ton; tonne

tâna border post

tanâb rope

tasâdom accident

tanbal lazy

tan-ba-tan hand to hand

tandur oven

tânestan to be able (to)

tang tight; narrow

tangi mountain pass

tanhâ only; alone

tânk tank; **tânk-e petrol** petrol tank

tânkar tanker; **tânkar-e têl** oil tanker

tapa hill

taqalobi counterfeit; **In paysa taqalobi hast.** This money is counterfeit.

taqâto' crossroads

ta'qib kardan to chase

taqriban approximately; nearly

taqsim kardan to divide; to share; to distribute

taqsim awqat timetable

tar damp; humid; wet

târ string

taraf-e from

tarâfik

tarâfik traffic
tarâfiki: eshâra-ye tarâfiki traffic lights
tarkidan to burst
tarâsh kardan to shave
tarbuz watermelon
tarh-e khâna sâzi housing project
târik dark
târikh date; history; **târikh-e khoruj** date of departure; **târikh-e tawalod** date of birth; **târikh-e worud** date of arrival; **Târikh-e emruz chist?** What date is it today?
târikhi historical
târikh-nawis historian
târiki darkness
tarjih dâdan to prefer
tarjoma translation; interpretation; **tarjoma kardan** to translate; to interpret
tarjoman translator; interpreter
tark kardan to leave; to quit; to desert
tarkâri vegetables
tarkib composition; make-up; syntax
tarmêm repair; **tarmêm kardan** to fix; to repair
tars fear; **tars dâshtan** to be afraid
tarsândan to frighten
tarsendôk afraid
tarsidan to be afraid (of)
tartib order; **tartib kardan/dâdan** to arrange
tasalyat condolence
tasbê(h) rosary
tasfiya kardan to filter
tasfiyakhâna refinery; **tasfiyakhâna-ye têl** oil refinery
tashakor thank you; thanks; **tashakor!** thank you!; **tashakor kardan** to thank

tashkhis-e tebi diagnosis *medical*
tashkil dadan form *official*
tashna thirsty
tashnâb bathroom; toilet(s); **tashnâb kardan** to have a bath
tashrefât etiquette; protocol
tashrêh explanation; **tashrêh kardan** to explain; to describe
tashwesh dâshtan to be worried
tashy-e jenâza funeral
ta'sis kardan establish
tasmim decision; **tasmim gereftan** to decide
taswir image; portrait
tâtil; tâtilât holiday; vacation
taw fever
tâwa frying pan
tawajô kardan to pay attention
tawalod birth; **tasdeqnâma-ye tawalod** birth certificate; **tawalod kardan** to give birth to
tawalodi birth
tawân strength
tawânâ able; strong
tawânâyi ability
tawânestan to be able
tawaqof brake; **tawaqof kardan** to stop
taw-e syâgak tweezers
ta'wiz amulet
tawqif kardan to seize
tawsêya development
tawsif kardan to describe
tawzih dâdan to explain
tawzihât explanation
tayâr ready; **tayâr kardan** to prepare
tayâra airplane
tayâri preparation
tâyr tire/tyre; **tâyr-e eshtapni** spare tire; **tâyr-e panchar** flat tire

tâza fresh; recent

tazâhor konendagân demonstrators *political*

tazâhorât demonstration *political*

tasbê rosary

tazkera I.D.

tazriq kardan to give an injection

teb-e atfâl pediatrics

tebi medical

tefel; tefl baby; infant

tekrâr kardan to repeat

têl oil; têl parâganda shoda oil spill; têl-e dizel diesel; têl-e petrôl gas/petrol

telâ gold; telâ-ye safêd silver

têla kardan to push

têlar trailer

telefun telephone; telefun kardan to telephone; telefun-e satilâyt satellite phone; telefun-e omumi pay/public phone

telegerâm telegram

teleks telex

teleskôp telescope

teliwizyun television; teliwizyun-e sayâr portable T.V.

telifun *see* telefun

telâ gold

teli rate

tenis tennis

tarâktor tractor

têr: têr-e kamar spine; spinal column; têr kardan/shodan to pass

teror kardan assassination

test *academic* emtehân; *medical* test

teyori theory

têz fast; sharp

tiket ticket; tiket-e yak tarafa one-way ticket; tiket-e do tarafa return ticket

tiket-e posti *postage* stamp

tim team

tira dark *adjective*

tirandâzi kardan to shoot

tof saliva; tof andâkhtan/ kardan to spit

tofang rifle; gun

tofangcha pistol

tofâni blizzard

tôhfa gift; tôhfa-ye yâdgâri souvenir

tokhom egg

tokma button

tolu' sunrise

tombân trousers *traditional*

tond rapid; spicy

tôp ball; gun; cannon; tôp khâna artillery

Torki Turk; Turkish

Torkiya Turkey

torsh sour

toshak mattress

tota-ye kâghaz sheet of paper

trak truck

tu you *singular*

tufân storm

tufâni windy; stormy

tulâni long; tulâni kardan to lengthen

tunal tunnel

tup ball; gun; cannon; tup khâna artillery

turân lieutenant

tur-e mâhi giri net: fishing net

tut berry; mulberry; tut farangi strawberry

tyâra airplane

tyâter theater

tyub tube; inner-tube

U

u he/she/it; him/her/it

urdu army

ustâd; ustâz professor

usu thereabouts

utu iron *for clothes*

W

wa; -w and
wâ they; those
wabâ cholera
wa'da; wâda promise; **wâda dâdan** to promise
wâhed-e puli currency
wahshat nâk terrible
wakht *see* **waqt**
wakil lawyer
wâksin vaccination; **wâksin kardan** to vaccinate
wâledayn parents
walê but
wâli governor
wâqê shodan to occur
wâqêyi real
wâqêyat reality
waqt time; already; **waqt-e ruz** daytime
warag; waraq sheet *of paper*
waram kardan to swell
war-dâshtan to remove
wâred kardan to import
warzesh athletics; sports; **warzesh kardan** to exercise
warzesh-kâr sportsman
wasâyel equipment; tools; **wasâyel-e sawti** sound equipment
wasâyel-e tashnâb/ hamâm toiletries
wâskat waiscoat; vest
wât street
watan homeland
wayrân destroyed; ruined
wâyres-e kâmpyutar computer virus
wâz open; **wâz kardan** to open
wazifa profession; duty
wazir minister
waz'iyat situation
wazn weight
wêdyô video player
welâyat province

wêto kardan to veto
wêza visa
wezârat ministry
wiski whiskey
wo and
wobâ cholera
worud arrival; check-in
worudi arrival(s)

Y

yâ or; these; they
yâd memory; **yâd budan/ dâshtan** to remember; **yâd gereftan** to learn; **yâd na-budan** to be forgotten
yâd-dâsht record
yâftan to find
yag *see* **yak**
yagâna only
yâghi bandit; rebel
Yahud Jew
Yahudi Jew; Jewish
Yahudiyat Judaism
yak one; a/an; **yak bâr** once; **yak bâr-e digar** again; **yak chiz** something; **yak jâyi** somewhere; **yak nafar** someone/somebody; **yak jây** together; **yak kame** a little bit; **yak lehâf-e ezâfi** an extra blanket; **yak paw** one-quarter; *and see* **yakh**
yakh ice; **yakh bandân** frost; **yakh zadan** to freeze
yakhchâl refrigerator; glacier
yaki single; a/an; **yaki digar** another
yakjâ-sâkhtan unification
Yakshambê Sunday
yaktâ unique
yâl mane
yâne... that's to say...; I mean...
yaqin sure; **yaqin dâshtan** to be sure
yaqinan certainly

yârd yard *distance*
yatim orphan
yâzda eleven
yek *see* yak
Yunân Greece
Yunâni Greek
yuro euro *currency*

Z

zabân tongue; language; **zabân shenâs** linguist; **zabân shenâsi** linguistics
zadan to hit; to beat; to knock
zâgh crow
zâhed saint
zâher shodan to appear
zâhmat dâdan to disturb
zâhr poison; toxin; **zâhr-dâr** poisonous; toxic
zayif weak
zakhim thick; wide
zakhira supplies
zakham injury; wound; **zakham-e mêda** stomach ulcer
zakhmi injured; wounded; **zakhmi shodan** to be injured/wounded; to bruise
zâlem cruel; unjust; tyrannical
zamân time; period; **zamâni ke** while
zambur wasp; bee
zamestân winter
zamin land; earth; ground; **zamin shenâs** geologist
zan woman; wife
zan-dâr married *said by a man*
zang bell; **zang zadan** to ring
zang-zada rust
zanjir chain
zanjirak zip; zipper
zânu knee; **zânu zadan** to kneel
zar gold
zarabin lens
zarba concussion *medical*;

zarba zadan to strike
zarb-ol-masal proverb
zard yellow
zardak carrot
zardâlu apricot
zâre' farmer
zarf dish; **zarf-e âsh pazi** cooker/stove
zarfâ dishes; crockery
zari-kardan gravel
zara particle
zarorat dâshtan to need
zarur necessary
zâyidan to give birth (to)
zayif weak
zaytun olive
zêbâyi beauty
zed-e against; **zed-e yakh** anti-freeze; **zed-e ofôni/zed-e mikrôb** sterile/antiseptic
Zelând-e Jadid New Zealand
zelzela earthquake
zenâ adultery
zenakh chin
zenda alive; live; **zenda budan** to be alive
zendagi life; **zendagi kardan** to live
zendân prison
zendâni prisoner
zêr; zêr-e under; **zêr gozar** underpass; **zêr zamin** underground
zerâ (ke) because (of)
zerê-push; zerê-posh armored car; tank *military*
zêr-khâna cellar
zêrpôshi underwear
zêwarât jewelry
zeyârat agriculture; farming
zhornâlist journalist
zid-e *see* zed-e
zina ladder; stairs; **zina-ye barqi** escalator
ziyâd much; many; **meqdâr-e ziyâd** a lot
zobân language

zôf faint(ing); unconsciousness

zoghâl coal

zohr noon

zokâm influenza

zolm tyranny

zud; zut fast; early; **zut shodan** to hurry

zukur male

zyâd; zyât very; many; more; much; *& see* ziyâd

zyârat tomb

ENGLISH—DARI
INGLISI—DARI

A

ability tawânâyi
able lâyeq; **to be able** tawânestan; tânestan
about hodudan, taqriban; *regarding* râjê-ba; **about 50 miles** hodudan penjâ mêl; **about town** atrâf-e shâr; **just about** taqriban
above bâlâ-ye; **above all** khosusan
abroad khârej
absent ghâyeb; ghayrhâzer
absolutely bêkhi
abundance ferâwân
academy akâdemi
accept qabul kardan
acceptable monâseb
accident hâdesa; tasâdom
accommodation manzel
accordance: in accordance with motâbeq (-e)
according to motâbeq-e
account hesâb
accurately daqiqan
accuse motaham kardan
accustomed: to be accustomed to âmokhta shodan
ache kôft; dard
acre êkar
adapter *electric* adâptar
add jama kardan
address âdras
adjutant dagarman
administrator modir
admire sayl kardan
adultery zenâ
advance: in advance az pêsh
advert e'lân

advertise e'lân kardan
advertising e'lânât
advice nasyât
afghani *currency* afghâni
Afghan *person* Afghân; *thing* Afghâni
Afghanistan Afghânestân
afraid tarsendôk; **to be afraid (of)** tarsidan
after ba'd; bâd; pas az (ân ke); pas(-e); **after supper** bâd az nân-shaw
afternoon bâd az zohr; pêshen; **this afternoon** ba'd az zohr-e emruz; **good afternoon!** ba'd az zohr ba khayr!
afterwards bâdan
again bâz
against zed-e
age omor
ago pêsh; **a year ago** yek sâl pêsh
agreement qarârdâd
agriculture zeyârat
agronomist motakhases-e zerâyat
aid *noun* komak; *verb* komak kardan; **first aid** komak-e awaliya
AIDS Eydz
air hawâ
air conditioner; air conditioning êrkândêshan
air base pâygâh-e hawâyi
air drop partâb
air force qowâ-ye hawâyi
air mail pôst-e hawâyi
airfield maydân-e hawâyi
airline shêrkat-e hawâyi
airplane tayâra

airport maydân-e hawâyi

alcohol alkôl

alive zenda; **to be alive** zenda budan

all hama; ama; **all together** hama bâ ham

allergic: I'm allergic to antibiotics. Man bâ antibayâtik hasiyat dârom.

alliance khêshâ

allow ejâza dâdan

allowed halâl

alright mowâfeq

almond bâdâm

almost taqriban

alms barây khodâ

alone tanhâ

along pâlu-ye

already tâ ba hâl; wakht

also âm; ham

although agarchi; garchi

altitude sickness bêmâri-e ertefa'

always hamêsha

a.m. sobh

ambassador safir

ambulance ambulâns

ambush khas-pôshak

America Amrikâ

American Amrikâyi

among dar bayn-e

amount meqdâr

amputation qat'a-ye kardan ozw badan

amulet ta'wiz

amusement sât-têri

ancient qadim(i)

and wa; o; **both... and** hardo... wa

anesthetic dawâ-ye bêhushi

angry khafa; **to get angry** qâhr shodan

animal haywân

ankle bojolak

annoyed khafa

annual sâlâna

another digar; yeki digar; **another bottle** yek bôtal-e digar

answer *noun* jawâb; *verb* jawâb dâdan

antibiotic antibayâtik

anti-freeze zed-e yakh

antique qadim(i)

antiseptic dawâ-ye zed-e ofôni

any har yaki; **not any** hêch yak

anyone har kas

anyway bê az u

anywhere kodâm jây

apart from ghayr-e

apartment apartmân

appear zâher shodan

appetite eshtehâ

apple sêb

approximately taqriban

apricot zardâlu

April Epril

Arab Arab

Arabic Arabi

architect me'mâr

area manteqa

argument ghâl-ma-ghâl

arm bâzu; *weapon* salâh

armored car zerê-push

arms aslehâ

army ordu; lashkar

arrange tartib kardan

arrest dastger kardan

arrival worud

arrive rasidan

art fan; honar

artery shâh rag

articulation *of bones* band-e ostokhân

artificial masnuyi; **artificial leg** pâ-ye masnuyi; **artificial arm** bâzu-ye masnuyi

artillery tup khâna

artist honarmand

ashamed sharmida; **to feel ashamed** ehsâs-e sharmindagi kardan

Asia Âsyâ

ask for porsân kardan

aspirin âyspiren

assassin qâtel

assassinate koshtan; teror kardan

assembly majles; anjoman; shôrâ; **assemblies** majâles

assist komak kardan

assistance komak

asthma astmâ; nafas-tangi

at ba; tâ

athletics warzesh

atmosphere hawâ

attack *noun* hamla; *verb* hamla kardan

attempt kôshesh kardan

attention ehtyât; **to pay attention** tawajô kardan

attractive maghbul; maqbul

aubergine bâdenjân; bânjân

August Âgest

Australia Âstaraliyâ

Australian Âstaraliyâyi

author nawisenda

authorization ejâza; **without authorization** bedun-e ejâza

automatic awtomât

automobile môtar

autumn khazân

avalanche barf kuch

average *adjective* motawaset

awake bêdâr; **to be awake** bêdâr budan

ax tabar

B

baby tefel

back *noun* kamar; posht; *verb* hemâyat kardan

backache kamar dard

backpack bukhcha

backwards pas; **to go backwards** pas raftan

bacteria bâkteri

bad bad; kharâb

badly sakht; kharâb

bag baks desti

baggage baks

baker nânbây

bakery nânwâyi

balcony bâlâ khâna; balkoni

bald kal

ball tôp

ballpoint khodkâr

bandage bandâzh

Band-Aid *plaster* palaster; bandâzh

bandit yâghi

bank bânk

banker bânk dâr

bar bâr

barbecue kabâb-e sikhi

barbed wire sim-e khârdâr

barber salmâni; dalâk

barely nâ-chandân

bargain jagra kardan

bark *verb* ghaw-ghaw kardan

barley jaw

barrel bêlar; bêral

barren khoshk

base pây-gâh

basin lagan

basket sabad

basketball bâsketbâl

bath: to have a bath tashnâb kardan

bathe hamâm kardan

bathroom tashnâb

baths; public baths hamâm

battery bêtri

battle jang; paykâr

be budan

beak nôl

bean(s) lubiyâ

bear *noun* khers

beard rish

beat *verb* zadan

beautiful qashang

beauty zêbâyi

beauty salon salmâni; ârâyishgâh

because chun ke; cherâ ke; zerâ ke; **because of** ba khâtiri ke

become shodan

bed takht-e khâb; bestar; **bed and breakfast** hojra; **to be confined to bed** bestar

budan; **to go to bed** khaw kardan
bedridden bestari
bedroom otâq-e khaw
bee zanbur
beef gôsht-e gaw
beer bir
before: pêsh(-e); pêsh az (ân ke)...
before(hand) pêshtar
begin âghâz kardan; shorô kardan
beginning ebtedâ; aghaz
behind pas; aqab; posht-e
believe bâwar dâshtan/kardan
bell zang
below pâyin
belt kamarband
bend *verb* kham shodan
beneficial fâyedamand
berry tut
beside pahlu(-ye)
besides ghayr-e
best bêhtarin; bêtarin
betray khyânat kardan
better bêhtar; bêtar
better: I feel better. *health* bêhtar astom.
between mâ bayn; (mâ) bayne; myâna-ye; myânê
Bible Enjil
bicycle bâysekel
big bozorg; kalân
biggest bozorgtarin
bill bel
binoculars dôrbin
biography sar gozasht; biyogrâfi
bird parenda
biro khodkâr
birth tawalodi; **to give birth to** tawalod kardan
birth certificate taseqnâma-ye tawalod
birth control kontorol-e nufus
birthday ruz-e tawalod
bit: a little bit meqdâr-e kam
bite gazidan

bitter talkh
black syâh; **black market** bâzâr-e syâh
blackboard takhta
blameworthy makrô; makruh
blanket kampal
bleeding khun rêzi
blessed mobârak
blind kôr
blizzard kulâk; tofâni
blocked masdud; **The toilet is blocked.** Tashnâb masdud ast.
blood khun; **blood group** gorup-e khun; **blood pressure** feshâr-e khun; **blood transfusion** enteqâl-e khun; **blood test** test-e khun; **to give blood** khun dâdan
blow damidan
blow up *explode* enfejâr kardan
blue âbi
boar khuk
boarding pass kârt-e sawâr shodan dar tayâra
boat keshti
body jân; tan; badan; **dead body** jasad
boil *medical* dombal; *verb* jôshidan
boiling water âb-e jôsh
bomb bam; **bomb disposal** khonsâ kardan-e bam
bombardment bam bâran
bon voyage! Safar ba khayr.
bond band
bone ostoghân; ostokhân
bonnet *of car* bânat
booby trap talak-e enfejâri
book ketâb
bookshop ketâb forôshi
boot *of car* tul baks; **boots** moza
booth: cashier's booth ghorfa-ye mahâseb
border sarhad; **border crossing** gozargâh-e sarhad; **border guard** gârd-e sarhadi; **border post** tâna

born: Where were you born?
Dar kojâ motawaled shodêd?;
I was born in London. Man
dar Landan motawaled
shodam.
borrow qarz gereftan
boss ra'is
both har do; **both... and** har
do... wa
bottle bôtal; **bottle of water**
bôtal-e âb
bottle-opener sar bâz kon
bottom ta; bêkh
bowl kâsa
box baks
boxing boks
boy bacha; pesar
boyfriend dôst-e bacha; dôst-e
pesar
bracelet destband; disband;
chori
brain(s) maghz
brake(s) brêk
brandy brandi
brave delâwar
brazier sandali
bread nân
break *for refreshments* esterâhat;
verb shekastan; shekastândan;
to take a break dam
gereftan; **to break down**
kharâb shodan; **Our car has
broken down.** Môtar-e mâ
kharâb shodast.
breakfast chây-sob(h)
breast(s) sina
breast-feeding woman shir-
dâr
breath nafas
brick *adjective* kheshti; *noun*
khesht
bridge pol
bridle lagâm
briefcase baks
bright rôshan
bring âwordan
Britain Britânyâ

British; Briton Britânyâyi
brother berâdar; byâdar
brown naswâri
bruise *verb* zakhmi shodan
brush bors
bucket satel
budget budeja
bug *noun* khanak
build sâkhtan
building *action* sâkhtomân;
house khâna; tâmir
bulb gorup
bull gâw-e nar
bullet gôla; golôlâ
bumper *fender* bâmper
bureaucracy kâghaz parâni
burial jenâza
burn *noun* sôzesh; *verb* sôkhtan;
something sôkhtândan
burning hot dâgh
burst tarkidan
bury dafan kardan
bus bas; sarwês; **bus station**
estâdgâh-e bas/sarwês; **bus
stop** estâdgâh-e bas/sarwês
business *work* kâr/shoghol;
enterprise mo'âmela
businessman/woman tâjer;
darây shoghol
busy mashghul; **The line is
busy.** Khat mashghul ast.
but walê; amâ; lâken
butane canister kapsul-e gâz
butcher qasâb
butter maska
butterfly parwâna; shâh-parak
button dokma; tokma
buy kharidan
by ba; az; pêsh; **by means of** ba
wasila-ye; **by bus** ba wasila-ye
bas/sarwês; **by post** ba wasila-
ye pôst; **by way of** az râh-

C

cabbage karam
cabin kôta; kâben

cabinet *cupboard* almâri; *political* kâbena
cable sim; kêbal
cage qafas
cake kêk; kolcha
calculator mâshin-hesâb
calendar jantari
calf gôsâla; *of body* delak-e pây
call sadâ kardan; **call to prayer** *Islamic* âzân; **What are you called?** Nâm-e shomâ chist?; **I'm called Andy.** Nâm-e man Andy hast.; **Call the police!** Pôlis râ khabar kon!
calm ârâm; bêgham
camel shotor; **camel driver** shotorwân
camera kâmra
camouflage palpot
camp kamp; **Can we camp here?** Âyâ da injâ kamp zada mêtawânêm?
camping mêlakardan
campsite kamp
campus mohawata
can *noun* quti; **can opener** sar bâz kon; **I can...** man mêtawânam...;
Canada Kânâdâ
Canadian Kânâdâyi
canal majrâ; kânâl; kârêz
cancel faskha kardan; kensel kardan; **The plane is canceled.** Parwâz kensel shodast.
cancer saratân
candle sham'a; **candles** sham'a-hâ
candlestick sham'adân
candy shirini
canister quti
cannon tôp
capable lâyeq
capital *city* pâytakht; markaz; *financial* sarmâya
car môtar; **car park** pârking-e môtar; **car papers** asnâd-e môtar; **car registration** sabt-e môtar
caravan kârwân
care mowâzebat; morâqebat; ehtiyât
careful: be careful! mowâzeb bâsh!; ehtiyât ku!
cargo bâr
carpenter najâr
carpet farsh; *knotted* qâlen; *woven* gelam; gelim
carrot zardak
carry haml kardan; **to carry away** bôrdan
cart gâdi; karâchi
carton kârton
cartoon kârikâtor
case *bag* baks; **in any case** bê az u; **in case of...** dar surat-ê ke...; **in case** dar surati
cashier hesâb-dâr; mahâseb
cashier's booth ghorfa-ye mahâseb
casino qemâr khâna
cassette kaset; fita
castle qasar
cat peshak
catch gereftan
caterpillar kerm-e darakht
cathedral kalisâ
Catholic Kâtolik
cattle galaye gâw
cause *noun* dalil; elat
cave ghâr
CD player dastgâh-e si-di/ musik
cease bas kardan
ceasefire âtesh bas
ceiling chat
cellar zêr-khâna
cemetery qabrestân; hadira
center markaz
centimeter sânti
century qarn
ceramics sarâmek
certain yaqin; **to be certain** yaqin dâshtan
certainly yaqinan
chain zanjir; chên

chair chawki

chalk tabâshir

champagne shampâyn

change tabdil; *money* pul-e syâh; **to get change** *money* mayda kardan; **I want to change some dollars.** Man mêkhâhom meqdari dâlar tabdil konom.

channel kânâl; **TV channel** kânâl-e teliwizyun

chaps *medical* lagâmak

chapter fasl; fasel

character shakhs

charge kharch; **What is the charge?** Cheqadar kharch dârad?

charity *action* khayriya; *organization* mo'asesa-ye khayriya

chase ta'qib kardan

chauffeur môtar-wân

cheap arzân

cheaper arzântar

check *bank* chek; *bill* bel; **Check the oil please.** Lotfan, têl râ bobenêd.; **May I have the check?** Bel, lotfan.

check-in worud; **check-in counter** darwâza-ye worudi

cheers! salâmati!

cheese panêr; *hard* qorut

chemical mawâd-e kimiyawi

chemistry dawa khâna

cherry âlubâlu

chess shatranj

chest *body* sina; *box* sanduq

chew jawidan

chewing gum sâjeq

chicken morgh; *meat* gôsht-e morgh

chickenpox chechach

chickpea(s) nakhot

chief khân; ra'is

child tefel; kodak; awlâd

children atfâl; kodakân

chimney dudraw

chin châna; zenakh

China chin

Chinese Chinâyi

chives gandana

chocolate châklêt

choir goruh-e koras

choke khafa shodan; **He/ She is choking!** Khafa mêshawad!

cholera kolarâ

choose khosh kardan

chop *verb* khord kardan

Christian Isawi

Christianity Isawiyat

Christmas Kresmes

church kalisâ

cigar sigâr

cigarette(s) segrêt; **cigarette papers** kâghaz-e segâret

cinema sênamâ

circle dâyera

circumcision khatna; sonat

citizen tab'a

citizenship tâbe'iyat

citrus mewa hay hara-i

city shâr; **city center** markaz-e shâr; **city hall** shârwâli; **city map** naqsha-ye shâr

civil rights hoquq-e madani

civil war jang-e dâkheli

civilian madani; molki; shakhsi

clan khêl; qawm

class senf; *lesson* dars

classical music museqi-ye klâsik

claw chang

clay gel

clean *adjective* pâk; **clean sheets** rojây-e pâk; *verb* pâk kardan

clear *adjective* sâf; **to clear (up)** pâk kardan

climate eqlêm; hawâ

clinic klenik

clock sâ'at

close (to) nazdik(-e);

close *verb* basta kardan

closed basta; **to be closed** basta budan

clothes kâlâ; lebâs; **clothes shop** forôsh gâh-e lebâs
cloud abr
clown dalqhak; maskhara
club klab
clutch *of car* kalach
coach sarwês
coal zoghâl; **coal mine** mâdan-e zoghâl
coast sâhel
coat bâlâpôsh
cobbler but-dôz
cock *rooster* khorus
cockroach mâdar-e kayk-hâ; susk
code kôd; **international code** kôd-e baynolmelali
coffee qahwa
cognac konyak
coins seka-hâ
cold *adjective* sard; khonok; *noun, medical* rêzesh; **cold water** âb-e sard; **I am cold.** Sarda astom.; **It is cold.** Sard ast.
colleague hamkâr
college kâlej
colonel dagar-wâl
color rang; **color film** film-e ranga
colorless bê rang
comb shâna
combat paykâr
combine harvester kambâyn
come âmadan; **to come back** pas âmadan; **come in!** dâkhel shawêd!; **come!** byâ!
comfort râhat
comfortable: **to be comfortable** râhat budan; **The seat is comfortable.** Kawch râhat ast.
coming *next* âyenda
commander qomândân
commission kamêshan
common sense dark-e ebtedâyi; manteq
common âdi

commonwealth keshwarhâ-ye moshtarak-ol-manâfê
communications ertebâtât; mokhâberât
community jâme'a
companion rafiq; hamrâh
compare moqâyesa kardan
compass qotb namâ
compensation gherâmat; tâwân
competent qâbel
competition raqâbat; mosâbeqa
complain shekâyat kardan
complaint shekâyat
complete pura
completely bêkhi; belkol; tamâm
composer mo'alef
composition tarkib
computer kâmpyutar
computer program progrâm-e kâmpyutari
computer virus wâyres-e kâmpyutar
concert kânsart; **concert hall** sâlon-e museqi
concussion *medical* zarba
condition hâl; *term* shart; **on condition that** ba shart-ê ke
condolence tasalyat
condom kândom
conference kânfarâns; **conference room** otâq-e moshâwerat
confidence bâwar; **to have confidence** bâwar dâshtan
confirm kanfarm dâdan; **I want to confirm my flight.** Man mêkhâham parwâzam râ kanfarm konom.
confuse maghshush shodan
congestion birôbar
congress majles; **congresses** majâles
connection ertebât
consequently az i/u khâter
conserve kansarf kardan

consideration lehâz

constipation qabz

constitution qânun-e asâsi

construct sâkhtan

consulate qonsulgari

consultant moshâwer

contact lenses lenz-e chashm

contact tamâs gereftan; **I want to contact my embassy.** Man mêkhâhom bâ sefârat am tamâs bogirom.

contagion sarâyat

contagious sâri

contain shâmel budan

container *freight* kontenar; baks

contemplate sayr/sayl kardan

contemporary mo'âser

contest jang; nezâ

continue edâma dâdan

contract qarâr dâd

control *verb* kontorol kardan

conversation mokâlema

conversation gap; sohbat

cook *noun* âshpaz; *verb* pokhtan; pokhta kardan

cooked pokhta

cooker manqal; dâsh; **pressure cooker** dêg-e bokhâr

cooking vegetables sabzijât

cool khonok

cooperation ham kâri

copper mes

copy *noun* noskha; kâpi; *verb* kâpi kardan

coriander gashniz

corkscrew sar bâz kon

corn jawâri; *medical* mêkhak

corner konj

corpse jasad

correct *adjective* dorost; râst; sahih; *verb* sahih kardan

corridor dahlêz

corrupt fâsed

corruption fasâd

cost narkh; qêmat; **How much does this cost?** Qêmat-e in chand ast?

costs kharch; kharch

cosy narn

cotton pomba; pakhta; nakhi; **cotton wool** pomba

cough *noun* sorfa; *verb* sorfa kardan

council shura

count *verb* shomordan

counterfeit taqalobi; sâkhtagi; ja'li; **This money is counterfeit.** In paysa ja'li hast.

country mamlakat

countryside khârej az shâr/dêh

coup d'etat kudatâ

couple jôra

courageous delâwar

court *law* mahkama; **supreme court** stara-mahkama

cow gaw

craftsman kasaba

crane *machine* krên; jarsaqel

crash *verb* soqut kardan

crazy dêwâna

cream firni; qaymâq; *ointment* malam; marham; krim

create ba wojud âwardan

credit e'tebâr; **credit card** kredet-kârt

crescent êlâl; helâl

crime jenâyat

criminal jennayat kâr

crisis bohrân

crockery zarfâ

crooked kaj

cross *verb* gozashtan; têr shodan

crossing gozar-gâh

crossroads châr-râhi

crow *bird* zâgh

crowd(s) birôbar

cruel zâlem

cry gerya kardan

cucumber bâdrang

cuff desghir

culpable makrô; makruh

culture

culture koltur; farhang
cup pyâla
cupboard almâri
cure *noun* elâj; *verb* elâj kardan
curfew quyud(-e shab)
currency paysa; wâhed-e puli
curtain parda
custom *tradition* rasm
customs rasm-o rawâj; *border* gomrok
cut boridan; **to cut in two** nesf kardan; **The electricity has been cut off.** Barq qat'a shodast.; **The gas has been cut off.** Gâz qat'a shodast.; **The water has been cut off.** Âb qat'a shodast.

D

dagger khanjar
daily rôzâna
dairy labaniyât
dam band
damage kharâb shodan
damp martub; tar
dance; dancing raqs; raqsidan; **national dance** *of Afghanistan* atanemeli
Dane Denmârki
danger khatar
dangerous khatarnâk
Danish Denmârki
Dari Dari
dark *adjective* târik
darkness târiki
date târikh; **date of birth** târikh-e tawalod; **date of arrival** târikh-e worud; **date of departure** târikh-e khoruj; **What date is it today?** Târikh-e emruz chist?
daughter dokhtar
dawn *noun* sobh dam
day rôz; **night and day** rôz-o-shaw
daytime waqt-e ruz

dead morda
deaf kar
dear *loved* aziz; jân
death marg
debt qarz
decade daha
deceased: to be deceased fawt shodan
December Disambar
decide faysala kardan
decision tasmim; faysala
decorator rangmâl
deep choqor; amiq
deer âhu
defeat shekast
defend defâ kardan
delay *noun* mâtali; ta'khir; *verb* dêr kardan
delayed mâtal shoda; **The plane is delayed.** Tayâra ta'khir dârad.
delicate nâzok
democracy demokrâsi; hokômat-e mardom
demonstration *political* mozahera
demonstrators *political* mozâhera konendagân
dentist daktar-e dandân
deodorant atir
department store suparmârkêt
departures khoruj
deport ekhrâj kardan
deportation ekhrâj
depot godâm
deprive mahrum kardan
derrick jarsaqil
descend pâyin shodan; tâ shodan
describe tashrêh kardan; tawsif kardan
desert *noun* sahrâ; rêgistân; beyâbân
desert *verb* tark kardan
desire *verb* ârezu dâshtan
desk mêz
despite bâ wojud-e; har chand ke

dessert shirini-e bâd az nân

destroy nâbud kardan

destroyed wayrân; kharâb

destruction kharâbi

detergent *powder* podar-e kâlâ shôyi

development tawsêya; roshd

devil shaytân

diabetes maraz-e qand/shakar

diabetic marizi shakar

diagnosis *medical* tashkhis-e tebi

dial dâyl kardan; shomâra gereftan

dialect lahja

dialing code kôd-e telefuni; **dialing code for Kabul** kôd-e telefuni-ye Kâbol

diaper gol-kashedan; parcha-ye qondaq; **I need to change my baby's diaper.** Bayad qondaq-e bacha râ ewaz konom.

diarrhea es-hâl

diaspora jamiyat-e parâganda

dictator hâkem-e motlaq

dictatorship hokômat-e motlaqa

dictionary farhang; dekishnari

die môrdan

diesel têl-e dêzal

diet parêzâna; **to go on a diet** rezhim gereftan

difference farq; **to make a difference** farq kardan

different mokhtalef; **to be different** farq dâshtan

difficult dashwâr; moshkel

dig kandan

digestion hazm

dining room otâq-e nân

dinner nân-e shab

diphtheria syâ sorfa

diplomat diplomât

diplomatic ties rawâbet-e diplomâtik

direct râst; mostaqim; **Can I dial direct?** Mêtawânom bâ shomâ rasan telefun konom?

direction su; **in the direction of** sôy-e; son-e

directions masir; jehât

directly mostaqiman

directory ketâb-e râhnamâ

dirty cherk; chatal

disabled mayub; nâtawân

disaster mosibat

disco disko

discover kashf kardan

discuss goftogôy kardan; bahs kardan

discussion goftogôy; bahs

disease bêmâri; marizi

dish zarf; **dishes** zarfâ

dispensary dawâ-khâna

Displaced Person Shakhs-e Âwâra

dispute nezâ

dissolve hal kardan

distant dur

distressing ghamnâk

distribute tawzê kardan; taqsim kardan

district bakhsh; oloswâli; *of city* nâheya;

disturb zâhmat dâdan

diver awbâz

divide taqsim kardan

divorce *noun* talâq

dizziness ganksiyat

dizzy ganks

do kardan; kadan

dock langargâh

doctor dâktar; *traditional* hakim

document sanad

dog sag

doll godi; arusak

dollar dâlar

donkey khar

door darwâza; **door lock** qofl-e darwâza

double do chand; do barâbar; **double bed** bastar-e do nafara; **double room** otâq-e do nafara

doubt

doubt *noun* shak
down pâyin
dozen darjan
drag kashidan
drain khâli kardan
draw *a picture* rasm kardan
drawer almâri-ye mêz
dream *noun* khâb; royâ; *verb* khaw didan
dress *noun* jâma; lebâs; **traditional dress** pêrâhân-o tombân; **to dress** pôshândan
dressed pôshida; **to get dressed** lebâs pôshidan
dressmaker khayât
drill *verb* barma kardan; **to drill a well** châh kandan
drink *noun* nushidani; *verb* nushidan
drinking water âb-e nushidani
drive *verb* rândan
driver môtarwân; derêwar
driver's license lâysens
dropper qatra-chakân
drown gharq shodan
drug dawâ; **drug addict** mo'tâd
drum dôl
drunk mast; nasha; **drunk person** shakhs-e mast; **to be drunk** mast budan; **I am drunk.** Man mastom.; Nasha hastom.
dry *noun* khoshk; *verb* khoshk kardan
duck morghâbi
dump khâkandâz
dumplings âshak
during hangâm-e
dusk shâm
dust khâk
Dutch Hâlandi
duty: customs duty mâlyât-e gomrok
duvet lehâf; leyâf
dwell sâken shodan; sheshtan
dynamo daynamo

E

each har (yek)
eagle oqâb
ear gôsh; **ear infection** gôsh-dardi
early zud; pêshtar
earrings darâmad-hâ; awâyed
earth zamin
earthquake zelzela
east *noun* mashreq; sharq; *adjective* sharqi
Easter Id-e Masihi-hâ
eastern sharqi
easy âsân
eat khôrdan
economic eqtesâdi
economics eqtesâd
economist eqtesâd-dân
economy eqtesâd
edge laba; **on the edge of** da(r) lab-e
editor *newspaper* modêr; *program* edêtar; tahya koninda
education tahsilât; mo'aref
egg tokhom
eight hasht
eighteen hazhda
eighty hashtâd
elastic kashak
elbow âronj
elder *adjective* bozorgtar; *noun* pir; bâbâ; **village elder(s)** rish safêd
elect entekhâb kardan
election entekhâbât
electric barqi; **electric shock** shâk-e barqi
electrical goods store dokân-e sâmân âlât barqi
electrician barqi
electricity barq
element shâmel
elephant fil
elevator left
eleven yâzda
else: or else aga(r) nê
elsewhere digar jâ; jâ-ye diga(r)

e-mail imêl; **e-mail address** âdras-e elektroniki
embassy sefârat
emergency hâlat-e ezterâri; **emergency exit** khoruj-e ezterâri
employee mâmor
empty *adjective* khâli; *verb* khâli kardan
end *noun* pâyân; *verb* khalâs kardan
enemy doshman
engine enjin; mâshen
engineer enjinyar
England Inglestân
English *person* Inglis; *language* Inglisi
enough bas; kâfi; **enough!** bas!; **to be enough** bas kardan; **That's enough!** Kâfist!
enquiry tahqiq; taftish
enter darâmadan
enterprise kâr-e mohem
entertainment sât-têri
entire hama
entirely tamâm; ba-koli
entrance; entry (râh-e) dokhul
envelope pâkat(-e khat)
environs châr taraf
epidemic sâri
epilepsy mergi
equal to barâbar-e
equally hamchonin
equipment wasâyel
era dawrân
error gonâ
escalator zina-ye barqi
escape farâr kardan
especially makhsusan; especially as chi-khasâ-ye
espionage jasusi
essay maqâla
establish ta'sis kardan
etiquette tashrefât; âdâb
euro *currency* yuro
Europe Ôrôpâ; Yôrop

European Ôrôpâyi
European Union Etehâdi-ye Orupâyi
even âm; ham; hatâ
evening shab; **good evening!** shab ba khayr!; **in the evening** shawaki; **this evening** emshab
every ham(a); har; kol-e; **every time that...** har wakht ke...
everybody; everyone hamagi
everything hama chiz
evidence madrak; sobot
evil bad; kharâb
exact daqiq;
exactly pura
exam; examination emtehân; emtyân
examine *medically* mo'âyena kardan
example mesâl; **for example** masalan
excellent âli
except bedun-e; **except for...** ba joz az
excess ezâfa
exchange tabdil kardan; **Do you exchange money?** Shomâ paysa tabdil mêkonêd?
excuse *noun* bahâna; **excuse me!** bobakhshêd!
execute *carry out* tamrin kardan; *kill* ejrâ kardan;
exhaust-pipe *of car* ekzâst; salânsar
exhibit namâyesh dâdan
exhibition namâyesh-gâh
exile mohâjer; **exiles** mohâjerin
existing mawjud
exit khoruj
expect entezâr dâshtan
expel ekhrâj kardan
expenditure; expenses kharch
expensive qêmat
explain fâhmândan
explanation tawzihât
explode monfajer shodan
exploration jostoju

explosion enfejâr

explosives mawâd-e monfajera

export *noun* jens-e sâderâti; *verb* sâder kardan

express *fast* sari'; **express post** post-ekspres; **express vehicle** têzraftâr; **express train** ekspres

extend gostâresh dâdan

extinguish gol kardan

extra ezâfi; **an extra blanket** yak lehâf-e ezâfi

extract kashedan

extraordinary fawq-ol-âda

eye chashm

eyeglasses âynak

eyes chashmân

eyesight binâyi; ed

F

face ruy

facing moqâbel(-e)

fact haqiqat

factory kârkhâna; fâbrika

faculty pôhanzay

failure nâkâmi/nâ tawâni

faint; fainting zôf

fair *just* dorost

falcon bâz

fall *autumn* khazân; *verb* aftâdan; **to fall down** ghaltidan

false nâ-drost

family fâmel

famine goresnagi

famous mash-hur

fan paka

far dur; **How far is the next village?** Tâ dêh-e ba'di cheqadar râh ast?; **so far** az i pêsh

fare kerâya; **What is the fare?** Kerâya cheqadar ast?

farm mazre'a; kesht; fârm

farmer dêhqân

farming zeyârat

Farsi Fârsi

fashion mod

fast têz; zut; *adverb* ba-zudi; *noun* rôza; *verb* rôza gereftan

fat *adjective* châgh; *noun* charbi; **cooking fat** rôghan

father padar

fatigue khastagi; mândagi

faucet nal

fax faks; **fax machine** mâshin-e faks

fear *noun* tars; *verb* tarsidan

feast *religious* id; êd

feather par

February Febriwari

federation etehâdiya; fedrâsyôn

feeble zayif

feed ghezâ dâdan

feeding bottle chôshak

feeding station ghezâ khori

feel ehsâs kardan

female mâda

femur ostokhân-e rân

fence katara; hesâr

fender *of car* gel gir

ferret mush khormâ

ferry keshti; gozargâh

fertile hâsel khêz

fertilizer kud

festival festiwal; **music festival** festiwal-e museqi

feud kina; doshmani

fever tab

field maydân

fifteen pânzda

fifty penjâ

fig anjir

fight jang kardan

fighter jangju

file dosiya

fill por kardan

filling station têlitânk

film film; **film festival** festiwal-e film

filmmaker film-sâz

filter tasfiya kardan

filth cherk

filthy cherk

final *adjective* âkher; *noun* âkheri; *sports* fâynal

finance hesâbat-e mâli; mâlya

find yâftan; paydâ kardan; **to find out** mâlum kardan

fine *good* khub; âli; *thin* nâzok; *of money* jarima

finger angôsht; kelk; **little finger** kelkak

finish khalâs kardan

fire âtesh

firewood hizom

first awal

firstly awalan

fish mâhi

fisherman mâhiger

fishing mâhigeri

fist musht

five panj

fix mahkam kardan; shândan; feks shodan

flame sho'la; shôla

flash barq-e sari; *camera* falash

flashlight cherâgh

flat tire panchar; **I have a flat tire.** Yak tâyr-e môtaram panchar shodast.

flavour maza

flea kayk

flee gorêkhtan; panâ bordan

flight *plane* parwâz

float shenâwar budan

flock gala

flood sêl

floor *ground* zamin; *story* manzel

florist gol forôsh

flour ârd

flower gol

flu zokâm

flute nay

fly *noun* magas; *verb* parwâz kardan

fog ghobâr

foggy ghobâr alud

folk *noun* mardom; **folk dancing** raqs-e mahali; **folk music** museqi-ye mahali

folklore rosum-e mahali

food ghezâ; nân

fool *noun* nâdân; ahmaq

foolish ghul

foot pâ; pây; *measurement* fut

football futbâl

footpath peyâda raw

for barây-e; barê

forbid man' kardan

forbidden mana'; harâm

ford gozar

forehead pêshâni

foreign; foreigner khâreji

forest jangal

forget farâmush kardan; **to be forgotten** az yâd raftan

forgive bakhshidan

forgiveness bakhshesh

fork panja

form *shape* shakal; *official* forma; *verb* tashkil dadan

formula noskha

fort qalâ

fortnight do hafta

forty chel

forum mêz-e modawar

forward(s) pêsh

foundation *organization* bonyâd; mo'asesa

four châr

fourteen chârda

fourth chârom

fox rôbâ

fracture *noun* shekastagi; *verb* shekastan

fragrant buynâk

free âzâd; *of charge* moft; **Is this seat free?** Âyâ in chawki khâli ast?

freedom âzâdi

freeze yakh zadan

freezing besyâr sard

freight container kontenar

French Farânsawi

fresh tâza; *cool* khonok

Friday Jom'a

fridge yakhchâl

friend dôst

frighten tarsândan
frog baqa
from az; **from now on** az i pas
front muqâbel; pêsh; **in front of** dar muqâbel-e
frontier sarhad
frost yakh bandân
frostbite yakh zadagi; sarmâ gazidagi
fruit mêwa; **fruit juice** âb-e mêwa
frying pan tokhom paz
fuel mawad-e sukht; **fuel dump** makhzan-e sukht
full por; **full moon** mâh-e kâmel; **to be full** sêr budan; **I am full up!** Man sêr astom!
funeral jenâza
funny khanda dâr; mozhik
fur hat kolâ
furniture farnechar; mêz-o-chawki
future âyenda

G

gala jashn; mêla
gallon gêlan
game bâzi
gangrene gazak
garage garâzh; warakshop; & see filling station
garage-owner mestari
garbage khâkjâro
garden bâgh
garlic sêr
garrison gârnizun
gas gâz; petrol têl-e petrôl; **gas bottle/canister** balun-e gâz
gate darwâza
gear gêr
general noun ganrâl; adjective omumi
generally omuman
genitals ozw-e tanasol
genocide qatl-e âm
gently âstâ

geologist zamin shenâs
German Âlmâni
Germany Âlmân; Jarmani
germs mikrôb-hâ
get gereftan; **to get up** khêstan
ghee rôghan
gift hadya; tôhfa
girl dokhtar
girlfriend dôst-e dokhtar
give dâdan; **to give birth (to)** ba donyâ âwardan; zâyidan; **give me...** ...râ ba man botê.
glacier yakh châl
gland ghodud
glass substance shisha; drinking gelâs; **glass of water** gelâs-e âb
glasses âynak
gloves dest kash
go raftan; **to go in** darâmadan; **to go out** barâmadan; **to go down** tâ shodan; **to go up** bâlâ shodan; **go!** boro!
goal aim hadaf; football gol
goat boz
goatskin mashk
God Khodâ
gold telâ
golf golf
good khô; khub; khayr
goodbye! khodâ hâfez! or bâmân-e khodâ!; response khodâ hâfez!
goods mâl
goose qâz
government hokômat
governor wâli
grain dâna
gram gerâm
grammar sarf-o nahw; gerâmar
grandchild nawâsa
grandfather padar kalân
grandmother mâdar kalân
grape(s) angur
grass chaman
grateful mamnun; **I am grateful.** Mamnun-am.

gratis moft
grave *serious* besyâr mohem; *noun* qaber
gravel jaghal
great bozorg
greatest bozorgtarin
Greece Yunân
Greek Yunâni
green sabz
greengrocer sabzi forôsh
greens sabzi
grind khord kardan; mayda kardan
groan nâlesh kardan
groom *for horses* mêhtar; negahban-e asb
ground zamin; *sports field* maydân
group gorup
grow roshd kardan; **to grow crops** kâshtan; **to grow up** bozorg shodan
gruel âb-e jôsh dâdagi
guard *noun* mahâfez; *verb* negahbâni kardan; **border guard** negahbân-e sarhadi
guerrilla pârtizân; cherek
guest mêhmân; **guest speaker** sokhanrân-e dawat shoda
guesthouse mêhmân khâna
guide râhbar; *book* (ketâb-e) râhnamâ; *verb* râhnamâyi kardan
gum bira
gum: chewing gum sâjeq
gun tôp
gutter jôy; badraft
gynecologist dâktar-e zanân

H

habits rasm-o rawâj
hair mo; muy
hairbrush boros-e mo
haircut: I want a haircut please. Lotfan mo-ye ma râ kutâh konêd.

hairdresser salmâni
hairdryer mo khoshkun
halal halâl
half nesf; nim
halt tawaqof kardan
hamburger hambargar
hammer chakosh
hand dast; dest; **to hand out** tawzê kardan; **to hand over** tahwil dâdan; **hand to hand** tan-ba-tan
handbag baks desti; destkawl
handicraft kâr-e desti
handkerchief destmâl-e bini
handle desta
hang âwêzân kardan
hangar âshiyâna
hanger *clothes* kot band
hangover sardardi bâd az sharâb noshi
happen gap shodan; wâqê shodan
happiness khoshi
happy khosh
haram harâm
harbor panâh-gâh
hard sakht
hardly nâ-chandân
hardware store khorda forôshi
harmful mozer
harmful: to be harmful nokhs kardan
harvest hâsel; daraw
hashish chars
hat *fur* kolâ; *Nuristani* pakôl
hate *verb* nafrat dâshtan
have dâshtan; **to have to** bâyad
hawk bâz
hay kâh
he ô
head sar; *boss* ra'is; **head of state** ra'is-e dawlat
head-ache sar-dard
headman dar râs; ra'is
headquarters markaz
heal shafâ dâdan
health juri; salâmat; sehât

healthcare hefzolseha; morâqebat sehi; bedâsht
healthy sâlem; sehatmand
hear shonidan
heart del; qalb; **heart attack** hamla-ye qalbi; **heart condition** bêmâri-ye qalbi
heat *noun* garmi; *verb* garm kardan
heatwave mawj-e garmi
heaven behesht
heavy gerang
heel kori
height belandi
helicopter helikôptar
hell jahanom
hello! salâm!; salâm alêkom! *to which the response is* wâlêkom asalâm!
help *noun* komak; *verb* komak kardan; **help!** komak, komak!; **Can you help me?** Mêta-wânêd bâ man komak konêd?
hemorrhage khun-rêzi
hen morgh
henceforth az i bâd; az i pas
hepatitis hepâtet
her ô
herb giyâh
herd gala
here injâ; **here is/are** êna
hereabouts isu
hernia *inguinal* chora; *umbilical* nâf-raftagi
hero qahrumân
hers -esh; az ô
herself khodesh
hidden pot
hide pot shodan
high beland; boland; **high blood pressure** feshâr-e khun-e bâlâ
highway shâh râh
hijack rabudan
hijacker robâyenda
hijacking rabudan
hike gardesh kardan
hill tapa

him ô
himself khodesh
Hindi Hendi
Hindu Hendu; Ondu
Hinduism dên-e Hendu
hip bâlâ-ye râ
hire kerâya kardan
his -esh; az ô
historian târikh-nawis
historical târikhi
history târikh
hit zadan
hold negah dâshtan
hole surâkh
holiday rokhsati; *religious* id
homeland watan
homeless bêkhâna
honey asal
honeymoon mâh-e asal
honor ghayrat
hoof somb
hook changak
hookah chelam; chelem
hooping-cough khorâsak
hope omêd
horse asb; asp; **horse racing** asb dawâni; **horse show** na'l-e asb
horseback riding asb swâri
hose lola
hospital shafâ-khâna
host mêzbân
hostage gerôgân; **to take hostage** gerôgân gereftan
hostel laylya
hostile doshman
hot garm; **boiling hot** dâgh; **hot water** âb-e garm; **I am hot.** Garm astom.; **It is hot.** Garm ast.
hotel hôtal
hour sâ'at; sât
house khâna; *& see* parliament
how? chetôr? **how much?** cheqadar?; **how many?** chand dâna?; **how far?** cheqadar râh ast?; **how are you?** hâl-e shomâ chetor ast?; **how old**

are you? chand sâl dârêd?
however sar az i/u ham
H.Q. markaz
human ensân; **human being** bashar; **human rights** hoquq-e bashar
humanitarian ensâni; **humanitarian aid** komak-e ensâni
humid tar; martub
humor shukhi
humorous mazaqi; shukh
hundred sad
hunger goresnagi
hungry goresna; **to be hungry** goshna budan; **I'm hungry.** Goresna hastom.
hunt shekâr kardan
hurry *noun* ajala; *verb* zut shodan; **I'm in a hurry.** Man ajala dârom.
hurt *noun* dard; *verb* dard kardan; **Where does it hurt?** Kojây shomâ dard mêkonad?; **It hurts here.** Man râ nârâhat mêkonad.
husband shawhar; shoy
hut kôta
hyena kaftâr
hygiene pâki; hefzolseha; nezâfat
hypocrite monâfeq

I

I man; ma
ice yakh
ice-cream fâluda; shiriyakh
I.D. kârt-hoyat; tazkera
idea nazar; aqida
identification shenâsâyi
idiom estelâh-e âmiyâna
slang estelâh-e âmiyâna
idle bêkâr
if agar; **if possible** agar momken bâshad
ill bêmâr; mariz; **to be ill** bêmâr budan; **I am ill.** Man bêmâr

astom.; **ill health** nâ-juri
illegal ghayr-e qânuni
illicit harâm
illness bêmâri
image taswir
imam emâm
immediate fawri
immediately fawran; desti
immigrant mohâjer
immigration mohâjerat
import *verb* wâred kardan
importance ahamiyat
important mohem
impossible nâ-momken
improve bêhtar kardan
in dar; da; **in front (of)** pêsh-e ruy(e); **in the country** dar in keshwar
included shâmel shoda
inconvenient nokhs
independence esteqlâl
independent mostaqel; **independent state** keshwar-e mostaqel
India Hendustân; Hend
Indian Hendi
indicator light eshâra-ye alâmat/môtar
indigestible saqel
indigestion bad-hazmi
industry san'at
infant tefel
infection ofunat; **ear infection** gôsh-dardi
influenza zokâm
inform khabar kardan
information mâlumât; khabar(â); etelâyât; **information office** daftar-e mâlumât
informed: **to be informed** khabar dâshtan
injection nês
injure masdum kardan
injured zakhmi; **slightly injured** awgâr; **to be injured** zakhmi shodan
injury zakham

ink

ink rang
inner-tube tyup
innocent bêgonâh
inquiry tahqiq
insane dêwâna
inscription naweshta
insect hashara; insects hasharât
insecticide hashara kosh
inside daru(n); darun-e
inside-out chapa
insomnia bê-khawi
instead (of) êwaz(-e)
institute mo'asesa
insult tawhên
insurance bêma; I have medical insurance. Man bêma-ye tebi dârom.; My possessions are insured. Dârâyi-ye man bêma shodast.
insured bêma shoda
intellectual rôshan-feker
intelligent hushyâr
intend qasd dâshtan
intense shadid
intention maqsad; with the intention of az khâter-e
interest alâqa; *financial* sud; *verb* alâqa dâshtan
interesting jâleb
interior *adjective* dâkheli; *noun* dâkhel
internal dâkheli
international baynolmelali; international code rasm-e baynolmelali; international flight parwâz-e baynolmelali; international operator aprêtar-e telefun
internet entarnet
internet café klub-entarnet
interpreter tarjomân
interval fâsela
interview mosâheba
intestine(s) rôda; large intestine kata rôda
into darun-e
intoxicated mast

introduce mo'arefi kardan
invalid bestari
invasion tahâjom
invention ekhterâ
inventor mokhtarê'
investigate tahqiq kardan
investigation tahqiq
invitation dâwat
invite dâwat kardan
Iran Irân
Iranian Irâni
Ireland Âyrlaynd
Irish Âyrishi
iron âhan; âyin; *for clothes* utu
Islam Eslâm
Islamic Eslâmi
Israel Esrâyil
Israeli Esrâyili
it in; ô
Italian *person* Itâlawi
Italy Itâlyâ
itch *noun* khâresh; *verb* khâridan
item dâna; tâ
its -esh

J

jack *of car* jak-e môtar
January Jenwari
Japan Jâpân
Japanese Jâpâni
jar kôza
jaw alâsha
jazz jâz
jeans kawbây
Jew Yahud
jeweler zargar
jeweler's shop; jewelry zargari
jewelry zêwarât
Jewish Yahudi
jihad jehâd
job kâr
joint gôla; golôla
joke mazâq; shokhi
journal jarêda

leader

journalist zhornâlist
joy khoshi
Judaism Yahudiyat
judge qâzi
jug kôza
July Julây
jumper jâkat
June Jun
junior kuchaktar
just *adjective*dorost; **just about**
    taqriban
justice adâlat

K

kebab kabâb
keep negâ kardan
ketchup kechup
kettle chây-jôsh
key kelid; keli
kidnap rabudan
kidnapper robâyenda
kidnapping rabudan
kidney gorda
kill koshtan
killer qâtel
kilogram kilô; kilôgerâm
kilometer kilômeter
kind *adjective* mêhrabân; *noun*
    qesem; **to be kind** mêhrabâni
    kardan
kindness mêhrabâni
king shâh
kiosk ghorfa; **news kiosk**
    akhbâr forôshi
kiss bosidan; mâch kardan
kitchen âshpaz-khâna
kite *paper* godi-parân
knee zânu
kneel zânu zadan
knife châqu; kârd
knock zadan
knot gerê; gereh
know *something* dânestan;
    someone shenâkhtan; **I know.**
    Mêdânom.; **I don't know.**
    Man namêdânom.; **Do you**

know him/her? Âyâ shomâ ô
    râ mêshenâsêd ?
knowledge âgâhi
known: well-known shenâkhta
    shoda; sarshenâs
Koran Qorân

L

laboratory laborâtwâr
labor kâr
laborer mozdur
lack *noun* kambud
ladder zina
lake jahel
lamb bara
lame lang
lamp cherâgh; lampa; **oil-lamp**
    cherâgh-e têli
lancet nêshtar
land *noun* zamin; *verb (airplane)*
    neshastan
landslide laghzesh-e zamin
language zabân
lap dâman
lapis lazuli lâjward
laptop computer kâmpyutar-
    e syâr
large bozorg; beland; kalân
larger bozorgtar
larynx halq
last âkher; **last night** dishab
late dêr; nâ-wakht; **to be late**
    dêr kardan
later pasântar
laugh *noun* khanda; *verb* khanda
    kardan
laughter khanda
laundry *washing* khoshka-shôyi
law qânun; **law court** mahkama
lawful rawâ; halâl
lawyer wakil
lay nehâdan
lazy kâhel
lead *verb* rahbari kardan
leader rahbar; khân; **spiritual**
    leader shaykh; pir

leaf

leaf barg
leak *noun* chakak; *verb* chakidan
lean *adjective* bârik; *verb* takya kardan
leap khêz zadan
leap year sâl-e kabisa
learn yâd gereftan
leather charm
leave mândan
lecture lekchar
leech jôk
leek gandana
left chap; **to the left** dest-e chap
left-over mânda
left-wing chap gerâ
leg pâ; pây
legal qânuni
legend afsâna
lemon lêmu
lend qarz dâdan
length darâzi
lengthen darâz kardan
lens lenz; zarabin; **contact lenses** lenz-e kontâkt
lentils dâl
less kam; kamtar
lesson dars
let's go! byâ borawêm!
letter *written* maktub; khat; *of alphabet* harf
lettuce kâhu
level *adjective* hamwâr; *noun* mêzân
lever shahin-e tarâzu
liar dorôgh-gôy
liberation âzâdi
library ketâb khâna
lice shepesh
lie *noun* dorugh; **to lie down** darâz kashedan
lieutenant turân
life zendagi
lift *elevator* left; *verb* boland kardan
light *noun* rôshani; *not dark* rôshan; *not heavy* sobok; **to light** *a fire* dar dâdan; **to light**

(up) rôshan kardan; **Do you have a light?** Segrêt-lêtar dârêd?
light meter nur sanj
lightbulb cherâgh; grup
lighter lêtar; **lighter fluid** gâz-e lêtar
lighting rôshan sâkhtan
lightning ra'd-o barq/almasak
like mesl-e; chun; **like that/ this** otto(r); *verb* dôst dâshtan; khosh dâshtan; **I like...** Man ... dôst dârom.; **I don't like...** Man ... dôst nadârom.
likely mohtamal; **to be likely** mohtamal budan; ehtemal dâshtan
likewise hamchonin
limbs dest-o pâ
lime *fruit* lêmu; *mineral* chuna
limit had; andâza
line khat
linguist zabân shenâs
linguistics zabân shenâsi
link band
lion shêr
lip lab
lipstick lab serin
list lest; jadwal
listen gôsh kardan; shonidan
liter lêtar
literature adabiyât
little khord; chucha; **a little** kambê; kame
live *adjective* zenda; *verb* zendagi kardan; **to live (in)** sheshtan
lively têz
liver jegar
living *adjective* zenda
lizard chalpâsa
load bâr
local mahali; **a local shop for local people** maghâza-ye mahali barâye mardom-e mahal
location mahal
lock *noun* qofl; *verb* qofl kardan
locomotive lokamôtiv; mâshin

long darâz
look didan; **to look for** pâlidan
loose change pul-e syâh
lord khodâwand
lorry lâri
lose gom kardan; **I have lost my key.** Man kelidam râ gom kardom.; **I am lost.** Man râh râ gom kardâm.
lot; a lot besyâr; zyâd; zyât
loud; loudly boland
louse eshpesh
love *noun* eshq; *verb* dôst dâshtan
low pâyin; **low blood pressure** feshâr-e khun-e pâyin
lower pâyin kardan
luck bakht; tale
lucky kâmyâb
lunar qamari
lunch nân-e châsht
lung shosh

M

machete kârd
machine mâshin
madame Khânom; Mêrman
made in... sâkht-e...
madrasa *religious school* madrasa
magazine mojala
magnetic meqnâtisi
mail post
mailbox post-baks
main asli; **main square** chawk-e markazi
maintain negah dâshtan; mo'âzebat kardan
maize jawâri; jwâri
majority aksariyat
make kardan; sâkhtan
make-up tarkib
malaria malaryâ
male mozakar; mozakar
mammal pestân dâr
man mard; âdam; ensân

manager modir
mane yâl
manoeuver châl
manual *book* ketâb rahnama
manufacture *verb* sâkhtan
many zyâd; zyât; besyâr
map naqsha; **map of Kabul** naqsha-ye Kâbol
March Mârch
mare kâbus; malikholya
mark neshân
market bâzâr
marriage nekâh
married *said by a man* zan-dâr; *said by a woman* shoy-dâr; **I am married.** *said by a man* Man zan dârom.; *said by a woman* Man shawhar dârom.
marsh bâtlâq; jabazâr
martyr shahid; **martyrs** shohadâ
mascara surma
massage *verb* mâlesh
mat chuti
match *football* mosâbeqa; *lighter* gogerd
material mâda; shay
mathematics riyâzyât
matter: It doesn't matter! Mohem nêst!
mattress doshak; toshak
mature pokhta
mausoleum maqbara
May May
may I? momken hast man...?
maybe momken; shâyad
mayor shârwâl
me man; ma
meal nân
mean mânâ dâdan; **What does this mean?** mânâ-ye in chist?
meaning mânâ
means: by means of az râh-e
measles sorkhakân
measure *verb* andâza gereftan
measurement andâza
meat gôsht; **ground meat** kôfta

mechanic mêkhânik; mestari
media *the press* matbu'ât; **mass media** wasâyil etelâ'at-e jam'i; rasâna-hâ-ye jam'i
medical tebi; **medical insurance** bêma-ye tebi
medication dawâ
medicine dawâ
meet molâqât kardan
meeting majles; molâqât; **meetings** majâles
melon kharbuza
member ozw
memory yâd
menstruation nâ-juri mâhâna
menu mênyu
mercenary mozdur
message payghâm
metal felez
meter *measure* mitar; **light meter** nur sanj
midday châsht
middle miyân; **in the middle of** mâ bayn-e
Middle East Sharq-e Myâna
midnight nesf-e shab
midwife qâbela
mile mâyl; mêl
military *adjective* nezâmi; **military university** harbi pôhantun
milk shir
mill: watermill âsyâ
millet arzan
million melyun
minaret monâr
mince; minced meat kôfta
mine *explosive* mayn; *mineral* mâdan
minefield sâha-ye mayn; maydân-e mayn
miner mâdanchi
mineral mâdani
mineral water âb-e mâdani
minister wazir
ministry wezârat
minority aqaliyat
minute *noun* daqiqa; daqa
miracle mo'jeza

mirror âyina
miss *verb* az dest dadan
Miss Pêghla
missile râkêt; mezâyl; marmi
mist ghobâr
mistake ghalat; error; gonâ; **to make a mistake** eshtebâh kardan
mobile phone mobâyl
model *example* mâdal; namuna
modem mâdem
modern modern; jadid; asri
Mojahed Mojâhed
Mojahedin Mojâhedin
mollah molâ
moment lahza; **a moment!** yak sât!
monarch shâh
monarchy shâhi; saltanati
monastery mâbad
Monday Doshambê
money paysa; pul
month mâh
monthly mâhâna
monument âsar; yâdgâr
moon mâh; mâhtâb; **full moon** mâh-e kâmel; **new moon** mâh-e naw
more bêshtar; **more or less** kam-o-bêsh
more zyâd; zyât
moreover ghayr-e
morning sôb; sôbh; **in the morning** sôbaki; **this morning** emruz sobh; **good morning!** sobh ba khayr!
mosque masjed; mâjed
mosquito pasha; **mosquito net** pashakhâna
most bêshtarin
mother mâdar
motorbike môtarsaykel
motorway sarak; shahrâh
mountain kô; kôh; **mountain pass** kôtal; **mountain stream** sêl
mouse mush
mouth dahan; dân

move harakat kardan; **to move home** kôch kardan

movement harakat

movie film

Mr. Âqâ; Sâheb; Shâghâlay

Mrs. Khânom; Mêrman

Ms. Dokhtar; Pêghla

much zyâd; zyât; besyâr; **how much?** chand?; cheqadar? **how much is it?** cheqadar ast?; **not much** kam; **too much** besyâr zyâd

mud khâk; gel

mug *noun* pyâla; *verb* dozdi kardan

mugger dozd

mugging dozdi

mulberry tut; **dried mulberries** talkhân

mule qâter

mullah molâ

municipality shârwâli

murder *noun* qatl; *verb* qatl kardan

murderer qâtel

museum mozyam

music museqi; mozik; **music festival** festiwal-ye museqi

Muslim *person* Mosolmân; *thing* Eslâmi

must bâyad

mustache burut

mutton gôsht-e gospand

my -em

myself khodam

N

nail clippers nâkhon gir

nail *metal* mêkh; *of finger/toe* nâkhun

naked loch

name nâm; esm; **family name** esm-e fâmel; **What is your name?** Nâm-e shomâ chê-st?; **My name is Fred.** Nâm-e man Fered hast.

napkin destmâl; ruypâk

nappy qondâq; **I need to change my baby's nappy.** Man bâyad qondâq-e teflam râ ewaz konom.

narrow tang

nation *people* melat; *state* mamlakat

national meli

nationality meliyat; tabiyat

natural tabiyi; **natural disaster** balâ-ye tabiyi; **natural resources** manâbê-ye tabiyi

nature tabiyat

nausea del-badi

navel nâf

navy qowâ-ye bahri

near nazdik

near (to) nazdik(-e)

nearby nazdiki

nearly taqrêban

necessary lâzem; zarur; **to be necessary** kâr budan; **It's necessary.** Lâzem ast.

neck gardan

necklace gardan band

necktie nektây

need niyâz dâshtan; kâr dâshtan; zarorat dâshtan; **I need...** Man niyâz ba ... dârom.

needle sôzan; suzan; **Do you have needle and thread?** Shomâ suzan wa târ dârêd?

negotiator mozâkera konenda

neighbor hamsâya

neither hêch kodâm

nerve(s) asâb

net: **fishing net** tur-e mâhi giri; **mosquito net** pashakhâna

never hargez; hêch wakht

nevertheless sar az i ham; sar az ô ham

new naw; **new moon** mâh-e naw; **new year** sâl-e naw

New Year's Day Nawrôz

New Zealand Zelând-e Jadid

news akhbâr; khabar(â); mâlumât

newspaper akhbâr; rôz-nâma; newspaper in English akhbâr-e Inglisi

next ba'di; âyenda; next week hafta-ye âyenda

nice khosh

niceness khoshi

night shab; night and day shabânarôz; at night shawaki; last night dishab; good night! shab ba khayr!

nightclub disko

nightguard; nightwatchman gazmê shab

nine no

nineteen nozda

ninety nawad

no nê; na; *not any* hêch kodâm/yak; no one hêch kas; no entry dâkhel shodan mamnu ast; no problem! Moshkel nêst!; no smoking segrêt kashedan mana' ast; no sugar bê bôra

nobody hêch kas

noise ghâlmaghâl

noisy ghâlmaghâli

nomad kuchi

none hêch kodâm; hêch yak

noon châsht

normal âdi

north *noun* shamâl

north(ern) *adjective* shamâli

Northern Ireland Âyrlaynd-e Shamâli

nose bini

not na; ne; do not...! ... nakon!

note: bank note bânknot

notebook ketâbcha

nothing hêch

nought sefer

noun nâm; esim

novel ketâb-e dâstân; nâwel; a novel in English ketâb dâstân-e Inglisi

November Nowambar

now âle; hâlâ; hâle; from now on az i pas; till now az i pêsh

nowhere hêch jây

nude loch

number nomra

nurse nars; parastâr

nut mêwa-ye khoshk; khasta

O

obese châq

objective maqsad

obligation ta'ahod; masuliyat

obliged majbur

observer nâzer

obviously mâlumdâr

occupation *job* kâr; pêsha; kesb; occupation of a country eshghâl-e yak keshwar; occupying forces nêru-hâ-ye eshghâl gar

occur wâqê shodan; etefaq oftadan

o'clock: It is six o'clock. Sâ'at: sâ'at shesh ast.

October Aktobar

odor buy

of az

offer bakhshidan

office daftar; office worker kârmand dafter

officer afsar; karmand

official *adjective* rasmi

often besyâr

oil têl; cooking oil rôghan; oil pipeline pâyp-lâyn-e têl; oil production estekhrâj-e têl; oil refinery tasfiyakhâna-ye têl; oil spill lâya têl; têl parâganda shoda; oil tanker tânkar-e têl; oil well châh-e têl; oil worker kârgar estekhrâj-e têl; oil can quti-ye têl; oil field maydân-e têl; oil-lamp cherâgh-e têli

ointment malam; marham

okay mowâfeq

okra bâmyâ

old kôhna; pir; **old man** bâbâ; pir; **old city** shâr-e kohna; **How old are you?** Chand sâla asti?; **How old is he/she?** Chand sâla hast?; **I am ... years old.** Man ... sâla hastom.

olive zaytun; **wild olive** senjed

on balâ-ye ruy-e; **Is the bus on time?** Âyâ bas sar-e waqt myâyad?

one yak; **one-quarter** yak paw

oneself khod

one-way yak tarafa; **one-way street** sarak-e yak tarafa; **one-way ticket** tiket-e yak tarafa

onion pyâz

only yagâna; tanhâ

onto *preposition* ba suy-e

open *noun* bâz; *verb* bâz kardan

opera operâ

operating theater/room otâq-e amaliyât/jarâhi

operation *surgical* amaliyât

operator aprêtar

opinion khyâl; **in my opinion** ba khyâlem

opposite (to) moqâbel(-e)

opposition mokhâlefat

or yâ

orange *fruit* nârenj; mâlta; kêno; *color* nârenji

orchard bâgh

order *verb:* **to order a meal** ghezâ sefâresh dâdan; **to order someone** sefâresh/farmâyesh dâdan; **to put in order** tartib kardan/dâdan

ordinary âdi

origin asl

original asli

orphan yatim

orphanage mrastun

other digar; dega

otherwise agar nê

our -emâ

ours az mâ

ourselves mâyân

out bêrun

outbreak *skin* mêda

outside bêrun

oven tandur; dâsh

overcoat bâlâpôsh

overtake sebqat kardan

owing to az khâter-e

owl bum

own *adjective* khod; *verb* az mâlek budan

owner mâlek; sâheb; dârâ

oxygen âksêjan

P

package basta

padlock qofl; qolf

page safa

pail satel

pain dard

painful dardmand; dardnâk

painkiller mosaken; **painkillers** mosakenhâ

paint *noun* rang; *verb* rang kardan

painter rangmâl; naqâsh

painting *action* rangmâli; *picture* tâblo

pair jôra

Pakistan Pâkestân

Pakistani Pâkestâni

palace qasar

pale rang parida

pantyhose barjis

paper *substance* kâghaz; *article* maqâla; *newspaper* akhbâr; **sheet of paper** tota-ye kâghaz

parachute parâshot

paradise behesht; janat

paralyze falaj kardan

parcel basta; pârsal

pardon *noun* ozor; *verb* bakhshidan; **to beg pardon** ozor khâstan

parents

parents wâledayn; padar-mâdar
park *noun* pârk; *verb* pârk kardan
parliament pârlemân; *lower house* olosi-jerga; *upper house* meshrâno-jerga
part qesmat
participate shêrkat kardan
particle zara
partridge kabk
party mêhmâni; *political* hezb; **parties** *political* azhâb
Pashto *language* Pashtô
Pashto; Pashtun Pashtun
pass *noun* gozargâh; *mountain* kôtal; tangi; *verb* gozashtan; têr shodan
passable qâbel-e gozar; **Is the road passable?** Ayâ in sarak qâbel-e gozar kardan ast?
passage gozar; dahlêz
passenger mosâfer; **passengers** mosâferin
passport pâsport; **passport number** shomâra-ye pâsport
past *adjective/noun* gozashta; **in the past** dar sâbeq
pasta makaroni
path râh
patience saber
patient *medical* mariz
pause *verb* dam gereftan
pay *noun* mo'âsh; mozd; *verb* pardâkhtan; **pay phone** telifun-e omumi
payment pardâkht
peace solh; **peace talks** mozâkerât-e solh; **peace-keeping troops** qowâ-ye hâfez-e solh
peach shaftâlu
peak qola
pear nâk
pearl morwârid
peasant zâre'; dêhqân
pebble sangchel
pediatrician dâktar-e atfâl

pediatrics teb-e atfâl
pelvis lagan-e khâsera
pen qalam
pencil pensel
penicillin pensilin
penknife châqu-ye jêbi
people mardom
pepper morch
perfect âli
perform amali kardan; ejrâ kardan
performance ejrâ
perfume ater
perhaps shâyad
period *of time* zamân; *menstrual* âdat-e mâhâna
permission ejâza
permitted rawâ; halâl
Persian Irâni; *language* Fârsi
person âdam; ensân; shakhs
personal shakhsi
perspiration khôy
petrol petrol
pharmacy dawâ-khâna
phone *noun* telefun; *verb* telefun kardan
photo aks; foto
photocopier mâshin-e fotokâpi
photocopy *noun* fotokâpi; *verb* fotokâpi kardan
photograph *noun* foto; aks; *verb* foto/aks gereftan
photographer akâs
photography akâsi
physics fizik
physiotherapy fizyotrâpi
piano pyâno
pickax kolang
pickles âchâr
picture aks; tâblo
pig khuk
pigeon kaftar
pilaf/pilau rice palaw
pilgrim hâji
pill goli
pillow bâlesh; bâlesht
pilot pêlat
pin peng; senjâq

pink golâbi

pipe *tube* pâyp; *smoking* nal

pipeline pâyp-lâyn; *oil pipeline* pâyp-lâyn-e têl

pirate dozd

pistachio pesta

pistol tofangcha

pitch *football* maydan-e futbâl

pizza pitsa

place jây; mahal; **place of birth** mahal-e tawalod; **in place of** êwaz-e; **to take place** gap shodan

plain *noun* dasht

plan naqsha; plân

plane *airplane* tayâra

plane tree chenâr

plank takhta

plant geyâ; gyâ

planting kâshtan

plaster *Band-Aid* palaster

plastic palastik

plate bêshqâb

play *theater* nammâyesh; *verb* bâzi kardan; *a musical instrument* nawâkhtan

please *verb* khosh âmadan; **please!** lotfan!

pleasure lezat

plow *noun* qolba; *verb* qolba zadan

plug *electric* palag

plum âlu

plumber nâldawân

p.m. ba'd az zohr

pneumonia sina-o-baghal

poaching *animals/game* shekâr-e ghayr-e qânuni

poacher; game poacher shekârchi-ye ghayr-e qânuni

pocket jêb

podium loj-e saltanati

poem she'r

poet shâyer

pointed têz

poison zâhr

poisonous zâhr-dâr

police pôlis; **police station** mâmoryat-e pôlis

policeman pôlis

polite mo'adab

political siyâsi

politician siyâsat madâr

politics siyâsat

pollute âluda kardan

polo chogân

pony yâbo

pool hawz

poor gharib; bêchâra; nâdâr

population nufus

pork gôsht-e khuk

port bandar

portable T.V. teliwizyun-e sayâr

portion qesmat

portrait taswir

position makân; mawqiyat

possessions mâl

possible momken; **if possible** agar momken bâshad

post *mail* post; **border post** tâna

postbox post-baks

postcard postkârd

post office posta-khâna

postpone mâtel kardan

pot dêg

potato kachâlu

pottery kolâli

pound *weight* pawnd; *sterling* pawnd

pour rêkhtan

powder *noun* podar; *verb* mayda kardan

power qodrat

practice; practise *noun* prêktes; *verb* prêktes kardan

praise tamjid kardan; sifat kardan

pray do'â kardan

prayer namâz

precise dorost; daqiq

precisely pura

prefer khosh kardan

pregnant shekam-dâr; hâmela; **I'm pregnant.** Man hâmela hastom.

premier sadr-e a'zam

preparation tayâri
prepare âmâdagi gereftan; tayâr kardan
prepared tayâr
prescription *medical* noskha
present *gift* hadyâ; tôhfa; *time* hâzer
president ra'is-e jamhur
presidential guard gârd-e reyasate-e jamhuri
press: the press matbu'ât
pressure feshâr
pressure cooker dêg-e bokhâr
previously pêshtar
price qêmat; qêmat; narkh
pride ghorur
priest kashish
prime minister sadr-e a'zam
print châp kardan
printer matbo'a; *computer* printer
printer's châp-khâna
prison zendân; bandi-khâna
prisoner asir; bandi; **prisoner-of-war** asir-e jangi
prize jâyeza
probable mohtamal; **it is probable** emkân dârad; mohtamal ast
probably ehtemâlan; **most probably** hatman
problem moshkel
product mahsul
profession kesb; kesp; wazifa
professional *person* herfawi; maslaki
professor profaysar; ustâd; pôhând
profit fâyeda; **to make a profit** fâyeda kardan
program progrâm; **radio program** progrâm-e râdyôyi
prohibited mana'; harâm
projectile gôla; marmi
projector projektor
promise *noun* wa'da; wâda; *verb* wâda dâdan

pronounce talafoz kardan
pronunciation talafoz
proof sobut; dalil
prophet payghâmbar; rasul
prosthesis masnuyi
prostration sajda
protect mohâfezat kardan
protection mohâfezat
protest *noun* mokhâlefat; *verb* mokhâlefat kardan
protocol tashrefât
proud maghrur
prove sâbet kardan
proverb zarb-ol-masal
provided that ba shart-ê ke
province welâyat
pub bâr
public *adjective* omumi; **public phone** telifun-e omumi
publication châp
publish enteshâr dâdan; pakhsh kardan
publisher nâsher
pul *currency* pul
pull kashedan
pull-over jâkat
pump *noun* pamp; *verb* pamp kardan
pumpkin kaddu
puncture panchar; **I have a puncture.** Yak tâyr-e môtaram panchar ast.
punish jazâ dâdan
pupil shâgerd
pure pâk; sâf
purple arghawâni
push tela kardan
put gozâshtan; mândan; **to put on clothes** lebâs pushidan; **to put out** gol kardan

Q

quadruped châr-pây
quail bôdana
quarter *area* mahal; *town* kârta
queen maleka

question *noun* porsân; sawâl; *verb* porsân kardan; porsidan
queue qatâr; dom; domb
quick têz; zud; zut
quickly ba-zudi
quiet *adjective* khâmôsh
quietly âhesta
quilt lehâf
quince behi
quit tark kardan
quiz mosâbeqa-ye zehni

R

rabbit khargôsh
rabies bêmâri-ye sag-e dêwâna
radar râdâr
radiator râdiyâtor-e markaz garmi; *of car* râdiyâtor
radio râdyô; **radio broadcast** nashrât-e râdyôyi; **radio program** progerâm-e râdyôyi; **radio station** estêshan-e râdyôyi
radiography râdyôgrâfi
radish moli
rag sâfi
raid hamla; hojum
railway khat-e rêl; **railway station** estêshan
rain *noun* bârân; *verb* bâridan; **it is raining** bârân mêbârad
rainbow kamân-e rostam; rangin kamân
raisins keshmesh
ram kubidan
Ramadan Ramazân; Rôza
range reshta; selsela
rape tajâwoz kardan; **I've been raped.** Ba man tajâwoz shodast.
rapid sari'; zod
rapidly sari'an
rarely besyâr kam
rash dâna
rat mush
rate telli; *speed* andâza-ye sor'at

ravine tangi
raw khâm
razor; razor blade pâki; pal rish; **electric razor** mâshin-e rish
reach (dest) rasidan
reactionary mortajê
read khândan
reading khândan
ready âmâda; tayâr; **I am ready.** Man âmâda astom.
real wâqêyi
reality wâqêyat
realize dark kardan
reaping daraw kardan
reason dalil; **reason for travel** dalil-e/hadaf-e mosâferat; **for that reason** ba ân dalil
reasonable mâqul
rebel *noun* yâghi
recall yâd dâdan
receipt noskha; rasid
receive qabul kardan
recent âkherin; tâza
recently jadidan; âkhiran
reception desk mêz-e pazirâyi
recipe noskha
recognize shenâkhtan
record *noun* rekârd; *verb* sabt kardan
recovery *medical* jôrâyi
red sorkh
Red Cross salib-e sorkh
reed nay
referee hakam; refri
refinery tasfiyakhâna
refrigerator yakhchâl
refugee panâhenda; mohâjer; **refugees** panâhendagân
refugee camp kamp-e panâhendagan
regarding râjê-ba
regime rezhim
region manteqa
registered mail post-e râjistar
reign *noun* saltanat; dawra
relationship *alliance* khêshâ; *blood* qawmi

relative khêshâwand; **relatives** aqâreb

relax esterâhat kardan

release rehâ kardan; khalâs kardan

relief aid komak-e emdâdi

religion dên

religious scholar mawlawi

remain bâqi mândan

remaining mânda

remember yâd budan/dâshtan

remove pas kardan

repair *noun* tarmim; *verb* tarmim kardan

repeat tekrâr kardan

replace jâneshin kardan

reply *noun* jawâb; *verb* jawâb dâdan

report gozâresh dâdan

represent namâyendagi kardan

representation namâyendagi

representative namâyenda

republic jamhuri

research tahqiq kardan

reservation *ticket* rezarf; **I have a reservation.** Man rezarf karda-om.

reserve *verb* rezarf kardan; **Can I reserve a place/seat?** Mêtawânom yak ja rezarf konom?

reservoir aw-dân

responsibility mas'uliyat

responsible mas'ul

rest *noun* esterâhat; *remainder* bâqimânda; *verb* esterâhat kardan

restaurant rastôrân

restore pas dâdan

restricted majbur

result natija

return *noun* bazgasht; **return ticket** tiket-e do tarafa; *verb* (bâz) âmadan

reverse mâkus; sarchapa; *of vehicle* rêwars

reversed chapa

review *newspaper* tabsera

revolution enqelâb

rheumatism româtizom

rhubarb rawâsh

rib qaborgha

rice *raw* brenj; *plain cooked* chalaw; *pilau/pilaf* palaw; **rice water** aw-brenj; **rice pudding** shir-brenj

rich serwatmand; puldâr

ride *a horse* sawâr shodan

rifle tofang

right râst; *correct* dorost; **right now** hamin lahza; **right way up** râsta

rights hoquq; **civil rights** hoquq-e madani; **human rights** hoquq-e bashar

right-wing dest-rasti dar syâsat

ring *noun* halqa; angôshtar; *verb* zang zadan; **I want to ring Emma.** Man mêkhâhom ba Emma zang bozanom.

riot âshub; eghteshâsh

ripe pokhta

rise boland shodan; qyâm karda; khêstan

risk *noun* khatar; *verb* khatar kardan

river daryâ; **river bank** lab-e daryâ

road râh; sarak; **road map** naqsha-ye râh; **road sign** eshârât/alâmât-e tarâfiki

roadblock râh-e band

rob dozi kardan; **I've been robbed.** Az nazd-e man dozdi shodast.

robbery dozi

rock sang

roof bâm

room otâq; **room number** shomâra-ye otâq; **room service** khedamat-e otâq; **double room** otâq-e do nafara; **single room** otâq-e yak nafara

rooster khorus
rope rêsmân; rêspân
rosary tasbê
rose golâb
rotten ganda
round gerd
roundabout châr-râhi; chawk
route râh
row *line* radif; qatâr
royal saltanati
rubber râbar; **eraser** penselpâk
rubbish khâkjâro; **rubbish dump** khâkandâz
rubble kharâba
rude khashan; gostâkh
rug farsh
rugby râgbi
ruined bêrân; kharâb
ruins kharâba
ruler *measure* khat kash; *person* hâkem
run dawidan; **to run away** gorêkhtan; **to run out** tamâm kardan; **I have run out of petrol.** Têli môtaram khalâs shodast.
run dawidan
Russia Rus; Rusiya
Russian *person* Rus; *thing* Rusi
rust *noun* zang zada

S

sack *noun* kharita; khalta; *verb* barkenâr kardan
sad deq
safe bêkhatar; mahfuz
safety amneyat
safety pin peng
saffron zâfarân
sail *verb* keshtirâni kardan
sailboat keshti-e bâdi
saint zâhed
salad salâta
salary ma'âsh
sales assistant forôsh
salesperson forôshenda

saline shôr
saliva tof
salon: beauty salon salmâni
salt namak
salty shôr
same âm; ham
samovar samâwâr
sand rêg
sandal(s) chapli
sandwich sandewich
sanitary towels jan pâk
satellite qamar masnoye; **satellite phone** telifun-e satilâyt
satisfactory rezâyat bakhsh
satisfied râzi
Saturday Shambê
saucepan rôghan-dân
sausage sâsej
save *rescue* nejât dâdan; *money* pasandâz kardan
saw *noun* ara; *verb* ara kardan
say goftan
scabies garg
scales mêzân
scar dâgh-e zarm
scarcely nâ-chandân
scarf châdar
scatter parâganda kardan
scholar: religious scholar mawlawi
school maktab; **religious school** madrasa
sciatica negres
science olum
scientific elmi
scientist sâynsdân
scissors qaychi
score *noun* emteyâz; nomra; *football* gol; **What's the score?** Natija-ye mosâbeqa chist?; *verb* sabt kardan; **Who scored?** Ki emteyâz dârad?
scorpion gazhdom
Scot Eskâtlayndi
Scotland Eskâtlaynd
Scottish Eskâtlayndi
screw *noun* pêch; *verb* pechedan; pechândan

screwdriver pêch-kash; pêch-taw

scuba-diving awbâzi

scythe dâs

sea bahera

search jostoju kardan

season fasl

seat chawki; *political* korsi; post

second *adjective* dôwom; *noun* sânya

secondhand dest-e dôwom

secret *adjective* seri; *noun* ser

secret police pôlis-e makhfi

secretary sekartar

section qesmat; bakhsh

security salâmat; amniyat

see didan

seed dâna

seek pâlidan

seem mâlum shodan

seize tawqif kardan; dastger kardan

seldom besyâr kam

self khod

sell forôkhtan

seller forôsh

send ersâl kardan; rasândan

sender ferestinda

senior arshad; bâlâ

sense *meaning* mâni

sentence jomla

separately alâyda

September Septâmbar

septic gandida

series *TV/radio* selsela; seryâl

serious jeddi

servant nôkar

service khedmat

serviette destmâl; ruypâk

session jalsa

set shândan

seven haft

seventeen hafda; abda

seventy haftâd

several chandin

severe shadid; **severe heat** garmi-ye shadid

sew dôkhtan

sewing machine mâshin-e khayâti

sex *gender* jens; *act* joftgiri

shade sâya

shah shâh

shake takân dâdan

shame sharm

shampoo shâmpu

shape shakl

share *noun* sahm; *verb* taqsim kardan

sharp têz

shave tarâsh kardan

shaving cream krim-e rish

shawl shâl

she u

sheep gospan; gospand

sheepdog sag-e gala

sheet *bed* rojây; *of paper* tota-ye kâghaz

shell *military* marmi; *snail/sea* sadaf

shelter panâh gâh

shepherd chôpân

shine dorokhshidan

ship keshti

shirt pêrâhân

shiver *noun* larzesh

shivering larza

shock *medical* shâk

shoe(s) but

shoeshop but forôshi

shoot fâyr kardan; **Don't shoot! Fâyr nakon!**

shooting *film* film-giri

shop maghâza; dokân

shop assistant forôsh

shopkeeper dôkândâr

shopping kharid kardan; **to go shopping** sawdâ kharidan

shore sâhel

short kutâ(h)

shortage kambud

shoulder shâna; **shoulder blade** bêlak-e shâna

shout faryâd zadan

shovel bêl; pâru

show *noun* nomâyesh; *verb* neshân dâdan

shower hamâm kardan
shut *adjective* basta; *verb* bastan; basta kardan
sick bêmâr; mariz; **to be sick** mariz budan; **I am sick.** Man mariz astom.
sickness bêmâri; marizi
side: on the side of da(r) lab-e; **side by side** pâlu-ba-pâlu
sideways kaj
sight nazar
sign *noun* eshâra; alâma; *verb* emzâ kardan; **sign language** lesân-e alâmat
signal eshâra
signature emzâ
significance ahamiyat
significant mohem
silence khâmoshi
silent khâmôsh
silk abrêshom
silly ahmaq
silver noqra
similar shabê; **to be similar** shabê budan
simmer dam kardan
simple sâda
sin gonâ
since az; *because* chun (ke); **ever since** az sar-e
sing khândan; sorudan
single tak; **single room** otâq-e yak nafara
sink *noun* dastshu; *verb* gharq shodan; pâyin raftan
sinner gonâgâr
sister khwâr; khâhar
sit neshastan; sheshtan
situation hâl; hâlat
six shash
sixteen shânzda
sixth shashom
sixty shast
size andâza; qad
skeleton eskelêt
ski ski zadan
skill mahârat
skilled mâher

skin pôst
skirt dâman
sky âsmâm
sleep *noun* khâb; khaw; *verb* khâbidan; **to go to sleep** (dar) khaw budan
sleeping bag kharita-ye khâb
sleeping car môtar-e khâb
sleeping pill(s) dawâ-ye khâb; guli-ye khâb âwar
sleepy khâb âlud; **I am sleepy.** Man khâb âlud astom.
sleet barf-o-bârân
slender nâzok
slip laghzidan
slope sarâshêbi
slow; slowly âhesta; âyesta; âsta
small khord; kochak; chucha
smaller khordtar; kochaktar
smallpox chechak
smell *noun* bu; buy
smoke *noun* dud; *verb* dud kardan; *tobacco* segrêt kashedan
smoked *food* dud
smoking *tobacco* segrêt kashedan
smooth lashem
smuggler qâchâq bar
snack asrya
snail gawak
snake mâr
snakebite mâr gazidagi
snow barf; **It is snowing.** Barf mêbârad.
so khay; **so far** az i pêsh; **so much/many** inqadar; zyâd
soap sâbun
soccer futbâl; **soccer match** mosâbeqa-ye futbâl
social ejtemâyi
society jâme'a
sock(s) jorâb
sodium bicarbonate poli
soft narm
softly âhesta; âyesta; âsta

solar shamsi
soldier askar
solve hal kardan
some ba'zi
somebody kase; kasê
somehow ba yak qesm
someone kase; kasê
something chize
sometimes gâhe; gây
somewhere kodâm jây; somewhere else dega jây; digar jâ
son pesar
song âwâz
son-in-law dâmâd; dâmât
soon ba zudi; as soon as har wakht ke
sorbet shir-yakh
sore throat golu(n) dardi
sorrow gham
sorry! Mo'azerat mêkhahom!; I'm sorry! mota'asefam!
sort *noun* qesem; *verb* jodâ kardan
soul jan; ruh
sound sadâ; sound equipment wasâyel-e sawti
soup shorwâ; sup
sour torsh
source manba'
south *noun* jonub
south(ern) *adjective* jonubi
souvenir tohfa-ye yâdgâri
soviet shurawi
sow kâshtan
space fazâ
spade bêl; pâru
Spaniard Haspânawi
spanner rench
spare ezâfi; spare tire tâyr-e eshtapni; spare parts store porza forôshi
sparkle jaraqa zadan
sparrow gonjeshk
speak gap zadan; Do you speak English? Shomâ Inglisi mêfahmêd?; I speak... Man ... gap mêzanom.

speaker sokhansara
special makhsus
specialist motakhases
spectacles âynak
speed sor'at
spell *verb* naweshtan; How do you spell it? In râ chetor mênawisêd?
spend kharch kardan; masraf kardan
spending kharch; kharch
spicy *hot* tond; masâla dâr; talkh
spider ankabut
spill rêkhtan
spin charkhidan
spinach pâlak
spinal column stun-e foqarât; têr-e kamar
spine *back* sotun-e foqarât; têr-e kamar
spiritual leader pir; shaykh
spit tof kardan
spite: in spite of har chand ke
splint *medical* takhta
split jodâ kardan
spoil kharâb shodan
sponge esfanj
spoon qâshoq
sports warzesh
sportsman warzesh kâr
sprain *medical* barâmadagi
spread *verb* tet kardan
spring *of water* cheshma; *metal* fanar; *season* bahâr
spy jâsus; râpôrchi
square chawk; town square chawk-e shâr
stadium estâdyum
staff kârmandân
stage marhala
stairs zina
stale kohna
stallion asb-e nar
stamp *postal* tiket-e posti; *official* mohr
stand istâdan
star setâra**

start shorô kardan; **to start up** châlân kardan

state *condition* hâl; *federal* iyâlat; *nation* dawlat

station estêshan

stationer's qertâsya foroshi

stationery qertâsi-ye naweshtan

statue mojâsema

stay (bâqi) mândan; pâyidan

steak stêk

steal dozi kardan; **My wallet has been stolen.** Baksakam râ dozdidand.

steam bokhâr

steel fôlâd

steering wheel eshtireng

sterile *antiseptic* zed-e ofôni

sterling pawnd estarling

stethoscope estâtiskop

stew âsh; qorma

stick *noun* asâ; *walking* chub desti; *verb* chaspidan

still *adverb* hanôz

sting *noun* nêsh; *verb* nêsh zadan; gazidan

stink *verb* bu-ye bad dâdan

stire *shop* maghâza

stitch *surgical* kok khordan

stolen dozdi; **My car has been stolen.** Môtaram dozdi shoda.

stomach shekam; mêda

stomachache shekam dard

stone *noun* sang; *of fruit* khasta; *adjective* sangi

stop istâdan; estâd kardan; tawaqof kardan; **stop!** estâd shaw!; **don't stop!** estâd nashaw!

store *shop* maghâza; *for storage* godâm; *warehouse* tahwil-khâna

storm tufân

story dâstan; *floor* manzel

stove ojâq; *for heating* bokhâri

stove-pipe dudraw

straight râst; mostaqim; **straight on** râst; **Go straight ahead.** Mostaqim pêsh boro.; **straight on** ru-ba-ru

straightaway desti; fawran

strange ajib

stranger bêgâna; nâ-âshnâ

straw kâh

strawberry tut farangi

stream jôy; **mountain stream** sêl

street kocha

strength tawân; qodrat

strengthen mahkam kardan

strike *noun, from work* e'tesâb; *verb* e'tesâb kardan

string târ; sim

strong tawâna; qawi

structure sâkhtomân; emârat

struggle kushesh kardan

stuck: to be stuck gir mândan; **Our car is stuck.** Môtar-e mâ band mânda.

student shâgerd; mota'alem

study *noun* motale'a; *verb* motale'a kardan; khândan

subject matlab; mawzu; mazmun

suburb huma; atrâf

success pêruzi

such chenin

sudden; suddenly dafatan

sufficient kâfi; bas; **to be sufficient** bas kardan

sugar *granulated* bôra; **sugar cane** nay shakar; **sugar lump** qand

suit *of clothes* dereshi

suitable monâseb

suitcase baks

sultan soltân

summer tâbestân

summit qola

sun âftâb; âftaw

sunbathe hamâm-e âftâb

sunblock âftâb gir

sunburn âftâb zadagi

Sunday Yakshambê

sunglasses âynak-e âftâbi

sunny âftâbi; **It is sunny.** Hawâ âftâbi hast.

sunrise tolu'
sunset ghorub
supermarket suparmârkêt
supervise negâ kardan
supper nân-shaw; nân-e shaw
supplies zakhira
supply *noun* sâmân; *verb* rasândan
suppose farz kardan
sure *adjective* motmayen; yaqin; *adverb* motmayenan; **to be sure** yaqin dâshtan
surgeon jarâh
surgery *operation* jarâhi
surname nâm-e fâmeli; khânawâdagi
surprising ghayr-e montazera; ta'ojob âwar; **to be surprising** ta'ojob âwar budan
survey *noun* moshâheda; *verb* moshâheda kardan
surveyor moshâheda gar; takhmin konenda
swallow *verb* bal'idan; khôrdan
swamp bâtlâq; jabazâr
swear *oath* qasam khordan; *curse* bad-rad goftan; nasaza goftan
sweat *noun* araq; *verb* araq kardan
sweater jâkat
sweep *verb* jâru kardan
sweet shirin
swell waram kardan; pondendan
swelling barâmadagi
swim awbâzi kardan
swimming awbâzi
swimming pool hawz
swimsuit lebâs-e awbâzi
swindler lochak
swing *noun* tâb khordan
switch *electric* switch; **to switch off** gôl kardan; **to switch on** roshan kardan
symbol neshân; sambôl
symptom alâmat; alâyem
synagogue mâbad-e Yahudi; kanesht

syntax nahwa; tarkib
syphilis âtashak
syringe pêchkâri
syrup sharbat
system sistam

T

table mêz
tablecloth sar-mêzi
tablet goli; tâblêt
tailor khayât
take bôrdan; gereftan; **to take off** *something* boland shodan; **What time does the plane take off?** Che waqt tayâra parwâz mêkonad?
talk gap zadan; hafr zadan
tall boland
tampon kotekh; tampôn
tank makhzan; *military* tânk; zerê-posh; **petrol tank** tânk-petrol
tanker tânkar
tap *faucet* shêrdân
tape nawâr; *cassette* kâset; **tape recorder** nawâr zabt
target maqsad
taste *noun* maza; *verb* maza kardan
tasteless bêmaza
tasty mazadâr
tax *noun* mâliyât; teks; mâhsul; *verb* mâliyât waza kardan
tax-free bedun-e mâliyât
taxi taksi
tea chây; **tea with lemon** chây bâ lêmu; **tea with milk** sher-chây; **herbal tea** jôshanda
teach dars dâdan
teacher mo'alem; mwalem
tea-house chây-khâna
team tim
teapot châynak
tear *noun* ashk
tear *verb* pâra kardan
teaspoon qâshoq-e chây khori
technical fanni; takhasosi

technique fan; takhnik

teeth dandânhâ

telecommunications mokhâberât

telegram telegerâm

telephone *noun* telefun; telifun; *verb* telefun kardan; **telephone operator** aprêtar-e telefun

telescope teleskôp

television teliwizyun

telex teleks

tell goftan

temperature *atmospheric* harârat; medical daraja-ye tab; **The temperature is high.** Harârat bâlâ ast.; **The temperature is low.** Harârat pâyin ast.; **I have a temperature.** Man tab dârom.

temple mâbad

ten da; dâ; dah

tender narm

tennis tenis

tent khayma

tenth dahom

term *condition* shart

termite muriyâna

terrible wahshat nâk

territory qalamro

test *noun* emtehân; test; *verb* azmâyesh kardan; **blood test** test-e khun

text matn

than nesbat ba; dar moqayesa bâ

thank *verb* tashakor kardan; **thank you!** tashakor!

that ân; ô; *conjunction* ke

theater teyâter

theft dozi

their -eshân

theirs az ânhâ

them ânhâ râ

themselves khodeshân

then bâd

theory nazari'ya; teyori

there onja; **there is/are** ôna

thereabouts usu

therefore bênehâyat

thermometer tarmamêtar; mêzân-ol-harâra

these; they inhâ; ânhâ

thick *wide* zakhim; **thick forest** jangal-e anbuh

thief dozd

thigh rân

thin nâzok

thing chiz; dâna; tâ

think feker kardan; **I think that...** Man feker mêkonom ke...

third sêwom; **one-third** yak sêwom

thirsty tashna; **I'm thirsty.** Tashna hastom.

thirteen sêzda

thirty si

this i; in; **this way; in this way** hamchonin

thorn khâr

those ânhâ

thought feker; tafakor

thousand hazâr

thread rêsmân; târ; **Do you have needle and thread?** Suzan wa târ dârêd?

three sê; **three times** sê bâr; **three-quarters** sê paw

throat golu; golun

thrombosis gerê khordan khun dar rag

throne takht-e shâhi

through az bayni

throw andâkhtan; partâftan

thumb shast

thunder ra'd

thunderstorm tufân

Thursday Panjshambê; Paynjshambê

thus hamchonin

tick *insect* kana

ticket ticket; **one-way ticket** tiket-e yak tarafa; **return ticket** tiket-e do tarafa; **ticket office** daftar-e forôsh-e tiket

tie

tie *necktie* nektây; *verb* bastan
ties rawâbet; **diplomatic ties** rawâbet-e diplomâtik
tight tang
tights jorâb-e zanâna
till tâ; **till now** az i pêsh
time waqt/wakht; *hour* sât; *period* zamân; **two times** do bâr; **for a long time** barâye zamân-e zyâd; **free time** waqt-e tafrê(h); **What time is it?** Sâ'at chand ast?
timetable taqsim awqat; barnâma; **timetable for travel** barnâma-ye parwâzhâ
tip *noun, money* bakhshesh
tire *noun* tayr; *verb* khasta bodan
tired khasta
tiredness khastagi
tiring khastagi-âwar
tissues kâghaz; destmâl kâghazi
to ba; tâ
toast *bread* nân-e sorkh karda/ bereshta
tobacco tambâku
today emrôz
toe panja-ye pa
together yak jây
toilet(s) tashnâb; *outside* khâkandâz; **toilet paper** kâghaz-e tashnâb
toiletries wasâyel-e tashnâb/ hamam
tomato bânjân-e rumi
tomb qaber; *saint's* zyârat
tomorrow fardâ; sabâh; **the day after tomorrow** pas-fardâ
ton; tonne tan
tongue zabân
tonight emshab; emshaw
too âm; ham; **too little** besyâr kam; **too many/much** besyâr zyâd
tools wasâyel
tooth dandân
toothache dandân dard

toothbrush bors-e dandân
toothpaste krim-dandân
toothpick khelâl-dandân
top bâlâ
torture *noun* shekanja; *verb* shekanja kardan
touch *verb* dest zadan
tourism sayâhat; torezam
tourist sayâh; garzandôy; **tourist office** daftar-e torezam
tow rope rêsmân; kêbal
tow kashedan môtar ba aqeb môtar digar; **Can you tow us?** Môtar-e mâ râ kash karda mêtawânêd?
toward(s) sôy-e
towel jan pâk; **hand-towel** dest-pâk
tower borj
town shâr; **town center** markaz-e shâr; **town hall** shâr wâli; welâyat
toxic zâhr-dâr
track dombâl kardan
tractor taráktor
trade *profession* kesb; kesp; **trade union** etehâdiya-ye tejârati
tradition rasm; rawâj
traditional an'anawi
traffic tarâfik
traffic lights eshâra-ye tarâfiki
traffic police polis-e tarâfik
trailer têlar
train terên; qatâr; **train station** estêshan
tranquilizer mosâken
transfer: **flight-transfer** parwâz-e enteqâl
transformer enteqâl dehenda
transfusion enteqâl; **blood transfusion** enteqâl-e khun
translate tarjoma kardan
translation tarjoma
translator tarjomân
transmit ferestâdan

transmitter ferestinda
transport enteqâl dâdan
trap dâm
trash khâkjâro
trauma âsib
travel *noun* mosâferat; *verb* safar kardan; **travel agency** daftar-e mosâferati; trêwal ejansi
traveler mosâfer; **travelers** mosâferin
traveler's checks chek-e mosâferati
treacherous khâyen
treasure khazâna
treasurer khazâna-dâr
treasury khazâna
treatment êlâj
tree darakht; **trees** darakhthâ
trial *legal* mahâkema; da'wâ; *test* azmâyesh
troops asâker
trouble *noun* moshkel; *verb* zâhmat dâdan; **What's the trouble?** Che moshkel wojud dârad ?
trousers patlun; *traditional* tombân
truce solh; môtareka; âtesh-bas
truck trak; lâri
true râst
trunk *of car* tôl-baks môtar
truth haqiqat
try azmâyesh kardan; kôshesh kardan
tube tyub
tuberculosis sel; *of the bones* sel-e ostokhân
Tuesday Sêshambê
tunnel tunal
turban longi
Turk Torki
turkey filmorgh
Turkey Torkiya
Turkish Torki
turn dawr zadan; gardidan; **to turn around** bar gashtan; **turn left!** taraf-e chap bagard!; **turn right!** taraf-e râst bagard!
turnip shalgham
T.V. teliwizyun
tweezers taw-e syâgak
twelve dowâzda
twenty bist
twice do bâr
twilight shâm
twins dogânagi
twisted kaj
two do; du
type *noun* qesm
typewriter tâyprâytar
typhoid; typhus mohreqa
tyrannical zâlem
tyranny zolm
tyre *noun* tâyr

U

ulcer zakham; **stomach ulcer** zakham-e mêda
umbrella chatri
uncle *maternal* mâmâ; *paternal* kâkâ
uncomfortable nâ râhat
unconsciousness zôf
under zêr-e
underground zêr zamin
underpass zêr gozar
understand fahmidan; **I understand.** Man mêfahmom.
undertake ta'ahod kardan; ejrâ kardan
underwear zêrpôshi
undo khonsâ kardan
unemployed bêkâr
unemployment bêkâri
unexploded bomb bam-e monfajer nashoda
unfortunate bad bakht
unfortunately bad bakhtâna; motâsefâna
unhappiness gham
unhappy nâ-râzi
unify motahed kardan

uniform *noun* lebâs
union etehâd; etehâdiya
unique yaktâ; behamtâ
United Nations Sâzmân-e Melal-e Motahed
United States of America Eyâlât-e Motaheda-ye Amrikâ
universal jahâni
university pôhantun; **military university** harbi pôhantun
unjust zâlem
unknown nâ-shenâs
unless magar
until tâ (ba); tâ wakht-e ke; **until now** az i pêsh
unwell bêmâr; nâ-jôr
up bâlâ; fawq
uproar ghâl-ma-ghâl
upset porayshân
urgent fawri
urine shâsha
us mâ
U.S.A. *see* United States
use estêmâl kardan
used to: to get used to âmokhta shodan
useful mofid
useless bêkâra
usual mâmuli
usually ghâleban

V

vacation rokhsat(i)
vaccinate wâksin kardan; **I have been vaccinated.** Man wâksin shodam.
vaccination wâksin
valley dara
van bârkash
variety anwâ
varnish jalâ dâdan
vase gol dân
vegetables sabzi (jât); tarkâri
vegetable shop sabzi forôshi
vegetarian sabzi khôr; **I am a vegetarian.** Man sabzi khôr astom.
veil châdar; **to put on a veil** ruy gereftan
vein rag; **jugular vein** shâh-rag
vendor forôsh
venereal disease maraz-e jensi
verb fe'l
very besyâr; zyâd/zyât; **very well** ba khubi; besyâr khub
vest *waistcoat* wâskat
veto rad kardan; wêto kardan
vice-president mo'âwen-e ra'is jamhur
victim qorbâni; **victims** qorbâniyân
victor pêrôz
victory pêruzi
video cassette; video player kaset-e wêdyô
view nazar; **in view of** az khâter-e
village dê
vine tâk
vinegar serka
violence khoshunat
virus wâyrus
visa wêza
visit *verb* molâqât kardan
visitor mêhmân
voice sadâ
vomit *verb* estefrâq kardan; **I have been vomiting.** Man estefrâq mêkardom.
vomiting estefrâq
vote *noun* ra'y; *verb* ra'y dâdan

W

wage war jang kardan
waist kamar
waistcoat wâskat
wait saber kardan; **to wait for** entezâr kashedan
waiter; waitress gârson; pêsh khedmat
wake bêdâr kardan; **Please**

wake me up at... Lotfan ma râ ... bêdâr konêd.

wall dêwâl; dêwâr

wallet baks-e jêbi

walnut châr-mâghz

want khâstan; **What do you want?** Che mêkhâyêd?; **I want...** Man ... mêkhâhom.; **I don't want...** Man ... na mêkhâhom.

war jang; **civil war** jang-e dâkheli

warehouse tahwil-khâna

warehouseman tahwil-dâr

warm garm

warped kaj

wash shostan

washing *laundry* kâlâ-shôyi; **washing powder** podar-e shostan

washroom tashnâb

wasp zambur

watch *noun* sât; *verb* morâqeb budan; **to watch (over)** negâ kardan; sayl kardan

water âw; âb; **water bottle** bôtal-e âw; **water carrier** saqaw; **Is there drinking water?** Âw-e nushidani hast?

waterfall âb shâr

watermelon tarbuz

watermill âs-e âb; âsyâ

way râh; **by way of** az râh-e; **that way** ân taraf; **this way** in taraf

we mâ

weak sost; zayif

weapon salâh; **weapons** aslehâ

wear pushidan

weasel râsu

weather hawâ

Wednesday Chârshambê

week hafta; **last week** hafta-ye gozashta; **this week** in hafta; **next week** hafta-ye âyenda

weekend âkher-e hafta

weekly haftawâr

weep geristan; gerya kardan

weight wazn

welcome! khosh âmadêd!

well *adjective/adverb* khub; *noun* châh; **oil well** châh-e têl; **very well** ba khubi

wellbeing juri

well-known mash-hur

west *noun* gharb; maghreb

west(ern) *adjective* gharbi

wet *adjective* tar

what? che?; chi?; **what kind?** che qesim?; **what's that?** ân chi-st?

wheat gandom

wheel charkh

wheelchair chawki-ye charkhi barâye mayub

when chun; kay; chi-waqt

where kojâ; **where from?** az kojâ?

whey dôgh

which *singular* kodâm; *plural* kodâmâ

while da(r) waqt-e ke

whiskey wiski

white safêd

who ke; ki?

whoever har ke; har kodâm

whole tamâm

whooping-cough khorâsak

why barây-e chi; bare chi; cherâ?

wide pahn; bardâr

wife zan

wild boar khuk

willow tree bêd

win bordan; **Who won?** Ki bord?

wind *noun* bâd

window kelken; panjara

windscreen; windshield kelken

windy tufâni

wine sharâb

wing bâl

winner pêrôz; kâmyâb

winter zamestân

wire sim; **barbed wire** sim-e khâr dâr

wisdom dânâyi
wish *verb* khâstan
with bâ
withdraw pas raftan
without bê-; bedun-e
witness shâhed
wolf gorg
woman zan
womb reham; batn
wood *substance* chob; *forest* jangal
wooden chubi
wool pashm
woolen pashmi
word kalema; loghat
work *noun* kâr; *verb* kâr kardan; **I work in a bank.** Man dar bânk kâr mêkonom.; **The phone doesn't work.** Telifun kâr namêkonad.
worker kârgar
world donyâ; jahân
worm kerm
worried nêgarân; **to be worried** tashwesh dâshtan
worry parwâ
worse badtar; **I feel worse.** Hâlem badtar ast.
worth arzesh
worthy lâyeq; **worthy of** barâbar-e
wound *noun* zakham; *verb* majruh kardan
wounded zakhmi; **slightly wounded** afgâr
wrap pushândan
wrench rench
wrestling pahlawâni; koshti
wrist band-e dest

write naweshtan; naweshta kardan
writer nawisenda
writing khat
wrong ghalat

X

X-ray(s) ekserê

Y

yard *garden* bâgh; *distance* gaz
year sâl; **last year** pâr-sâl
yellow zard
yes balê; hâ
yesterday dirôz; dina-rôz; **the day before yesterday** pare-rôz
yet hanôz
yogurt mâst
you *singular* tu; *polite/plural* shomâ
young jawân; jwân; **young person** shakhs-e jawân
your *singular* -et; *plural* -etân
yours *singular* az tu; *plural* az shomâ
yourself khodat
yourselves khodetân
youth jwâni

Z

zero sefer
zip; zipper zanjirak

DARI
Phrasebook

bedun istradar
wlv stupy

1. ETIQUETTE

Hello . . .

Salâm! ("peace!") is the Dari way of saying "hello!", to which the response is simply **salâm!** This greeting, which means "peace on you", is also used for the other greetings of the day, corresponding to English "good morning," "good afternoon," "good evening," and "good night." An extension of this becomes the more traditional Muslim greeting **Asalâmu alaykum!** ("peace on you!") to which the formal response is **alaykum asalâm** ("[and] on you peace!"). Some other common greetings used during the day are given below.

Hello!	**Salâm!**
—the response is:	**Salâm!**
How are you?	**Che hâl dâred?**
Fine, thank you!	**Khub astom, tashakor!**
Good morning!	**Sobh ba khayr!***
Good afternoon!	**Rôz ba khayr!***
Good evening!	**Shab tân khosh!***
Good night!	**Shab ba khayr!***
See you later!	**Ba'dan mêbinêm!**
See you tomorrow!	**Sabâ mêbinametân!**
Goodbye!	**Bâmâni khodâ!**
—the response is:	**Khodâ hâfez!**
Bon voyage!	**Safar ba khayr!**
Welcome!	**Khosh âmadêd!**
Please!	**Lotfan!**
Thank you!	**Tashakor!**
Excuse me!/Sorry!	**Mêbakhshêd!**

* You use the same greeting as the response.

2. QUICK REFERENCE

I	**man**
you *singular*	**tu**
he/she/it	**ô**
we	**mâ**
you *plural*	**shomâ**
they	**ânhâ; wâ**
yes	**balê**
no	**nê**
this	**in**
that	**ân**
these	**inhâ**
those	**ânhâ**
here	**injâ**
there	**ânjâ**
where?	**kojâ?**
who?	**ki?**
what?	**che?**
when?	**che waqt?**
which?	**kodâm?**
how?	**chetor?**
why?	**cherâ?**
how far?	**cheqadar dur?**
how near?	**cheqadar nazdik?**
how much *(price)*?	**chand?**
how many?	**chand dâna?**
what's that?	**ân chist?**
where is/are?	**kojâ hast/hastand?**
what must I do?	**man che bâyad bokonom?**
what do you want?	**shomâ che mêkhâhêd?**

very	**besyâr**
and	**wa; o**
or	**yâ**
but	**amâ; walê**
I like ...	**Man ... dôst dârom.**
I don't like ...	**Man ... dôst nadârom.**
I should like to ...	**Man mâyelom ...**
I want ...	**Man ... mêkhâhom.**
I don't want ...	**Man ... namêkhâhom.**
I know.	**Man mêdânom.**
I don't know.	**Man namêdânom.**
Do you understand?	**Shomâ fahmidêd?**
I understand.	**Man fahmidom.**
I don't understand.	**Man nafahmidom.**
I am sorry (to hear that).	**Man mota'asefam (az shanidan-e ân).**
I am grateful.	**Sepâs gozâr astom.**
It's important.	**In mohem ast.**
It doesn't matter.	**Mohem nêst.** or **Parwâ nadârad.**
No problem!	**Hêch moshkele nêst!**
more or less	**kam-o bêsh**
here is/are	**injâ ... hast/hastand**
Is everything OK?	**Hama chiz khub?** or **Sahi ast?**
Danger!	**Khatar!**
How do you spell that?	**Ânrâ chetor mênawisêd?**

I am ...

	Man . . . astom.
cold	**sard**
hot	**garm**
sleepy	**khâb âlud**
hungry	**goresna**
thirsty	**tashna**
angry	**khashamgin**
happy	**khosh hâl**
sad	**ghamgin**
tired	**khasta**
well	**khub**

—Colors

black	**syâh**
pink	**golâbi**
blue	**âbi**
purple	**benafsh**
brown	**naswâri**
red	**sorkh**
green	**sabz**
white	**safêd**
orange	**nârenji**
yellow	**zard**

3. INTRODUCTIONS

What is your name?	**Nâm-e shomâ chist?**
My name is ...	**Nâm-e man ... ast.**
May I introduce you to ...	**Mêtawânom shomâ râ ba ... mo'arefi konom.**
This is my ...	**In ...-e man ast.**
friend	**dôst**
colleague/companion	**hamkâr**
relative	**khêshâwand**

—Nationality

Afghanistan	**Afghânestân**
—Afghan *person*	**—Afghân**
Where are you from?	**Shomâ az kojâ hastêd?**
I am from ...	**Man az ... astom.**
America	**Amrikâ**
Australia	**Âstarâlyâ**
Britain	**Britânyâ**
Canada	**Kânâdâ**
China	**Chin**
England	**Inglestân**
Europe	**Oropâ**
France	**Faransâ**
Germany	**Âlmân**
India	**Hendustân**
Iran	**Irân**
Ireland	**Âyrlaynd**
Italy	**Itâlyâ**
Japan	**Jâpân**
New Zealand	**Zêland-e Jadid**
Pakistan	**Pâkestân**

Wales	**Weylz**
Scotland	**Eskâtlaynd**
Spain	**Haspânyâ**
the USA	**Amrikâ**
I am ...	**Man ... astom.**
American	**Amrikâyi**
Australian	**Âstarâlyâyi**
British	**Britânyâyi;**
	Bartânawi
Canadian	**Kânâdâyi**
Dutch	**Hâlandi**
English	**Inglis**
French	**Farânsawi**
German	**Âlmâni**
Indian	**Hendi**
Iranian	**Irâni**
Irish	**Âyrlayndi**
Israeli	**Esrâyili**
Italian	**Itâlawi**
Pakistani	**Pâkestâni**
Portuguese	**Portagâli**
Scottish	**Eskâtlayndi**
Spanish	**Haspânawi**
Welsh	**Weylzi**

Where were you born?	**Shomâ kojâ tawalod shodêd?**
I was born in ...	**Man dar ... tawalod shodam.**

—Regional nationalities

Kirgizstan	**Qerghizestân**
—Kirgiz	**—Qerghizi**
Tibet	**Tabat**
—Tibetan	**—Tebeti**

Tajikistan	**Tâjikestân**
—Tajik	**—Tâjik**
Turkmenistan	**Torkmanestân**
—Turkmen	**—Torkman**
Uzbekistan	**Ozbakestân**
—Uzbek	**—Ozbak**

—Occupations

What do you do?	**Shomâ che kâr mêkonêd?**
I am a/an ...	**Man ... astom.**
academic	**ostâd pôhantun**
accountant	**mohâseb**
administrator	**modir**
agronomist	**motakhases-e zerâyat**
aid worker	**kârmand-e emdâdi**
analyst	**mofaser**
architect	**me'mâr; mohandes**
artist	**honarmand**
banker	**bânk dâr**
business person	**tâjer**
carpenter	**najâr**
civil servant	**kârmand-e dawlat**
consultant	**moshâwer**
dentist	**dâktar-e dandân**
designer	**tarâh**
diplomat	**diplomât**
doctor	**dâktar**
economist	**eqtesâd-dân**
engineer	**enjinyar**
factory worker	**kârgar**
farmer	**dêhqân**
film-maker	**film-sâz**
journalist	**zhornâlist**
lawyer	**wakil**

mechanic	**mestari**
midwife	**qâbela**
nurse	**nars; parastâr**
office worker	**kârmand-e edâri**
pediatrician	**dâktar-e atfâl**
pilot	**pêlat**
relief worker	**kârmand-e emdâdi**
scientist	**sâynsdân**
secretary	**sekartar**
soldier	**askar; sarbâz**
student	**shâgerd**
surgeon	**jarâh**
teacher	**mo'alem**
therapist	**dâktar**
tourist	**sayâh; torist**
volunteer	**dâwatalab**
writer	**nawisenda**
I work in ...	**Man dar ... kâr mêkonom.**
advertising	**e'lânât**
a charity	**yak mo'asesa-ye khayriya**
computers	**kâmpani kâmpyutar**
insurance	**bêma**
I.T.	**kâmpyutar**
the leisure industry	**senf-e tafrêhâti**
marketing	**bâzâr yâbi**
an office	**yak daftar**
the retail industry	**pêsha-ye/senf-e khorda forôshi**
sales	**forôshendagi**
a shop	**yak dôkân**
telecommunications	**mokhâberât**
tourism	**sayâhat; torezam**
the hotel industry	**senf-e hôtal dâri**

INTRODUCTIONS

—Age

How old are you?	**Shomâ chand sâl dârêd?**
I am ... years old.	**Man ... sâl dârom.**

—Family

Are you married?	**Shomâ ezdewâj kardêd?**
said to a man	**Shomâ zan dârêd?**
said to a woman	**Shomâ shoy/ shawhar dârêd?**
How many children do you have?	**Chand farzand dârêd?**
I don't have any children.	**Man hêch farzand nadârom.**
I have a daughter.	**Man yak dokhtar dârom.**
I have a son.	**Man yak bacha dârom.**
How many sisters do you have?	**Chand khâhar dârêd?**
How many brothers do you have?	**Chand berâdar dârêd?**

father	**padar**
mother	**mâdar**
grandfather	**padar kalân**
grandmother	**mâdar kalân**
brother	**berâdar**
sister	**khwâr**
children	**atfâl**
daughter	**dokhtar**
son	**pesar; bacha**
girl	**dokhtar**
boy	**bacha**

twins	**dogânagi**
husband	**shawhar; shoy**
wife	**zan**
family	**khânawâda**
man	**mard**
woman	**zan**
person	**nafar**
people	**mardom**
orphan	**yatim**

—Religion

The people of Afghanistan are mainly Muslims, the majority of whom are Sunni, with a significant number who are Shi'i. (For more, see the note on "Religious Heritage" on page 169.)

I am (a) ...	**Man ... astom.**
Muslim	**Mosolmân**
Buddhist	**Budist; Budâyi**
Christian	**Isawi**
Catholic	**Kâtolik**
Hindu	**Hendu**
Jewish	**Yahudi**

I am not religious.	**Man maz-habi nêstom.**

4. LANGUAGE

Dari is one of the most widely used languages throughout Afghanistan, along with Pashto. Turkic languages such as Uzbek and Turkmen are spoken by large numbers of the population, particularly in the north. There are also numerous other languages spoken in the country such as Baluchi, Hazara, Brahui and Nuristani, and bilingualism is extremely common. Many people will also know Urdu and at least a smattering of one or more European languages — particularly English or Russian. As a result of the obvious influence of Islam, you will find widespread knowledge of Arabic. Because Dari speakers share a wide range of ethnic backgrounds, they are also scattered over a wide area outside of Afghanistan where their speech may be assimilated into Persian (Farsi) or Tajik.

Do you speak . . . ?	**Shomâ . . . gap mêzanêd?**
English	**Inglisi**
Hindi	**Hendi**
Urdu	**Ordu**
German	**Âlmâni; Jarmani**
Italian	**Itâlawi**
French	**Farânsawi**
Chinese	**Chinâyi**
Spanish	**Haspânawi**
Farsi	**Fârsi**
Arabic	**Arabi**
Russian	**Rusi**

Does anyone speak English?	**Kasi hast Inglisi gap bozanad?**
I speak a little ...	**Man kami ... mêdânom.**
I don't speak ...	**Man ... namêdânom.**
I understand.	**Man fahmidom.**
I don't understand.	**Man nafahmidom.**
What does this mean?	**In che mâni dârad?**

Please point to the word in the book.	**Lotfan in loghat râ dar ketâb neshan dehêd.**
Please wait while I look up the word.	**Lotfan sabr konêd tâ man loghat râ paydâ konom.**
Could you speak more slowly, please?	**Lotfan mêtawânêd âhestatar gap bozanêd.**
Could you repeat that?	**Mêtawânêd ân râ tekrâr konêd?**
How do you say ... in Dari/Pashto?	**Ba Dari/Pashtu chetor mêguyêd ...?**
What does ... mean?	**... che mâni dârad?**
How do you pronounce this word?	**In loghat chetor talafoz mêshawad.**
I speak ...	**Man ... gap mêzanom.**

Arabic	**Arabi**
Chinese	**Chinâyi**
Danish	**Denmârki**
Dari	**Dari**
Dutch	**Hâlandi**
English	**Inglisi**
Farsi	**Fârsi**
French	**Farânsawi**
Hindi	**Hendi**
Pashto	**Pashtu**
Urdu	**Ordu**
German	**Âlmâni; Jarmani**
Italian	**Itâlawi**
Japanese	**Jâpâni**
Spanish	**Haspânawi**
Russian	**Rusi**
Tajik	**Tâjiki**
Uzbek	**Ozbaki**

5. BUREAUCRACY

> Note that many forms you encounter may be written also in Pashto or English.

name	**nâm**
surname	**nâm-e fâmeli**
middle name	**nâm-e wasat**
address	**âdras**
date of birth	**târikh-e tawalod**
place of birth	**mahal-e tawalod**
nationality	**meliyat; tabiyat**
age	**sen**
sex: male/female	**mozakar/mo'anas**
religion	**dên**
reason for travel:	**dalil-e safar:**
business	**tejârat**
tourism	**sayâhat; torezam**
work	**kâr**
personal	**shakhsi**
profession	**shoghl; wazefa**
marital status	**waz'iyat-e tâhul**
single	**mojarad**
married	**mota'ahel**
divorced	**talâq shoda**
date	**târikh**
date of arrival	**târikh-e worud**
date of departure	**târikh-e khoruj**
passport	**pâsport**
passport number	**shomâra-ye pâsport**
visa	**wêza**
currency	**paysa**

BUREAUCRACY

Ministries

Ministry of Defense	**Wezârat-e Defâ**
Ministry of Agriculture	**Wezârat-e Zeyârat**
Ministry of Foreign Affairs	**Wezârat-e Omur-e Khâreja**
Ministry of Home Affairs	**Wezârat-e Omur-e Dâkhela**
Ministry of Tourism	**Wezârat-e Torezam**
Treasury	**Khazâna**
Ministry of Finance	**Wezârat-e Mâlya**
Ministry of Health	**Wezârat-e Sehati Âma**
Ministry of Education	**Wezârat-e Tâlimât**
Ministry of Higher Education	**Wezârat-e Tâlimâti Âli**
Ministry of Commerce and Industry	**Wezârat-e Tejârat wa Zârat-e Sanâye**
Ministry of Information and Culture	**Wezârat-e Etilâyât wa Koltor**

Appointments

Where is Mr./Ms. ...'s office?	**Daftar-e âqâ-ye/ khânom-e ... kojâ-st?**
Which floor is it on?	**Kodâm manzel ast?**
Does the lift/elevator work?	**Lift kâr mêkonad?**
Is Mr./Ms. ... in?	**Âqâ-ye/khâmom-e ... hastand?**
Please tell him/her that I am here.	**Lotfan ba ishân boguyêd ke man injâ astom.**
I can't wait, I have an appointment.	**Man namêtawânom montazer bomânom, man qarâr-e molâqât dârom.**
Tell him/her that I was here.	**Ba ishân boguyêd ke man injâ budom.**

6. TRAVEL

> **PUBLIC TRANSPORT** — When running, buses are generally too crammed for comfort. Far more practical are taxis or private cars hailed in the street or the minibuses called **minibas** (in Kabul you may hear them called **nisân-pikâp** "Nissan pick-up") which stop at pre-determined pickup points. You pay the driver or his assistant as you get out. When the railway lines are opened again, you will find rail travel slow, subject to long delays mid-journey and less safe than by road. Travel anywhere, even by air, is problematic due to the sustained and systematic destruction of Afghanistan's infrastructure. The railway system in particular has been affected and therefore we haven't included a railway section for this edition. Bicycles and motorbikes are not difficult to find but are not much use outside of the town spaces.

What time does the ...	**Che waqt ...**
airplane leave/arrive?	**tayâra harkat mêkonad/mêrasad?**
bus leave/arrive?	**bas harkat mêkonad/mêrasad?**
train leave/arrive?	**terên harkat mêkonad/mêrasad?**
minibus leave/arrive?	**minibas harkat mêkonad/mêrasad?**
The plane is delayed/ cancelled.	**Tayâra ta'khir dârad/kensel shoda.**
The train is delayed/ cancelled.	**Terên ta'khir dârad/kensel shoda.**
How long will it be delayed?	**Cheqadar ta'khir dârad?**
There is a delay of ... minutes.	**... deqiqa ta'khir dârad.**
There is a delay of ... hours.	**... sâ'at ta'khir dârad.**

—Buying tickets

Excuse me, where is the ticket office?	**Mêbakhshêd, daftar-e tiket kojâ-st?**
Where can I buy a ticket?	**Kojâ mêtawânom tiket kharidâri konom?**
I want to go to ...	**Man mêkhâhom ba ... borawom.**
I want a ticket to ...	**Man yak tiket ba ... mêkhâhom.**
I would like ...	**Man ... mêkhâhom.**
a one-way ticket	**yak tiket-e yak tarafa**
a return ticket	**yak tiket-e do tarafa**
Do I pay in afganis or in dollars?	**Ba afghâni bopardâzom yâ ba dâlar?**
You must pay in afghanis.	**Shomâ bâyad ba afghâni bopardâzêd.**
You must pay in dollars.	**Shomâ bâyad ba dâlar bopardâzêd.**
You can pay in either.	**Shomâ bâ har kodâm mêtawânêd bopardâzêd.**
Can I reserve a place?	**Mêtawânom yak jâ rezerv konom.**
How long does the trip take?	**In safar cheqadar tul mêkashad?**
Is it a direct route?	**Âyâ parwâz-e mostaqim ast?**

—Air

When is the Karachi flight arriving?	**Parwâz-e Karâchi che waqt mêrasad?**
Is it on time?	**Sar-e waqt myâyad?**
Is it late?	**Dêr ast?**

Do I have to change planes?	**Âyâ man bâyad tayâra râ ewaz konom?**
Has the plane left Karachi yet?	**Tayâra az Karâchi harkat karda?**
What time does the plane take off?	**Che waqt tayâra parwâz mêkonad?**
What time do we arrive in Kabul?	**Che waqt wâred-e Kâbol mêshawêm?**
I wish to confirm my flight.	**Man mêkhâhom parwâzam râ kanfarm konom.**

excess baggage	**bâr-e ezâfa**
international flight	**parwâz-e baynolmelali**
national/internal flight	**parwâz-e dâkheli**

—Bus

bus stop/bus station	**estâdgâh-e bas**
Which bus goes to ... ?	**Kodâm bas ba ... mêrawad?**
Does this bus go to ... ?	**Âyâ in bas ba ... mêrawad?**
How often do buses pass by?	**Dar che fasela-hâ bas az injâ mêgozarad?**
What time is the ... bus?	**Bas-e ... che waqt myâyad?**
first	**awal**
last	**âkher**
next	**ba'di**
Will you let me know when we get to ... ?	**Waqti ba ... residêm ba man boguyêd?**
Please let me off here.	**Lotfan ma râ injâ tâ konêd.**
How long is the journey?	**Cheqadar fasela ast?**
What is the fare?	**Kerâya cheqadar ast?**

—Taxí

Some taxis are marked, while others are not. You can also wave down and negotiate a fare with any private car willing to go your way, although this is not always as safe. To avoid unpleasant surprises, agree to fares in advance. It is useful to be able to tell the driver your destination in Dari or Pashto (or have it written down on a piece of paper). Be warned, however, that some drivers will have as little idea as you as to the precise whereabouts of your destination. A reliable option is to call up one of the growing number of radio taxi (**taksi telifun dar**) companies.

Taxi!	**Taksi!**
Where can I get a taxi?	**Kojâ yak taksi gerefta mêtawânom?**
Please could you get me a taxi.	**Lotfan barâye man taksi bogirêd?**
Can you take me to ... ?	**Mêtawânêd ma râ ba ... bobarêd?**
How much will it cost to ... ?	**Tâ ... cheqard mêshawad?**
To this address, please.	**Ba in âdras, lotfan.**
Turn left.	**Chap boro.**
Turn right.	**Râst boro.**
Go straight ahead.	**Rubaru boro.**
Stop!	**Estâd konêd!**
Don't stop!	**Estâd nakonêd!**
I'm in a hurry.	**Man ajala dârom.**
Please drive more slowly!	**Lotfan âhestatar harakat konêd.**
Here is fine, thank you.	**Injâ khub ast, tashakor.**
The next corner, please.	**Nawsh-e ba'di, lotfan.**
The next street to the left.	**Sarak-e ba'di, taraf-e chap.**

The next street to the right.	**Sarak-e ba'di, taraf-e râst.**
Stop here!	**Injâ estâd konêd!**
Stop the car, I want to get out.	**Môtar râ estâd konêd, man mêkhâhom tâ shawom.**
Please wait for me here.	**Lotfan injâ montazer-e man bâshêd.**
Take me to the airport.	**Ma râ ba maydân-e hawâyi bobarêd.**

—General phrases

I want to get off at ...	**Da ... tâ mêshawom.**
Excuse me!	**Mêbakhshêd!**
Excuse me, may I get by?	**Mêbakhshêd, momken ast bogozarom.**
These are my bags.	**Inhâ baks-hâ-ye man astand.**
Please put them there.	**Lotfan ânhâ râ injâ bogozârêd.**
Is this seat free?	**Âyâ injâ khâli hast?**
I think that's my seat.	**Fekr mêkonom ân jây-e man bâshad.**
I need my luggage, please.	**Man baksam râ mêkhâhom, lotfan.**

—Travel words

airport	**maydân-e hawâyi**
airport tax	**mâliyât-e maydân-e hawâyi**
ambulance	**ambulâns**
arrivals	**worud**
baggage counter	**qesmat-e bâr**
bicycle	**bâysikel**
boarding pass	**kârt sawâr shodan**
boat	**qâyeq**

bus stop	**estâdgâh-e bas**
camel	**shotor**
car	**môtar**
check-in counter	**qesmat kantrol**
closed	**basta**
customs	**gomrok**
delay	**ta'khir**
departures	**khoruj**
dining car	**môtar-e ghezâ khori**
donkey	**khar**
emergency exit	**khoruj-e ezterâri**
entrance	**worud**
exit	**khoruj**
express	**sari'**
ferry	**keshti**
4-wheel drive	**jip; pajero**
information	**etelâyât**
ladies/gents toilets	**tashnâb-e zanâna/mardâna**
local	**mahali**
helicopter	**helikoptar**
horse	**asb**
horse and cart	**asb wa gâdi**
motorbike	**môtarsaykel**
mule	**qâter**
no entry	**worud mamnu'**
no smoking	**segrêt kashedan mamnu' ast**
open	**bâz**
platform	**pletfârm**
pony	**yâbo**
railway	**râh âhan; rêl**
reserved	**rezarf shoda**
radio taxi	**taksi telifun dar**
road	**râh**
sign	**alâmat**
sleeping car	**môtar-e khâb**

station	**estêshan**
telephone	**telifun**
ticket office	**ghorfa-ye tiket**
timetable	**barnâma**
toilet(s)	**tashnâb(-hâ)**
town center	**markaz-e shâr**
train station	**estêshan**

ELECTRIC CURRENT — Afghanistan is 220-volt electric current. However, it may not be constantly at full voltage strength and lengthy power failures may be common, particularly away from the larger towns, where the local transformers of villages that have a supply can overload. Although many buildings and villages may now have their own back-up generators in case of power failure, be sure to keep a flashlight or supply of candles.

---

7. ACCOMMODATION

> The hotel and guesthouse network is slowly being built up again. Should adequate accommodation be found away from the major towns, you will find that room service is not available, and breakfast or other meals will have to be negotiated and paid for separately.

I am looking for a ...	**Man donbal-e ... mêgardom.**
guesthouse	**mêhmân khâna**
hotel	**hôtal**
hostel	**laylya**
Is there anywhere I can stay for the night?	**Jâyi hast ke man shab râ bomânom?**
Is there anywhere we can stay for the night?	**Jâyi hast ke mâ shab râ bomânêm?**
Where is ... ?	**... kojâ-st?**
a cheap hotel	**yak hôtal-e arzân**
a good hotel	**yak hôtal-e khub**
a nearby hotel	**yak hôtal-e nazdik**
a clean hotel	**yak hôtal-e pâk**
What is the address?	**Âdras ash kojâst?**
Could you write the address please?	**Mêtawânêd âdras râ bonawisêd?**

—At the hotel

Do you have any rooms free?	**Otâq-e khâli dârêd?**
I would like ...	**Man ... mêkhâhom.**
a single room	**yak otâq-e yak nafara**
a double room	**yak otâq-e do nafara**

We'd like a room.	**Mâ yak otâq mêkhâhêm.**
We'd like two rooms.	**Mâ do otâq mêkhâhêm.**
I want a room with ...	**Man yak otâq bâ ... mêkhâhom.**

a bathroom	**hamâm**
a shower	**shâwar**
a television	**teliwizyun**
a window	**kelken**
a double bed	**takht-e do nafara**
a balcony	**balkoni; tarâs**
a view	**manzara**

| I want a room that's quiet. | **Man yak otâq-e ârâm mêkhâhom.** |

—Booking in

How long will you be staying?	**Barâye che modat mêmânêd?**
How many nights?	**Chand shab?**
I'm going to stay for ...	**Man barâye ... mêmânom.**

one day	**yak ruz**
two days	**do ruz**
one week	**yak hafta**

Do you have any I.D.?	**Kârt-hoyat/pâsport dârêd?**
Sorry, we're full.	**Mêbakhshêd, mâ sêr hastêm.**
I have a reservation.	**Man qablan yak otâq rezarf karda budom.**
Is it ready?	**Âyâ âmada hast?**
My name is ...	**Nâm-e man ... hast.**
May I speak to the manager please?	**Momken ast bâ modir sohbat konom.**
I have to meet someone here.	**Man bâyad kasi râ injâ molâqât konom.**

How much is it per night?	**Shawi chand ast?**
How much is it per person?	**Nafari chand ast?**
How much is it per week?	**Hafta-ye chand ast?**
It's ... per day.	**... hast dar har ruz.**
It's ... per person.	**... hast barâye har nafar.**

—Choosing a room

Can I see it?	**Mêtawânom bobinom?**
Is there ... ?	**... ast?**
airconditioning	**er kândishan**
a telephone	**telifun**
a bar	**bâr**
Is there ... ?	**... ast?**
hot water	**âb-e garm**
laundry service	**khoshka-shôyi**
room service	**sarwês-e otâq**
It's fine, I'll take it.	**Khub ast, man in râ mêgerom.**
No, I don't like it.	**Nê, man in râ khosh nadârom.**
It's too ...	**Besyâr ... ast.**
cold	**sard**
hot	**garm**
big	**bozorg; kalân**
dark	**tira/tarik**
small	**khord**
noisy	**ghâlmaghâl**
dirty	**nâ pâk**
Where is the bathroom?	**Hamâm kojâ-st?**
Is there hot water all day?	**Tamâm-e rôz âb-e garm ast?**
Do you have a safe?	**Shomâ sayf dârêd?**
Is there anywhere to wash clothes?	**Jâyi barâye shostan-e lebâs ast?**

Can I use the telephone?	**Mêtawânom az telifun estêfâda konom?**

—Needs

I need ...	**Man ba ... zarorat dârom.**
candles	**sham'a**
toilet paper	**kâghaz-e tashnâb**
soap	**sâbun**
clean sheets	**rojây-e pâk**
an extra blanket	**kampal-e ezâfi**
drinking water	**âw-e nushidani**
a heater	**yak bokhâri**
a lightbulb	**yak grup barq**
a mosquito net	**pashakhâna**
mosquito repellant	**dawâ-ye pasha**
Do you have a needle and thread?	**Suzan wa târ dârêd?**
The shower won't work.	**Shâwar kâr namêkonad.**
How do I get hot water?	**Az kojâ âb-e garm bogirom?**
The water has been cut off.	**Âb qat'a shoda.**
The electricity has been cut off.	**Barq qat'a shoda.**
The gas has run out.	**Gâz tamâm shoda.**
The airconditioning doesn't work.	**Êrkândêshan kâr namêkonad.**
The heating doesn't work.	**Bokhâri kâr namêkonad.**
The phone doesn't work.	**Telifun kâr namêkonad.**

I can't flush the toilet.	**Kamôd kâr namêkonad.** *or* **Âb namêrêzad.**
The toilet is blocked.	**Tashnâb masdud shodast.**
I can't switch off the tap.	**Shêrdân basta namêshawad.**
I can't close the window.	**Kelken basta namêshawad.**
I can't lock the door.	**Darwâza qofl namêshawad.**
I need a plug for the bath.	**Barây hamâm ba yak sarposh zarorat dârom.**
Where is the plug socket?	**Sâket kojâ-st?**
There's a strange insect in my room.	**Yak jânwar-e ajib dar otâq-e man ast.**
There's an animal in my room.	**Yak haywân dar otâq-e man ast.**

—Leaving

wake-up call	**zang-e bêdâr shawid**
Could you please wake me up at ... o'clock?	**Lotfan ma râ ... baja bêdâr konêd?**
I am leaving now.	**Man hâlâ mêrawom.**
We are leaving now.	**Mâ hâlâ mêrawêm.**
May I pay the bill now?	**Paysa-ye bel râ hâlâ botom?**

—Hotel words

bathroom	**hamâm**
bed	**bestar; takht-e khâb**
blanket	**kampal**
candle	**sham'a**
chair	**chawki**

cold water	**âb-e sard**
cupboard	**almâri lebâs**
doorlock	**qofl-e darwâza**
electricity	**barq**
excluded	**bêrun mânda**
extra	**ezâfi**
fridge	**yakhchâl**
hot water	**âb-e garm**
included	**shâmel shoda**
key	**keli(d)**
laundry	**khoshka-shôyi**
mattress	**doshak; toshak**
meal	**khorâk**
mirror	**âyna**
name	**nâm**
noisy	**ghâlmaghâl; sarosadâ**
padlock	**qolf**
pillow	**bâlesht**
(bath) plug	**shêrdân**
(electric) plug	**palag**
quiet	**ârâm**
room	**otâq**
room number	**nomra-ye otâq**
sheet	**rojây; roykash**
shower	**shâwar**
suitcase	**baks safari**
surname	**nâm-e fâmel**
table	**mêz**
towel	**roy pâk; qadifa**
water	**âw**
window	**kelken**

8. FOOD & DRINK

Food plays an important part of Afghan life, and important events in all aspects of life and the year are marked with a feast of one form or another. Food is a very important part of Afghan hospitality — it is both the host's duty to make sure his guests are eating and the guest's duty to partake of what is offered. **Palaw** is king in Afghan cuisine, and new guests are traditionally fed this dish above all others. In normal times, you will be offered a dazzling variety of dishes, delicacies and drinks, which vary from area to area and from season to season. Any menu you may encounter may be written in Dari, Pashto or English.

breakfast	**chây-sob(h)**
lunch	**nân-e châsht**
afternoon snack	**asrya**
dinner, supper	**nân-shaw**

MEALS — Afghans do not use separate names for meals as in English. The terms given above are rather literal terms. Lunch and dinner are usually just called **nân** "food" or "meal".

I'm hungry.	**Man goresna hastom.**
I'm thirsty.	**Man tashna hastom.**
Do you know a good restaurant?	**Kodâm rastôrân-e khub râ mêshenâsêd?**

—At the restaurant

Do you have a table, please?	**Yak mêz dârêd, lotfan?**
I would like a table for ... people, please.	**Man yak mêz barâye ... nafar mêkhâhom, lotfan.**
Can I see the menu please?	**Lotfan, mênyu râ deda mêtawânom?**

I'm still looking at the menu.	**Hanôz mênyu râ mêbenom.**
I would like to order now.	**Man mêkhâhom hâlâ farmâyesh botom.**
What's this?	**In che hast?**
Is it spicy?	**Âyâ in talkh ast?**
Does it have meat in it?	**Âyâ in gusht dârad?**
Does it have alcohol in it?	**Âyâ in alkôl dârad?**
Do you have ... ?	**Shomâ ... dârêd?**
We don't have ...	**Mâ ... nadârim.**
What would you recommend?	**Shomâ che farmâyesh mêdehêd?**
Do you want ... ?	**... mêkhâhêd?**
Can I order some more ... ?	**Mêtawânom ... bêshtar farmâyesh botom?**
That's all, thank you.	**Kâfi-st, tashakor.**
That's enough, thanks.	**Bas, tashakor.**
I haven't finished yet.	**Man hanôz tamâm nakardom.**
I have finished eating.	**Man ghezâ râ tamâm kardom.**
I am full up!	**Man sêr astom!**
Where are the toilets?	**Tashnâb kojâ-st?**
I am a vegetarian.	**Man sabzi khôr astom.**
I don't eat meat.	**Man gusht namêkhorom.***
I don't eat chicken or fish.	**Man morgh yâ mâhi namêkhorom.**

* In Afghanistan you will not be offered pork since it is an Islamic country. For reference purposes or use abroad, "I don't eat pork" is **Man gusht-e khuk namêkhorom.**

I don't eat nuts.	**Man bâdâm namêkhorom.**
I don't drink alcohol.	**Man sharâb namênushom.**
I don't smoke.	**Man segrêt namêkashom.**

> **CULTURAL NOTE** — While in the West it is perfectly OK to state dietary preferences, in Afghan society this is interpreted as an insult to the host: you are in effect telling them that the food isn't good enough for you. In traditional Afghan society (and many other Asian societies) people will be baffled that someone would voluntarily choose not to eat meat. Better to say that you have medical reasons for doing so.

—Needs

I would like ...	**Man ... mêkhâhom.**
an ashtray	**yak khâkester dani**
the bill	**bel**
a glass of water	**yak gelâs-e âw**
a bottle of water	**yak bôtal-e âw**
a bottle of wine	**yak bôtal-e sharâb/wâyn**
a bottle of beer	**yak bôtal-e bir**
another bottle (of ...)	**yak bôtal-e digar (az ...)**
a bottle-opener	**yak sar bâz kon**
a corkscrew	**yak sar bâz kon**
a drink	**nushidani**
a fork	**panja**
another chair	**yak chawki-ye digar**
another plate	**yak bêshqâb-e digar**
another glass	**yak gelâs-e digar**
another cup	**yak peyâla-ye digar**

a napkin	**yak destmâl**
a glass	**yak gelâs**
a knife	**yak châqu**
a plate	**yak bêshqâb**
a spoon	**yak qâshoq**
a table	**yak mêz**
a teaspoon	**yak qâshoq-e chây khori**
a toothpick	**yak khelâl dandân**

too much	**besyâr zyâd**
too little	**besyâr kam**
not enough	**kâfi nêst**

—Tastes

fresh fruit	**mêwa-ye tâza**
fresh fish	**mâhiye tâza**
spicy (hot)	**tond; talkh**
stale	**kohna**
sour	**torsh**
sweet	**shirin**
bitter	**talkh**
hot	**garm**
cold	**sard**
salty	**namaken**
tasteless	**bê maza**
bad	**bad**
tasty	**khosh maza**

—At the table

bowl	**kâsa**
bread	**nân**
butter	**maska**
cup	**peyâla**
dessert	**shirini-e bad az ghezâ**

fork	**panja**
glass	**gelâs**
knife	**châqu**
main course	**ghezâ-ye asli**
margarine	**maska nabâti**
meat	**gusht**
menu	**mênyu**
pepper	**kâghaz**
plate	**bêshqâb**
sauce	**sâs**
spoon	**qâshoq**
starter	**âghâz gar**
table	**mêz**
tablecloth	**sar-mêzi**

—Food in general

bread	**nân**
candy	**shirini**
cheese	**panir**
chewing gum	**sâjeq**
egg	**tokhom**
flour	**ârd**
ginger	**zanjafil**
hamburger	**hambargar**
honey	**asal**
ice-cream	**âys-krim; fâluda**
ketchup	**kechâp**
nut	**khasta**
oil	**rôghan**
pasta	**makaroni**
pepper	**morch**
pickles	**âchâr**
pizza	**pitsa**
rice	**brenj**
salad	**salâd; salâta**

salt	**namak**
saffron	**zâfarân**
sandwich	**sandewich**
sesame seeds	**dâna-ye konjid**
soup	**sup; shorwâ**
sugar	**bôra**
vinegar	**serka**
yogurt	**mâst**

> **RICE** — **Brenj** is uncooked rice. All cooked rice in Dari cuisine becomes pilau (**palaw**) or some other term depending on the dish. It's not eaten as plain white rice.

—Vegetables

aubergine; eggplant	**bâdenjân syâh; banjân**
beans	**lubiyâ**
breadfruit	**mêwa**
cabbage	**karam; kalam**
carrots	**zardak**
chickpeas	**nakhod**
corn	**jawâri**
cucumber	**bâdrang**
garlic	**sêr**
lentils	**dâl nakhod**
lettuce	**kâhu**
millet	**arzan**
mushroom	**samâroq**
okra; lady's fingers	**bâmyâ**
olives	**zaytun**
onion/onions	**piyâz**
peas	**matar**
pepper(s)	**morch**
potato(es)	**kachâlu**
sweet potato(es)	**kachâlu**
tomato	**bâdenjân-e rumi**
vegetables	**sabzi; sabzijât**

—Fruit & nuts

almonds	**badom**
apricot	**zard âlu**
bananas	**kêla**
cherry	**gilâs**
sour cherry	**âlubolu**
dates	**khormâ**
fig	**anjir**
fruit	**mêwa**
grapefruit	**chako tara**
grapes	**angur**
lemon; lime	**lêmu**
mango	**âm**
melon	**kharbuza**
mulberry	**tut**
nuts	**khasta**
peanuts	**bâdâm-e zamini**
pine nuts	**jalghroza**
pistachios	**pesta**
plum	**âlu**
orange	**mâlta**
peach	**shaftâlu**
pear	**nâk**
pomegranate	**anâr**
quince	**behi**
raisins	**kishmish**
strawberries	**tut farangi**
walnuts	**chârmaghz**
watermelon	**tarboz**

—Meat & fish

beef	**gusht-e gâw**
chicken	**morgh**
fish	**mâhi**
goat	**boz**
kebab	**kabâb**

lamb	**bara; gosfand**
pork	**gusht-e khuk**

—Drinks

Remember to ask for modern soft drinks by brand name.

alcohol	**alkôl**
beer	**bir**
bottle	**bôtal**
half-bottle	**nim bôtal**
brandy	**brendi**
can	**quti**
coffee	**qahwa**
coffee with milk	**qahwa bâ shir**
cold	**sard**
cup	**peyâla**
fruit juice	**âb-e mêwa**
gin	**jin**
gin and tonic	**jin bâ sodâ**
glass	**gelâs**
ice	**yakh**
with ice	**bâ yakh**
no ice	**bedun-e yakh**
lemonade	**sharbat-e lêmu**
milk	**shir**
mineral water	**âb mâdani**
tea	**chây**
tea with lemon	**chây bâ lêmu**
tea with milk	**sher-chây**
no sugar	**bê bora**
herbal tea	**jôshanda**
vodka	**wodkâ**
whisky	**wiski**
wine	**sharâb**
water	**âb**

More on food & drink . . .

The traditional diet of Afghans consists mainly of unleavened flat bread called **nân**, soup (**shorwâ**), yogurt (**mâst**), vegetables, fruit, and chicken/meat. Tea is the favorite drink. There is also a wide variety of rice and noodle based dishes. Some common specialities include:

palaw — rice with lamb or chicken or vegetables

qâboli palaw — rice with carrots and sultanas plus meat

karayi — lamb kebabs with tomatoes and peppers

sabzi chalaw — spinach and white rice (and when made with short-grain rice it's called **sabzi bata**)

qorma chalaw — meat with peas or beans and white rice

bulani —vegetable or meat patties covered in flour and fried in oil

shami kabâb — a sausage-shaped mix of ground meat with onion, eggs and vegetables

chapli kabâb — chilli ground meat fried with onion, tomatoes and peppers, sometimes with eggs in oil, sometimes fat

mantu — steamed dumplings stuffed with sauteed onions and mince beef served with yogurt sauce and topped with yellow peas

borani banjan – sliced sauteed aubergine served with garlic yogurt sauce

borani kado – sliced sauteed pumpkin served with garlic yogurt sauce

kofta — ground beef, onion green paper garlic and salt

âsh — noodles with meat, beans and yogurt

chopâni kabâb — lamb kebab

lândi palaw — rice with dried, salted lamb normally served in winter or early spring

lândi shorwâ — soup made of dried salt meat

kichri qurat — well-done rice with yogurt and mince meat

tika kabâb — chunks of lamb kebab

Accompanying the above will be seasonal greens and other finger food, as well as side dishes or garnishes such as **chatni gashniz** (coriander chutney), **turshi banjân** (pickled stuffed aubergine), **sambosa/ samusa** (samosas), and **dogh** (yogurt with mint). A popular herb used throughout Afghanistan is the chive-like **gandana**. Finish off your meal with **ferni** (a light pudding made with milk and sugar), **halwâ** (halva, often with pistachio nuts), **goshfil** (sweet pastries), **shir brinj** (rice pudding), or fruit — all washed down with the ubiquitous Afghan **chây** (tea). During the spring and summer, Afghans will go off into the cooler hills for the extended **mayla**, a picnic for all the family that can last for several days.

9. DIRECTIONS

Where is ... ?	**... kojâ-st?**
the academy	**akâdemi**
the airport	**maydân-e hawâyi**
the art gallery	**gâlari-e honar naqâshi**
a bank	**bânk**
the church	**kalisâ**
the city center	**markaz-e shâr**
the consulate	**qonsulgari**
the embassy	**sefârat**
the American embassy	**sefârat-e Amrikâ**
the British embassy	**sefârat-e Britânyâ**
the ... hotel	**hôtal ...**
the information office	**daftar-e mâlumât**
the main square	**chawk-e shâr; markaz-e shâr**
the market	**bâzâr**
the Ministry of ...	**Wezârat-e ...**
the mosque	**masjed**
the museum	**mozyam**
parliament	**pârlemân**
the police station	**mâmoryat-e pôlis**
the post office	**postakhâna**
the station	**estêshan**
the telephone center	**markaz-e telifun**
a toilet/bathroom	**tashnâb; hamâm**
the university	**pôhantun; uniwersiti**
What ... is this?	**In kodâm ... ast?**
bridge	**pol**
building	**sâkhtomân**

district *in town*	**nâhiya**
district *in province*	**oloswâli**
river	**daryâ**
road	**râh; jâda**
street	**sarak**
suburb	**atrâf; huma**
town	**shâr**
village	**dê; rustâ**
What is this building?	**In kodâm sâkhtomân ast?**
What is that building?	**Ân kodâm sâkhtomân ast?**
What time does it open?	**Che waqt bâz mêshawad?**
What time does it close?	**Che waqt basta mêshawad?**

—Getting there

Can I park here?	**Mêtawânom injâ pârk konom?**
Are we on the right road for ... ?	**Âyâ mâ dar masir-e dorost hastêm barâye ...?**
How many kilometers is it to ... ?	**Tâ ... chand kilometr ast?**
It is ... kilometers away.	**... kilometr dur ast.**
How far is the next village?	**Dê-ye ba'di az injâ cheqadar dur ast?**
Where can I find this address?	**In âdras râ dar kojâ mêtawânom paydâ konom?**
Can you show me on the map?	**Mêtawânêd dar naqsha ba man neshân dehêd?**
How do I get to ... ?	**Chetor mêtawânom ba ... borawom?**

DIRECTIONS

I want to go to ...	**Man mêkhâhom ba ... borawom.**
Can I walk there?	**Ânjâ peyâda rafta mêtawânom?**
Is it far?	**Dur ast?**
Is it near?	**Nazdik ast?**
Is it far from here?	**Az injâ dur ast?**
Is it near here?	**Ba injâ nazdik ast?**
It is not far.	**Dur nêst.**
Go straight ahead.	**Mostaqim borawêd.**
Turn left.	**Ba taraf-e chap dawr bozanêd.**
Turn right.	**Râst bochakhêd.**
at the next corner	**dar gusha ba'adi; dar zawya-ye ba'adi**
at the traffic lights	**nazdik-e eshâra-ye tarâfiki**
behind	**posht**
far	**dur**
in front of	**pêsh-e**
left	**chap**
near	**nazdik**
opposite	**rubaru**
right	**râst**
straight on	**mostaqim; râstan pêsh**
bridge	**pol**
corner	**gusha**
crossroads	**châr-râh**
roundabout	**chawk**
north	**shamâl**
south	**jonub**
east	**sharq**
west	**gharb**

10. SHOPPING

Where can I find a ... ?	**Kojâ yak ... râ paydâ karda mêtawânom?**
Where can I buy ... ?	**Kojâ ... râ khareda mêtawânom?**
Where's the market?	**Bâzâr kojâ-st?**
Where's the nearest ... ?	**Nazdik tarin ... kojâ-st?**
Can you help me?	**Mêtawânêd ba man komak konêd?**
Can I help you?	**Mêtawânom bâ shomâ komak konom?**
I'm just looking.	**Faqat mêbinom.**
I'd like to buy ...	**Man mêkhâhom ... kharidâri konom.**
Could you show me some ... ?	**Momken ast chand dâna râ ... ba man neshân dehêd?**
Can I look at it?	**Mêtawânom bobinom?**
Do you have any ... ?	**Âyâ shomâ ... dârêd?**
This.	**In.**
That.	**Ân.**
These.	**Inhâ.**
Those.	**Ânhâ.**
I don't like it.	**In khosham namêyâyad.** or **Man in râ khosh nadârom.**
I like it.	**In râ khosh dârom.**
Do you have anything cheaper?	**Chiz-e arzântari dârêd?**

Do you have anything better?	**Chiz-e bêhtari dârêd?**
larger	**bozorgtar**
smaller	**khordtar**
Do you have anything else?	**Chiz-e digari dârêd?**
Do you have any others?	**Digar ham dârêd?**
Sorry, this is the only one.	**Mêbakhshêd, faqat yak dâna mânda-st.**
I'll take it.	**Man in râ mêgerom.**
How much/many do you want?	**Cheqadar/chand dâna mêkhâhêd?**
How much is it?	**Cheqadar ast?**
Can you write down the price?	**Mêtawânêd qêmatash râ bonawisêd?**
Could you lower the price?	**Mêtawânêd qêmatash râ kam konêd?**
I don't have much money.	**Man paysa zyâd nadârom.**
Do you take credit cards?	**Kredet-kârt râ qabul mêkonêd?**
Would you like it wrapped?	**Mêkhâhêd ân râ bopêchânom?**
Will that be all?	**Chiz-e digar mêkhâhêd?**
Thank you, good-bye.	**Tashakor, khodâ hâfez.**
I want to return this.	**Mêkhâhom in râ pas dehom.**

—Outlets

baker's	**nânwâyi**
bank	**bânk**

barber's	**salmâni**
I'd like a haircut please.	**Lotfan mo-ye saram râ kutâh konêd.**
bookshop/bookstore	**ketâb forôshi**
butcher's shop	**qasâbi**
car spares shop	**porzâ forôshi**
chemist's/pharmacy	**dawâ khâna**
clothes shop	**maghâza-ye lebâs**
dairy	**labaniyât**
dentist	**dâktar-e dandân**
department store	**suparmârkêt**
dressmaker	**khayât**
electrical goods store	**dôkân-a wasâyel-e barqi**
fabric shop	**bazâzi**
florist	**gol forôshi**
greengrocer	**sabzi forôsh**
hairdresser	**salmâni**
hardware store	**khorda forôshi**
hospital	**shafâ khâna**
kiosk	**ghorfa**
laundry	**khoshka-shôyi**
market	**bâzâr; mârkêt**
newsstand	**akhbâr forôshi**
shoeshop	**but forôshi**
shop	**dôkân**
souvenir shop	**soghât forôshi**
stationer's	**qertâsya forôshi**
supermarket	**suparmârkêt**
travel agency	**daftar-e mosâferati; trêwal ejansi**
vegetable shop	**sabzi forôshi**
watchmaker's	**sâ'at sâz**

—Gifts

ARTS & CRAFTS — Much of Afghanistan's traditions has been destroyed or lost in the invasions, wars and conflicts that have lasted to the present day. The art of making carpets has survived in some parts. Copperware and pottery used to be widespread, in the form of fine belts, decorative trays, ewers, coffee pots, samovars, and beakers. A number of craftsmen forced to leave Afghanistan, in particular carpet makers and artists, have managed to re-establish themselves in other countries with some success.

amber	**anbar**
basket	**sabad**
box	**quti; baks**
bracelet	**destband; chori**
brooch	**senjâq-e sina**
bowls	**kâsa-hâ**
candlestick	**sham'adân**
carpet	**farsh**
chain	**zanjir**
chest	**sanduq**
clock	**sâ'at**
copper	**mes**
crystal	**belawor**
earrings	**goshwâra**
gold	**telâ**
handicraft	**kâr-e desti**
iron	**âhan**
jewelry	**jawâher**
leather	**charm**
metal	**felez**
modern	**jadid; naw**
necklace	**gardan-band; lâket**
pot	**kuza**
pottery	**kolâli**
ring	**halqa**
rosary	**tasbê(h)**
shield	**separ**

silver	noqra
spear	nayza
spoon	qâshoq
steel	folâd
stone	sang
stool	korsi
traditional	an'anawi
tray	patnus
vase	goldân
watch	sâ'at
wood	chob
wood carvings	chob-kâri

—Clothes

bag	baks-e desti; bêg
belt	kamar band
boots	moza; but
cotton	teka-ye nakhi
dress	kalâ
gloves	dest kash
handbag	baks-e desti
hat	kolâh
jacket	jampar
jeans	kawbây
leather	charm
necktie	nektây
overcoat	bâlâposh
pocket	jêb
scarf	châdar
shirt	pirâhan
shoes	kbut
silk	abrêshom
socks	jorâb
suit	dereshi
sweater	jâkat
tights/pantyhose	jorâb-e zanâna

trousers	**patlun**
umbrella/parasol	**chatri; chatr**
underwear	**zêrpôshi**
uniform	**yuniform**
wool	**pashmi**

Traditional clothing . . .

Traditional Afghan costume takes on a variety of guises depending from region to region. Headgear is important in Afghan society and can be a good indicator of where the wearer comes from. Apart from the more conventional hats (**kolâh**), there's quite an assortment on offer, including the turban (**longi**), the big bell-shaped Astrakhan hat made from soft karakul lambswool (**qaraqol**), and the "roll-top" Nuristani cap (**pakol**). Traditional clothing and fabrics are still very much in evidence in towns as well as the countryside. Women in many areas wear a variety of headscarves and veils – a very common one is the **châdar**. Men also wear a large body scarf, called the **pato**.

—Toiletries

aspirin	**âyspiren**
Band-Aid; plaster	**palaster**
comb	**shâna**
condom	**kândom**
cotton wool	**pomba**
deodorant	**atir; khoshbo**
hairbrush	**bors-e mô**
insect repellant	**hashara kosh**
lipstick	**lab serin**
mascara	**surma**
mouthwash	**mâye'-e shostoshu-ye dahan**
nail-clippers	**nâkhon gir**
perfume	**ater**
plaster; Band-Aid	**palaster**
powder	**podar**
razor	**pal-e rish**
razor blade	**pal-e rish**
safety pin	**peng**

sanitary towels	**jan pâk**
shampoo	**shâmpu**
shaving cream	**krim-e rish**
soap	**sâbun**
sponge	**esfanj**
sunblock cream	**krim-e âftâb gir;**
	krim hemâya-ye
	jold az âftâb
tampons	**tampôn**
tissues	**destmâl-e kâghazi**
toilet paper	**kâghaz-e tashnâb**
toothbrush	**bors-e dandân**
toothpaste	**krim dandân**
washing powder; detergent	**podar-e kâlâ shôyi**

—Stationery

ballpoint	**khodkâr**
book	**ketâb**
dictionary	**farhang; dekishnari**
envelope	**pâkat(-e khat)**
guidebook	**ketâb-e râhnamâ**
ink	**rang**
magazine	**mojala**
map	**naqsha**
road map	**naqsha-ye râh**
a map of Kabul	**naqsha-ye Kâbol**
newspaper	**akhbâr**
newspaper in English	**akhbâr-e Inglisi**
notebook	**daftar;**
	ketâbcha-ye
	yâd-dâsht
novel	**ketâb-e dâstân;**
	nâwel
a novel in English	**ketâb-e dâstân-e**
	Inglisi
(piece of) paper	**(porza-ye) kâghaz**

pen	**qalam**
pencil	**pensel**
postcard	**post kârd**
scissors	**qaychi**
writing paper	**kâghaz barâye naweshtan**

| Do you have any foreign publications? | **Âyâ shomâ nasharat-e khâreji dârêd?** |

—Photography

How much is it to process (and print) this film?	**Shostan (wa châp kardan)-e in film chand mêshawad?**
When will it be ready?	**Che waqt âmada mêshawad?**
I'd like film for this camera.	**Man film barâye in kâmra mêkhâhom.**
B&W (film)	**syâh-o safêd**
camera	**kâmra**
color (film)	**film ranga**
film	**film**
flash	**falash**
lens	**lenz**
light meter	**nur sanj**

—Smoking

> Although technically frowned upon by Islam, smoking is permissible in most areas. It is advisable to avoid constricted enclosed spaces if smoking creates problems for your health or if you simply find it offensive.

A packet of cigarettes, please.	**Yak qoti-ye segrêt, lotfan.**
Are these cigarettes strong/mild?	**Âyâ in segrêt qawi/ khafif ast?**
Do you have a light?	**Segrêt lâyter dârêd?**

Do you have any American cigarettes?	**Segrêt-e Amrikâyi dârêd?**
cigar	**segrêt**
cigarette papers	**kâghaz-e segrêt**
cigarettes	**segrêt**
a carton of cigarettes	**yak baks-e segrêt**
filtered	**filtar dâr**
filterless	**bê filtar**
flint	**sang-e chaqmaq**
lighter fluid	**gâz-e lâyter**
lighter	**lâyter**
matches	**gogerd**
pipe	**pâyp**
tobacco	**tanbâku**

—Electrical equipment

adapter	**adâptar**
battery	**bêtri**
cassette	**kaset**
CD	**si-di**
CD player	**dastgâh-e si-di**
fan	**paka**
hairdryer	**mo khoshkun**
iron *for clothing*	**otu**
kettle	**chai josh barqi**
plug	**palag**
portable TV	**teliwizyun-e sayâr**
radio	**râdyo**
record	**rekârd**
tape (cassette)	**fita**
television	**teliwizyun**
videotape	**kaset wêdyô**
voltage regulator	**adâptar**

> **LANGUAGE TIP** — For hi-tech stuff like cassettes, videos/
> video-players or transformers you are more likely to be
> understood if you use the English terms.

—Sizes

small	**khord**
big	**bozorg**
heavy	**sangin; gerang**
light	**sobok**
more	**bêshtar**
less	**kamtar**
many	**zyâd**
too much/too many	**besyâr zyâd**
enough	**bas; kâfi**
that's enough	**bas ast; kâfi-st**
also	**ham**
a little bit	**meqdâr-e kam**
Do you have a carrier bag?	**Âyâ shomâ yak khalta dârêd?**

11. WHAT'S TO SEE

Afghanistan's position at the crossroads of the great empires and religions of the world means that many great civilizations have made their mark and blended with local customs and cultures. Recent centuries however have seen the systematic destruction of settlements and monuments throughout Afghanistan — most recently the blowing up of the giant Buddha statue complex in the Bamyan Valley. Some of these monuments have survived, however, although often they are difficult to get to. Some of the more historic towns have managed to preserve their architectural heritage. Many of the old mosques that still remain are impressive with domes and interiors beautifully carved in flowing Arabic characters, such as those in Herat, Mazar-e Sharif — a leading place of international Muslim pilgrimage — and Balkh. There are also still a few saints' shrines and caravanserais (traditional trade-route inns) dotted about. The stone mountain villages perched on rocky valley sides can be stunning. There is also the immense natural beauty of Afghanistan, particularly the forests, teeming with wildlife (although many areas, sadly, are now heavily mined and therefore no-go areas), the racing rivers flowing from the glaciers and majestic snow-capped peaks in the north and the great desert plains of the south. Despite centuries of destruction and invasion the Afghans still have good reason to be proud of their land.

Do you have a guide-book?	**Shomâ ketâb-e râhnamâ râ dârêd?**
Do you have a local map?	**Shomâ naqsha-ye mahali dârêd?**
Is there a guide who speaks English?	**Âyâ râhnamâyi ke Inglisi bodânad ast?**
I want to see ...	**Man mêkhâhom ... râ bobinom.**
I want to see/visit ...	**Man mêkhâhom ... bâ molâqat konom.**
We want to see/visit ...	**Mâ mêkhâhêm ... râ bobinêm.**
We want to see/visit ...	**Mâ mêkhâhêm ... bâ molâqat konêm.**

What is that?	**Ân chist?**
How old is it?	**Cheqadar qedmat dârad?**
What animal is that?	**Ân kodâm haywân ast?**
What fish is that?	**Ân kodâm mâhi-st?**
What insect is that?	**Ân kodâm jânwar ast?**
May I take a photograph?	**Mêtawânom aks bogirom?**
What time does it open?	**Che waqt wâz mêshawad?**
What time does it close?	**Che waqt basta mêshawad?**
What does that say?	**Ân che mafhum dârad?**
Who is that statue of?	**Ân mojasema-ye ki-st?**
Is there an entrance fee?	**Âyâ dâkhel shodan fis dârad?**
How much?	**Cheqadar?; Chand?**
Are there any nightclubs/ discos?	**Âyâ dar injâ disko wojud dârad?**
Where can I hear local folk music?	**Dar kojâ museqi-ye mahali shoneda mêtawânom?**
How much does it cost to get in?	**Tiket-e dokhol chand ast?**
When is the concert?	**Kânsart che waqt ast?**
When is the wedding?	**Arusi che waqt ast?**
What time does it begin?	**Che waqt âghâz mêshawad?**
Can we swim here?	**Injâ awbâzi karda mêtawânom?**

Is it safe to get out of the vehicle?	**Kodam khatar-e nêst agar az môtar khârej shawêm?**
Stay in the vehicle!	**Dar môtar bomân!**
The animals are dangerous.	**In haywânât khatarnâk hastand.**

—Events

dancing	**raqs**
disco	**disko**
disc jockey	**gardanenda-ye museqi**
exhibition	**nomâyesh gâh**
folk dancing	**raqs-e mahali**
folk music	**museqi-ye mahali**
jazz	**jâz**
music	**museqi; mozik**
party	**mêhmâni**
pop music	**museqi-ye pâp**
rock 'n' roll	**râk-en-rol**
safari	**pârk haywânât wahshi**
take-away food/take-out food	**ghezâ-ye ke bâ khod mêbarand**

—Venues

apartment	**apartmân**
apartment block/building	**blâk**
archaeological	**bâstâni**
art gallery	**gâlari(-e honar-hâ)**
bakery	**nânwâyi**
bar	**bâr**
building	**sâkhtomân**
café	**qahwa-khâna; kâfi**
casino	**qemâr khâna**
castle	**qasar**
cemetery	**qabrestân**

church	**kalisâ**
cinema	**sênamâ**
city map	**naqsha-ye shâr**
college	**fâkolta; pôhanzay**
concert hall	**sâlon-e museqi**
concert	**kânsart**
dispensary	**shafâ khâna**
embassy	**sefârat**
fort	**qalâ**
game park	**pârk-e tafrêhi**
hospital	**shafâ khâna**
house	**khâna**
housing estate	**manteqa-ye maskuni**
industrial estate	**manteqa-ye san'ati**
library	**ketâb-khâna**
lift/elevator	**lift**
lodge	**khâna-ye chobi**
main square	**chawk-e shâr;**
	markaz-e shâr
market	**bâzâr**
monument	**yâdgâr**
mosque	**masjed**
museum	**mozyam**
nightclub	**disko**
old city	**shâr-e kohna**
park	**pârk**
parliament (building)	**(sâkhtomân-e)**
	pârlemân
pharmacy	**dawâ khâna**
pub	**bâr**
restaurant	**rastôrân**
ruins	**kharâba**
school	**maktab**
shop	**dôkân**
stadium	**estâdyum**
statue	**mojasema; bot**

synagogue	**mâbad-e Yahudi; kanesht**
Hindu temple	**mâbad-e Hendu; daramsâl**
theatre	**teyâter**
tomb	**qaber**
tower	**borj**
university	**pôhantun; uniwersiti**
zoo	**bâgh-e wahsh**

—Occasions

birth	**tawalod**
death	**marg**
funeral	**jenâza; marâsim-e jenâza**
marriage	**ezdewâj**

Religious heritage ...

Afghans are Muslims, mostly Sunni with large Shi'i communities. Small groups of Hindus, Sikhs, Parsees, and Jews are also scattered in the towns. Mosques and madrasas (religious schools) have always played an important part in the development of the Afghan people and state, and Islam makes its presence felt through the often stunning religious buildings still standing throughout the country.

HOLIDAYS & FESTIVALS — There are a wide variety of traditional festivals celebrated in every village and area. Important dates in the national calendar are **Ramazân** (Ramadan, the month of fasting), **Id al-Fetr**, when the end of Ramadan and fasting is celebrated, and, three months later, **Id al-Hajj** or **Id al-Adhâ**, which is when pilgrims traditionally celebrate their return from visiting Mecca. Both are normally three or four days holiday. **Mawlûd-Nabbi**, the Prophet Muhammad's Birthday, is also celebrated. **Nawrôz** is the Afghan New Year or Spring Festival (March 21st).

---

12. FINANCE

CURRENCIES — The official currency in Afghanistan is the **afghâni** (Af), divided into 100 **pul**. Unofficially in use, but still accepted everywhere outside of government establishments and retail outlets, are U.S. dollars. These may be refused however if notes are creased, torn, old, or simply a low denomination. Be prepared to accept change in afghanis.

CHANGING MONEY — Aside from the banks, money can also be changed in any bureau de change, where you will find reliable, up-to-date exchange rates prominently displayed on a board. The cashiers will often know a European language or two, and almost all will show the workings of the exchange on a calculator for you and give you a receipt. Many shops and kiosks will also be happy to change money for you.

I want to change some dollars.	**Man mêkhâhom dâlar tabdil konom.**
I want to change some euros.	**Man mêkhâhom yuro tabdil konom.**
I want to change some pounds.	**Man mêkhâhom pawnd tabdil konom.**
Where can I change some money?	**Kojâ mêtawânom paysa tabdil konom?**
What is the exchange rate?	**Narkh-e tabdil cheqadar ast?**
What is the commission?	**Kamêshan-esh chand mêsha?**
Could you please check that again?	**Mêtawânêd lotfan dobâra ân râ sayl konêd?**
Could you write that down for me?	**Mêtawânêd ân râ barâye man bonawisêd?**

dollar	**dâlar**
euro	**yuro**
pound/sterling	**pawnd/estarling**
bank notes	**bânknôt**
bureau de change	**sarâfi**
calculator	**mâshin hesâb**
cashier	**hesâb dâr**
coins	**seka**
credit card	**kredet-kârt**
commission	**kamêshan**
exchange	**tabdil**
foreign exchange/currency	**as'âr**
loose change	**pul-e khord**
receipt	**rasid**
signature	**emzâ**

Courtesy . . .

Afghans pride themselves on being a courteous people and this is reflected in the expressions they use towards guests and superiors. Some related expressions you'll commonly hear and use are:

khôsh âmadêd!	welcome!
	To which the response is :
	khôsh bâshêd!
khâna âbâd!	may your home be forever!
tashakor!	thank you!
salâmat bâshêd!	health to you!
bofarmâyêd!	you're welcome!; please!;
	come to the table!; please eat!

13. COMMUNICATIONS

TELECOMMUNICATIONS — It is likely that when Afghnistan's new telephone system is fully connected up, cell phones will be the preferred way to talk to one another. Satellite telephone links are costly but represent a reliable and secure method of communication in and out of the region.

POSTAL SERVICES — When operational, the postal service in Afghanistan is not always reliable. For important messages it would be best to stick to fax, telex, the telephone, couriers or e-mail. If you expect to receive mail, have it sent to the nearest headquarters of a host organization.

—Post

Where is the post office?	**Postakhâna kojâ-st?**
What time does the post office open?	**Postakhâna che waqt bâz mêshawad?**
What time does the post office close?	**Postakhâna che waqt band mêshawad?**
Where is the mail box?	**Post-baks kojâ-st?**
Is there any mail for me?	**Âyâ man khat dârom?**
How long will it take for this to get there?	**Cheqadar waqt lazem ast tâ in borasad?**
How much does it cost to send this to ... ?	**Ferestâdan-e in cheqadar masraf dârad?**
I would like some stamps.	**Man chand dâna tiket-e posti mêkhâhom.**

I would like to send ...	**Man mêkhâhom ...**
	boferestom.
a letter	**yak khat/nâma**
a postcard	**yak post kârd**
a parcel	**yak pârsal**
a telegram	**telegrâm**
air mail	**post-e hawâyi**
envelope	**pâkat**
mailbox	**post-baks**
registered mail	**post-e râjistar**
stamp	**tiket-e posti**

—Tele-etiquette

I would like to make a phone call.	**Man mêkhâhom yak telifun konom?**
I would like to send a fax.	**Man mêkhâhom yak faks boferestom.**
I would like to send a telex.	**Man mêkhâhom yak teleks boferestom.**
Where is the telephone?	**Telifun kojâ-st?**
May I use your phone?	**Mêtawânom az telifun-e shomâ estêfâda konom?**
Can I telephone from here?	**Mêtawânom az injâ telifun konom?**
Can you help me get this number?	**Mêtawânêd in nomra râ barâye man rokh konêd?**
Can I dial direct?	**Mêtawânom ra'san nâmber shomâra bogirom?**
May I speak to Mr. ... ?	**Mêtawânom bâ Âqâ-ye ... gap bozanom?**

COMMUNICATIONS

May I speak to Ms/Mrs. ... ?	**Mêtawânom bâ khânom-e ... gap bozanam?**
Can I leave a message?	**Yak payghâm barâyash mânda mêtawânom?**
Who is calling, please?	**Shomâ, lotfan?**
Who are you calling?	**Bâ ke kâr dârêd?**
Can I take your name?	**Mêtawânom nâmetân râ boporsom?**
Which number are you dialing?	**Kodâm nomra râ dâyl kardayêd?**
He/She is not here at the moment — would you like to leave a message?	**Hâlâ injâ nêstand, mêkhâhêd payghâm barâyash bomânom?**
This is not ...	**Inja ... nêst.**
You are mistaken.	**Eshtebâh kardayêd.**
This is the ... office.	**In daftar-e ... ast.**
Hello, I need to speak to ...	**Salâm, man mêkhâhom bâ ... gap bozanom.**
Sorry wrong number.	**Nomra-ye ghalat râ rokh kardayêd.**
I am calling this number ...	**Man in nomra râ rokh mêkonom ...**
I want to ring ...	**Man mêkhâhom nomra-ye ... râ rokh konom.**
What is the code for ... ?	**Kod ... chand ast?**
What is the international code for ... ?	**Kod baynolmelali barâye ... chand ast?**
What do I dial for an outside line?	**Barâye lâyn-e khâreji che shomârayi râ bogirom?**
The number is ...	**In nomra ... ast.**

The extension is ...	**Nomra-ye faraye ... ast.**
It's engaged/busy.	**Masruf ast.**
There's no dialing/busy tone.	**Hêch sadâ nadârad.**
I've been cut off./The line has been cut off.	**Lâyn qat'a shoda.**
Where is the nearest public phone?	**Nazdektarin telifun omumi kojâ-st?**

> **LANGUAGE TIP** — When answering the phone, most people in Afghanistan first say **halo!** or **alo!** — "hello!" You will also hear **balê** — "yes?"

—Technical words

digital	**dijital**
e-mail	**imêl**
extension (number)	**nomra-ye faraye**
fax	**faks**
fax machine	**mâshin-e faks**
handset	**gushi**
international operator	**aprêtar-e baynolmelali**
internet	**internet; entarnet**
internet café	**klub-entarnet**
line	**khat**
mobile phone; cell phone	**mobâyl**
modem	**mâdem**
operator	**aprêtar**
satellite phone	**telifun-e satilâyt**
telecommunications	**mokhâberât**
telephone center	**markaz-e telifun**
telex	**teleks**
to transfer/put through	**wasl kardan**

—Faxing & e-mailing

Where can I send a fax from?	**Az kojâ mêtawânom faks boferestom?**
Can I fax from here?	**Mêtawânom az injâ faks konom?**
How much is it to fax?	**Faks cheqadar kharch dârad?**
Where can I find a place to e-mail from?	**Az kojâ mêtawânom imêl boferestom?**
Is there an internet café near here?	**Âyâ dar in nazdiki klub-entarnet ast?**
Can I e-mail from here?	**Mêtawânom az injâ imêl boferestom?**
How much is it to use a computer?	**Barây-e estêfâda az kâmpyutar cheqadar bayad bopardazom?**
How do you turn on this computer?	**Chetor in kâmpyutar râ bayad roshan konom?**
The computer has crashed.	**In kâmpyutar az kâr oftâd.**
I don't know how to use this program.	**Namêdânom chetor bâ in progrâm kâr konom.**
I know how to use this program.	**Man mêdânom ke chetor bâ in progrâm kâr konom.**
I want to print.	**Mêkhâhom châp konom.**

14. THE OFFICE

chair	**chawki**
computer	**kâmpyutar**
desk	**mêz**
drawer	**rawak**
fax	**faks**
file *paper/computer*	**dosiya**
meeting	**molâqât**
paper	**kâghaz**
pen	**qalam**
pencil	**pensel**
photocopier	**mâshin-e fotokâpi**
photocopy	**fotokâpi**
printer	**prentar**
(computer) program	**progrâm (-e kâmpyutar)**
report	**gozâresh**
ruler	**khat kash**
scanner	**eskanar**
telephone	**telefun**
telex	**teleks**
typewriter	**tâyprâytar**

15. THE CONFERENCE

agenda	**ejandâ**
article	**maqâla**
a break for refreshments	**esterâhat;**
	tafreh barâye khordan
chairman/chairwoman	**monshi**
conference	**kânfarâns**
conference room	**otâq-e kânfarâns**
copy	**noskha; kopi**
discussion	**bahs; goftogu**
forum	**mêz-e modawar**
guest speaker	**mêhmân-e sokhanrân**
a (written) paper	**maqâla**
projector	**projektar**
session	**jalasa**
a session chaired by ...	**yak jalasa ba**
	riyâsat-e ...
speaker	**sokhanrân**
subject	**mawzu**

16. EDUCATION

to add		**jama kardan**
addition		**jama**
bench		**korsi**
biro		**khodkâr**
blackboard		**takhta**
book		**ketâb**
calculation		**hesâb**
chalk		**tabâshir**
class		**senf**
to copy		**kâpi kardan**
to count		**shomordan**
crayon		**khod-rang**
difficult		**sakht; dashwâr**
to divide		**taqsim kardan**
division		**taqsim**
easy		**âsân**
eraser	*pen/pencil*	**penselpâk**
	board	**takhtapâk**
exam		**emtehân**
exercise book		**ketâbcha**
to explain		**fâhmândan**
felt-tip pen		**khod-rang**
geography		**joghrâfiya**
grammar		**serf-o nahw; gerâmar**
history		**târikh**
holidays		**rokhsati**
homework		**kâr-e khânagi**
illiterate		**bêsewâd**
language		**zabân**
lazy		**kâhel; tanbal**
to learn		**yâd gereftan**

lesson	**dars**
library	**ketâb-khâna**
literature	**adabiyât**
madrasa	**madrasa**
maths	**riyâzyât**
memory	**yâd**
multiplication	**zarb**
to multiply	**zarb kardan**
notebook	**ketâbcha**
page	**safa**
paper	**kâghaz**
to pass *an exam*	**kâmyâb shodan**
pen	**qalam**
pencil	**pensel**
progress	**pêshraft**
to punish	**jazâ dâdan**
pupil	**shâgerd**
to read	**khândan**
to repeat	**tekrâr kardan**
rubber *eraser*	**penselpâk**
ruler *instrument*	**khat-kash**
satchel	**baks**
school	**maktab**
sheet *of paper*	**waraq**
slate	**takhta**
student	**shâgerd;** **mota'alem**
to subtract	**manfi kardan**
subtraction	**manfi; tafreq**
sum	**mablagh; raqam**
table	**mêz**
teacher	**mo'alem;** **mwalem**
test *academic*	**emtehân**
time	**waqt**

17. AGRICULTURE

agriculture	**zeyârat**
barley	**jaw**
barn	**kahdân**
cattle	**galaye gaw**
to clear land	**pâk kardan**
combine harvester	**kambâyn**
corn	**jwâri; jawâri**
cotton	**pomba; pakhta**
crops	**hâsel; paydâwâr**
earth	**zamin**
fallowland	**zamin-e bâyer**
farm	**mazre'a; kesht; fârm**
farmer	**dehqân**
farming	**zeyârat**
(animal) feed	**ghezâ**
fertilizer	**kûd**
field	**maydân**
fruit	**mêwa**
garden	**bâgh**
to grow crops	**kâshtan**
harvest	**hâsel; daraw**
hay	**kâh**
haystack	**bêda**
irrigation	**âbyâri**
marsh	**mordâb; bâtlâq**
mill	**âsyâ**
orchard	**bâgh**
planting	**kâshtan**
plow	**qolba**
to plow	**qolba zadan**
to reap	**daraw kardan**
reaping	**daraw**

season	**fasl**
seed	**dâna**
silkworm	**kerm-e abrêshom**
to sow	**kâshtan**
tractor	**tarâktor**
well (of water)	**châh**
wheat	**gandom**

Social organization . . .

FAMILY — Afghans place great value on social bonds and their society teaches respect for tradition and one's elders. This has been carried over into the active mechanism of authority. Afghans have always traditionally turned to their elders for all major decisions, embodying as they do one of the three pillars of family, tradition and religion on which the nation has been built and which has helped it survive against all odds. The village elders are the **rish-safêdân** ("grey-beards"), and include the **olemâ** or **olemâ-eddin** ("wisemen [of religion]" or ulema, Muslim scholars), the **qâzi** ("qadi" or Muslim judge), the **molâ** ("mullah" or Muslim clergyman). There are various titles for the secular heads of the communities: the head or mayor of a village is the **qaryedâr**, in a town he is the **walaswâl**, and in a city he is the **wali**. Their smaller meetings are called **jerga-hâ** or **shorô-hâ**, while the great congress that is convoked from year to year to consult and make joint decisions on matters of national importance is called the **loya-jerga**.

LAW – The concept of law reflects this mixture. Normal law in the sense of law and order is **qânun**, while an individual law is called a **moqarara**. Many Afghans also appeal to **shariya**, Islamic law, or even the customary law of their forefathers.

18. ANIMALS

—Mammals

animal	**haywân**
animals	**haywânât**
antelope	**gawazn**
baboon	**maymun; shadi**
buffalo	**gâw mêsh-e wahshi**
bull	**gâw mêsh**
camel	**shotor**
cat	**peshak**
cow	**gâw**
deer	**âhu**
dog	**sag**
Beware of the dog!	**Motawaje sag bâsh!**
donkey	**khar**
elephant	**fil**
ferret	**râsu**
flock	**dasta**
fox	**rubâh**
gazelle	**ghezâl**
goat	**boz**
herd	**gala**
horse	**asb**
lamb	**bara**
lion	**shêr**
mare	**mâdiyân**
monkey	**maymun**
mouse	**mush**
mule	**qâter**
pig	**khuk**
pony	**yâbo**
rabbit	**khar gush**
ram	**mêsh**

rat	**mush-e sahrâyi**
sheep	**gusfand**
sheepdog	**sag-e gala**
squirrel	**mush khurmâ**
stallion	**asb-e nar**
water buffalo	**gâw mêsh-e âbi**

—Birds

bird(s)	**parenda(-hâ)**
chicken/hen	**morgh**
cock/rooster	**khorus**
crow	**zâgh**
duck	**morghabi**
eagle	**oqâb**
goose	**qâz**
guinea fowl	**tawus**
hawk	**shahin; bâz**
owl	**bum**
peacock	**tâwus**
turkey	**filmorgh**
vulture	**kargas**

—Insects & amphibians

ants	**mur; morcha**
bee	**zanbur**
butterfly	**parwâna; shahparak**
caterpillar	**kerm-e darakht**
centipede	**hazâr pâ**
chameleon	**susmâre kochak**
cobra	**mâr-e kobrâ**
cockroach	**mâder-e kayk-hâ**
crocodile	**temsâh**
firefly	**kerm-e shab tâb**
fish	**mâhi**
flea	**kayk**
fleas	**kayk-hâ**

fly	**magas**
frog	**baqa; qurbaqa**
gecko	**susmâr**
insect	**hashara**
insects	**hasharât**
lizard	**chalpâsa**
louse	**shepesh**
lice	**shepesh-hâ**
mosquito(es)	**pasha(-hâ)**
python	**mâr-e pâyton/affi**
scorpion	**gazhdom**
snail	**gawak**
snake	**mâr**
spider	**ankabut**
termite	**muriyâna**
tick	**kana**
tortoise; turtle	**sang posht**
wasp	**zanbur**
worm	**kerm**

19. COUNTRYSIDE

canal	**kânâl**
cave	**ghâr**
dam	**band (âbi)**
desert	**sahrâ**
earthquake	**zelzela**
fire	**âtesh**
flood	**sêl**
foothills	**kôh pâya;**
	damân-e kôh
footpath	**payâda râh**
forest	**jangal**
hill	**tapa**
lake	**jahel**
landslide	**laghzesh-e zamin**
mountain	**kôh**
mountain pass	**kôtal**
peak	**qola**
plain/plains	**dasht**
plant	**giyâh**
range/mountain range	**selsela jabâl;**
	kôhestan
ravine	**tangi**
river	**daryâ**
river bank	**labi daryâ**
rock	**sang**
slope	**shêb; sarâshêbi**
stream	**juy**
summit	**qola**
swamp	**jabazâr; mordâb**
tree	**darakht**
valley	**dara**
waterfall	**âb shâr**
a wood	**jangal**

20. WEATHER

What's the weather like?	**Hawâ chetor ast?**

The weather is ... today.	**Emruz hawâ ... ast.**
cold	**sard**
cool/fresh	**khonok/tâza**
cloudy	**abri**
freezing	**yakh bandân**
hot	**garm**
misty	**ghobâr alud**
very hot	**besyâr garm**
windy	**bâdâlud**

It's going to rain.	**Bârân khâhad bârid.**
It is raining.	**Bârân mêbârad.**
It's going to snow.	**Barf khâhad bârid.**
It is snowing.	**Barf mêbârad**
It is sunny.	**Âftâbi hast.**

The temperature is high.	**Harârat zyâd ast.**
The temperature is low.	**Harârat pâyin ast.**
The temperature is about to drop sharply.	**Harârat besyâr pâyin khâhad âmad.**

▬Weather words

air	**hawâ**
cloud	**abr**
blizzard	**bad-e shadid bâ barf**
drought	**khoshk sâli**
frost	**yakh bandân**
full moon	**mâh-e kâmel**
glacier	**yakhchâl; yakh bandân**
heatwave	**mowj-e garmi**

hailstorm	**tufân-e tegarg**
ice	**yakh**
black ice	**yakh-e syâh**
moon	**mâh**
new moon	**mâh-e naw**
planet	**sayâra**
rain	**bârân**
sleet	**zhâla; barf-o-bârân**
snow	**barf**
snowdrift	**barf-e anbâshta**
star	**setâra**
sun	**âftâb**
weather	**hawâ**

—Seasons

spring	**bahâr**
summer	**tabestân**
autumn; fall	**khazân**
winter	**zamestân**

21. CAMPING

Where can we camp?	**Kojâ khayma zada mêtawânêm?**
Can we camp here?	**Injâ khayma zada mêtawânêm?**
Is it safe to camp here?	**Âyâ injâ barâye khayma zadan amneyat ast?**
Is there danger of wild animals?	**Âyâ dar injâ khatar-e haywânat-e wahshi wojud dârad?**
Is there drinking water?	**Âb-e nushidani hast?**
May we light a fire?	**Mêtwânêm âtesh roshan konêm?**

—Kit

axe	**tabar**
backpack	**bukhcha**
bucket	**satl**
campsite	**kamp; khayma**
can opener	**sar bâz kon**
compass	**qotb namâ**
firewood	**hizom**
flashlight	**cherâgh-e desti**
gas canister	**balun-e gâz**
hammer	**chakosh**
ice ax; ice pick	**yakh shekan**
lamp	**cherâgh**
mattress	**doshak; toshak**
penknife	**châqu-ye jêbi**
rope	**rêsmân; rêspân**
sleeping bag	**kharita-ye khâb**

stove	**ojâq; manqal**
tent	**khayma**
tent pegs	**mêkh-e khayma**
water bottle	**bôtal-e âb**

Weights & measures . . .

Afghanistan uses the metric system. Here is a list of international units — for reference, translations are included for the most common imperial units:

kilometer	**kilometr**
meter	**metr**
mile	**mâyl; mêl**
foot	**fut**
yard	**gaz**
acre	**ekar**
gallon	**gelan**
liter	**lêtar**
kilogram	**kilogerâm**
ton; tonne	**tan**
pound	**pawnd**
gram	**gerâm**
ounce	**awns**

Special words used for units of weight in Afghanistan are:

pâw	pound/half kilo
chârak	4 pounds/2 kilos
sêr	16 pounds/7 kilos

22. EMERGENCY

COMPLAINING — If you really feel you have been cheated or misled, raise the matter first with your host or the proprietor of the establishment in question preferably with a smile. Afghans are proud but courteous, with a deeply felt tradition of hospitality, and consider it their duty to help any guest. Angry glares and shouting will get you nowhere.

CRIME — Without undue paranoia, take usual precautions: watch your wallet or purse, securely lock your equipment and baggage before handing it over to railway or airline porters, and don't leave valuables on display in your hotel room. On buses, look out for pickpockets – keep valuables in front pockets and your bag close to your side. If you are robbed, contact the police. Of course in the more remote areas, sensible precautions should be taken, and always ensure that you go with a guide. In general, follow the same rules as you would in your own country and you will run little risk of encountering crime.

LOST ITEMS — If you lose something, save time and energy by appealing only to senior members of staff or officials. If you have lost items in the street or left anything in public transport, the police may be able to help.

DISABLED FACILITIES — The terrain and conditions throughout most of Afghanistan do not make it easy for any visitor in a wheelchair or with mobility difficulties to get around even at the best of times. Access to most buildings in the towns is difficult, particularly since the majority of lifts function irregularly. Facilities are rarely available in hotels, airports or other public areas.

TOILETS — You will find public utilities located in any important or official building. You may use those in hotels or restaurants. You may sometimes encounter failed plumbing and absence of toilet paper. Similar to Pakistan, India and countries in the Middle East, people in Afghanistan tend to use any available paper as toilet paper, and occasionally a jug of water (rural areas).

wheelchair	**chawki-ye charkhi barâye mayub; korsi charkh dâr**
disabled	**mayub**
Do you have seats for the disabled?	**Jây neshastan barâye mayubân dârêd?**

Do you have access for the disabled?	**Dastrasi barâye mayub hast?**
Do you have facilities for the disabled?	**Emkânât lâzem barâye mayub dârêd?**
Help!	**Komak, komak!**
Could you help me, please?	**Mêtawânêd bâ man komak konêd, lotfan?**
Do you have a telephone?	**Shomâ telifun dârêd?**
Can I use your telephone?	**Mêtawânom az telifun-e shomâ estêfâda konom?**
Where is the nearest telephone?	**Nazdik tarin telifun kojâ-st?**
Does the phone work?	**In telifun kâr mêkonâ?**
Get help quickly!	**Komak âjel bokhâh!**
Call the police.	**Bâ polis tamâs bogir.**
I'll call the police!	**Man polis râ khabar mêkonom!**
Is there a doctor near here?	**Âyâ dar in nazdik-e ha dâktar ast?**
Call a doctor.	**Dâktar râ khabar kon.**
Call an ambulance.	**Yak ambulâns bokhâ.**
I'll get medical help!	**Man komak-e tebi mêgirom!**
Where is the doctor?	**Dâktar kojâ-st?**
Where is the hospital?	**Shafâ khâna kojâ-st?**
Where is the pharmacy?	**Dawâ khâna kojâ-st?**
Where is the dentist?	**Dâktar-e dandân kojâ-st?**

Where is the police station?	**Mâmoryat-e pôlis kojâ-st?**
Take me to a doctor.	**Ma râ nazde dâktar bobarêd.**
There's been an accident!	**Takar shodast!**
Is anyone hurt?	**Âyâ kase afgar shoda?**
This person is hurt.	**In shakhs afgar shoda.**
There are people injured.	**Chand nafar afgar shodand.**
Don't move!	**Harkat nakon!** *or* **Shor nakhor!**
Go away!	**Dur boro!**
I am lost.	**Man râh râ gom kardam.**
I am ill.	**Man mariz astom.**
I've been raped.	**Ba man tajâwoz shodast.**
I've been robbed.	**Ma râ dozd zada.**
Thief!	**Dozd!**
My ... has been stolen.	**...-e man dozdi shoda.**
I have lost ...	**... gom shoda.**
my bags	**baks-e man**
my camera equipment	**wasâyel-e filmbardâri-e man**
my handbag	**destkawl-e man**
my laptop computer	**kâmpyutar-e man**
my money	**paysa-ye man**
my passport	**pâsport-e man**
my sound equipment	**wasâyel-e sawt-e man**
my traveler's checks	**trêwalchek-hâ-ye man**
my wallet	**baksak-e jêbi-e man**
My possessions are insured.	**wasâyel-e man bêma shodand.**

I have a problem.	**Man yak moshkel dârom.**
I didn't do it.	**Man nakardam.**
I'm sorry.	**Man mota'asefam.**
I apologize.	**Man ozr mêkhâhom.** *or* **Mo' azerat mêkhahom.**
I didn't realize anything was wrong.	**Man motawajêh-e chiz-e nâdorosti nashodom.**
I want to contact my embassy/consulate.	**Man mêkhâhom bâ sefârat-am/ qonsulgari-yam khod tamâs bogirom.**
I speak English.	**Man Inglisi gap mêzanom.**
I need an interpreter.	**Man ba yak tarjomân zarurat dârom.**
Where are the toilets/ bathrooms?	**Tashnâb/hamâm kojâ-st?**

23. HEALTHCARE

> **INSURANCE** — Make sure any insurance policy you take out covers Afghanistan, although this will only help in flying you out in case of a serious accident or illness. Consult your doctor for any shots required or recommended when making any trip outside of North America and Western Europe.
>
> **PHARMACIES** — Chemists are not always easy to find and tend to be chronically understocked or simply empty even in peacetime. Particularly if planning to travel off the beaten track, it is probably best to bring a sufficient supply of any medication you require — even basics such as aspirin, cotton wool or sunscreen. But most of the familiar range of medicines can be found in the larger towns.
>
> Don't forget to check the "best before" date.

What's the trouble?	**Moshkel-e shomâ chist?**
I am sick.	**Man mariz astom.**
My companion is sick.	**Hamrâh-e man mariz ast.**
May I see a female doctor?	**Momken ast yak dâktar-e zan râ bobinom?**
I have medical insurance.	**Man bêma-ye tebi dârom.**
Please undress.	**Lotfan lebâsetân râ bokashêd.**
What's the problem?	**Chi nâ-juri dâshti?**
How long have you had this problem?	**Cheqadar waqt ast in moshkel râ dârêd?**
How long have you been feeling sick?	**Cheqadar waqt ast ehsâs-e marizi mêkonêd?**
Have you been ill before?	**Pêshtar nâjôr bodi?**
How many times?	**Chand dafa?**
Where does it hurt?	**Kojâyt dard mêkona?**
It hurts here.	**Injâ dard mêkona.**

Where?	**Kojâ?**
Here.	**Injâ.**
That hurts.	**Dard mêkona.**
For how many days?	**Chand rôz mêsha?**
I have been vomiting.	**Man estefrâq mêkardom.**
I feel dizzy.	**Ehsâs-e sarcharkhi mêkonom.**
I can't eat.	**Khorda namêtawânom.**
I can't sleep.	**Khâbeda namêtawânom.**
I fell.	**Oftâda'am.**
I had an accident.	**Man takar kardam.**
I feel worse.	**Hâlem bad ast.**
I feel better.	**Hâlem bêhtar ast.**
Do you have diabetes?	**Bêmâri-ye shakar dârêd?**
Do you have epilepsy?	**Bêmâri-ye mergi dârêd?**
Do you have asthma?	**Nafas-tangi dârêd?**
I have diabetes.	**Man bêmâri-ye shakar dârom.**
I have epilepsy.	**Man bêmâri-ye mergi dârom.**
I have asthma.	**Man nafas-tangi dârom.**
I'm pregnant.	**Man hâmela hastom.**
How many children do you have?	**Chand awlâd dârêd?**

I have ...	**Man ... dârom.**
You have ...	**Shomâ ... dârêd.**
a cold	**zokâm**
a cough	**sorfa**
a headache	**sar dard**
a pain	**dard**
a sore throat/tonsils	**golu dard/tânsal**
a temperature	**harârat/tab**
an allergy	**hasâsiyat**
an infection	**ofunat**
an itch	**khâresh**
backache	**kamar dard**
constipation	**qabziyat**
diarrhea	**es-hâl**
fever	**tab**
hepatitis	**hepâtet**
indigestion	**su'-e hâzema**
influenza	**zokâm; rêzesh**
a heart condition	**bêmâri-ye qalbi**
pins and needles	**sozish**
stomachache	**shekam dard**
a fracture	**shekastagi**
toothache	**dandân dard**

I take this medication.	**Man in dawâ râ mêkhorom.**
I need medication for ...	**Man barâye ... ba dawâ zarorat dârom.**
What type of medication is this?	**In che qesim dawâ-st?**
How many times a day must I take it?	**Chand bâr dar ruz bâyad in dawâ râ bokhorom?**
When should I stop?	**Che waqt masraf nakonom?**
I'm on antibiotics.	**Man antibayâtik masraf mêkonom.**

HEALTHCARE

I'm allergic to antibiotics.	**Man bâ antibayâtic hasâsiyat dârom.**
I'm allergic to penicillin.	**Man bâ pensilin hasâsiyat dârom.**
I have been vaccinated.	**Man wâksin shodam.**
I have my own syringe.	**Man pêchkâri-ye khodam râ dârom.**
Is it possible for me to travel?	**Mêtawânom mosâferat konom?**

—Eyesight

I have broken my glasses.	**Âynâk-ye man shekasta.**
Can you repair them?	**Mêtawânêd inhâ râ tarmêm konêd?**
I need new lenses.	**Man niyâz ba lenz-hâ-ye naw dârom.**
When will they be ready?	**Che waqt hâzer mêshawad?**
How much do I owe you?	**Cheqadar ba shomâ bodehom?**
sunglasses	**âynak âftâbi**
eyeglasses	**âynak**
contact lenses	**kântakt lenz**
contact lens solution	**mâye' barâye kântakt lenz**

—Extra health words

AIDS	**eydz**
airsick	**marizi-ye parwâz**
I am airsick.	**Man marizi-ye parwâz dârom.**
alcoholism	**âdat-e harâb khori**
altitude sickness	**bêmâri-ye ertefâ**
amputation	**qat'a-ye ozw**

anemia	**kam khuni**
anesthetic	**dawâ-ye bêhushi**
anesthetist	**motakhases-e bêhushi**
antibiotic	**antibayâtik**
antiseptic	**dawâ-ye zed-e ofôni**
aspirin	**âyspiren**
bandage	**bandâzh**
better	**bêhtar**
bite	**gazidagi**
insect bite	**hashara gazidagi**
mosquito bite	**pasha gazidagi**
snakebite	**mâr gazidagi**
This insect bit me.	**In hashara ma râ gazida.**
This snake bit me.	**In mâr ma râ gazida.**
blood	**khun**
blood group	**grup khun**
blood pressure:	**feshâr-e khun**
low blood pressure	**feshâr-e khun-e pâyin**
high blood pressure	**feshâr-e khun-e bâlâ**
blood transfusion	**enteqâl-e khun**
bone	**ostokhân**
cancer	**saratân**
choke	**khafa shodan**
He/She is choking!	**Khafa mêshawad!**
cholera	**kolerâ**
clinic	**klenik**
constipation	**qabziyat**
dehydration	**kam âbi**
dentist	**dâktar-e dandân**
diarrhea	**es-hâl**
drug *medical*	**dawâ**
narcotic	**mawâd-e mokhader**
epidemic	**sâri**
fever	**tab**
flu	**zokâm**

flying doctor	**dâktar-e sayâr**
food poisoning	**masmumiyat-e ghezâyi**
I ate this.	**Man in râ khordam.**
frostbite	**yakh zadagi**
germs	**mikrob-hâ**
healthcare	**hefzolseha; bedâsht**
heart attack	**sakta-ye qalbi**
heatstroke	**sakta-ye maghzi**
HIV	**ech-ây-wi**
hygiene	**pâki; hefzolseha**
infection	**ofunat**
limbs	**dest-o pâ**
malaria	**malaryâ**
needle	**suzan**
nurse	**nars; parastâr; qâbela**
operating theatre/room	**otâq-e amaliyât**
(surgical) operation	**amaliyât**
oxygen	**âksêjan**
painkiller	**mosaken**
physiotherapy	**fiziyotrâpi**
rabies	**bêmâri-ye sag-e dêwâna**
rash	**dâna**
sleeping pill	**dawâ-ye khâb**
snowblindness	**barf kuri**
spots	**laka-hâ**
stethoscope	**estâtiskop**
sunstroke	**âftâb zadagi**
surgeon	**jarâh**
(act of) surgery	**amaliyât**
syringe	**pêchkâri**
thermometer	**tarmamêtar**
tranquilizer	**mosâken**

24. RELIEF AID

Can you help me?	**Mêtawânêd ba man komak konêd?**
Do you speak English?	**Shomâ Inglisi gap mêzanêd?**
Who is in charge?	**Mas'ul-e injâ kest?**
Fetch the main person in charge.	**Ra'isetân râ biwârêd.**
What's the name of this town?	**Nâm-e in shâr chist?**
How many people live there?	**Nofus-e ânjâ cheqadar ast?**
What's the name of that river?	**Nâm-e ân daryâ chist?**
How deep is it?	**Cheqadar amiq ast?**
Is the bridge still standing?	**Âyâ pol hanôz ham dar jâyash ast?**
Is the bridge down?	**Pol wayrân shoda?**
Where can we ford the river?	**Az kojâ mêshawad az daryâ gozasht?**
What is the name of that mountain?	**Nâm-e ân kôh chist?**
How high is it?	**Ertefah-e ân cheqadar ast?**
Where is the border?	**Sarhad kojâ-st?**
Is it safe?	**Âyâ amneyat ast?**
Show me.	**Ba man neshân dehêd.**
Is there anyone trapped?	**Kasi ger mândâ-st?**

—Checkpoints

checkpoint	**posta-ye talâshi**
roadblock	**râh bandân;**
	râh-e band
Stop!	**Shor nakho!**
said by police/army	**Drish!**
Do not move!	**Harkat nakonêd!**
Go!	**Boro!**
Who are you?	**Shomâ ki hastêd?**
Don't shoot!	**Fâyr nakon!**
Help!	**Komak, komak!**
no entry	**worud mamnu'**
emergency exit	**khoruj-e ezterâri**
straight on	**mostaqim**
turn left	**taraf-e chap bagard**
turn right	**taraf-e râst bagard**
this way	**in taraf**
that way	**ân taraf**
Keep quiet!	**Ârâm bâshêd!**
You are right.	**Shomâ dorost mêgoyêd.**
You are wrong.	**Shomâ eshtebâh mêkonêd.**
I am ready.	**Man hâzeram.**
I am in a hurry.	**Man ajala dârom.**
Well, thank you!	**Khub, tashakor az shomâ!**
What's that?	**Ân chist?**
Come in!	**Dâkhel byâyêd!**
That's all!	**Bas khalas!**

—Food distribution

feeding station	**ghezâ khori**
Please form a queue here.	**Injâ qatâr shawêd.**
How many people are in your family?	**Khânawâda-ye shomâ chand nafar and?**

How many children?	**Chand farzand dârêd?**
You must come back this ...	**Shomâ bâyad ... injâ bargardêd.**
afternoon	**bâd az zohr; pêshen**
tonight	**emshaw**
tomorrow	**fardâ**
the day after	**pas fardâ**
next week	**hafta-ye âynda**
There is water for you.	**Âb barâye shomâ-st.**
There is grain for you.	**Gandom barâye shomâ-st.**
There is food for you.	**Ghezâ barâye shomâ-st.**
There is fuel for you.	**Mawâd-e sukht barâye shomâ-st.**

—Road repair

Is the road passable?	**Âyâ râh qâbel-e têr shodan ast?**
Is the road blocked?	**Âyâ râh basta ast?**
We are repairing the road.	**Mâ râh râ tarmêm mêkonêm.**
We are repairing the bridge.	**Mâ pol râ tarmêm mêkonêm.**
We need ...	**Mâ ba ... zarorat dârêm.**
wood	**chub**
rock	**sang**
gravel	**jaghal**
sand	**rêg**
fuel	**sukht**
Lift!	**Kashkô!**
Drop it!	**Partô!**

Now!	**Hâli!; Hâlâ!**
All together!	**Yakjâ!**

—Mines

mine *noun*	**mayn**
mines	**mayn-hâ**
minefield	**sâh-ye mayn;**
	maydân-e mayn
to lay mines	**mayn gozâri kardan**
to hit a mine	**ba mayn paridan**
to clear a mine	**pâk kari kardan-e**
	zamin az mayn
mine detector	**mayn pâl**
mine disposal	**khonsâ kardan-e**
	mayn
Are there any mines	**Âyâ dar in nazdiki**
near here?	**hâ mayn hast?**
What type are they?	**Che qesim**
	hastand?
anti-vehicle	**zed-e môtar**
anti-personnel	**zed-e nafar**
plastic	**palâstik**
floating	**shenâwar**
magnetic	**meqnâtisi**
What size are they?	**Che andâzayi**
	hastand?
What color are they?	**Che rang astand?**
Are they marked?	**Neshani shoda**
	hastand? *or*
	Moshakhas
	shodand?
How?	**Chetor?**
How many mines are	**Chand tâ mayn**
there?	**ast?**
When were they laid?	**Che waqt farsh**
	shodand?

Can you take me to the minefields?	**Mêtawânêd ma râ ba maydân-hâ-ye mayn bobarêd?**
Don't touch that!	**Ba ô dest nazan!**
Don't go near that!	**Nazdekash naro!**
Are there any booby traps near there?	**Âyâ dar ânjâ mayn-hâ-ye talak dar ast?**
Are they made from grenades, high explosives or something else?	**Âyâ az bamb desti sâkhta shodand, yâ az mawâd-e monfajeraye qawi, wa yâ chiz-e digar sakhta shodand?**
Are they in a building?	**Âyâ dar sâkhtomân astand?**
on tracks?	**dar râh-hâ?**
on roads?	**dar jâda-hâ?**
on bridges?	**ruye pol-hâ?**
or elsewhere?	**yâ jâ-ye digar?**
Can you show me?	**Mêtawânêd ba man neshân dehêd?**

—Other useful words

airdrop	**quyud**
airforce	**qowâ-ye hawâyi**
ambulance	**ambulâns**
armored car	**zerê-push**
army	**ordu**
artillery	**tup khâna**
barbed wire	**sim-e khâr dâr**
bomb	**bam**
cluster bomb	**bam-e khoshayi**
bomber	**tayâra-ye jangi**
bomblet	**pârcha-ye bam** ·

bullet	**marmi**
cannon	**tup**
disaster	**mosibat**
earthquake	**zelzela**
fighter *plane*	**tayâra-ye jangi**
gun	**tofang**
machine gun	**mâshindâr**
missile	**râkêt**
missiles	**râkêt-hâ**
mortar	**hâwân**
natural disaster	**mosibat-e tabiyi**
navy	**qowâ-ye bahri**
nuclear power	**nêru-ye atomi**
nuclear power station	**nêrugâh-e atomi**
officer	**afsar; sâheb mansab**
parachute	**parâshot**
peace	**solh**
peace-keeping force	**qowâ-ye hâfez-e solh**
people	**mardom**
pistol	**tofangcha**
refugee camp	**kamp-e panâhendagân**
refugee	**panâhenda; mohâjer**
refugees	**panâhendagân**
relief aid	**komak-e emdâdi**
rifle	**tofang**
sack	**kharita; khalta**
shell	**tup**
submachine gun	**mâshindâr-e saqil**
tank	**tânk**
troops	**asâker**
unexploded bomb	**bam-e monfajer nashoda**
unexploded ammunition/ ordnance	**mohemât-e monfajer nashoda**
war	**jang**
weapon	**salâh; aslehâ**

25. TOOLS

binoculars	**durbin**
brick	**khesht**
brush	**bors**
cable	**sim; kêbal**
cooker/stove	**ojâq**
drill	**barma**
gas bottle	**balun-e gâz**
hammer	**chakosh**
handle	**desta**
hose	**nal**
insecticide	**hashara kosh**
ladder	**zina**
machine	**mâshin**
microscope	**mikroskop**
nail	**mêkh**
padlock	**qofl; qolf**
paint	**rang**
pickaxe	**têsha**
plank	**takhta**
plastic	**palâstik**
pressure cooker	**dêg-e bokhâr**
rope	**rêsmân; rêspân**
rubber	**râbar**
saw	**ara**
scissors	**qaychi**
screw	**pêch**
screwdriver	**pêchkash**
sewing machine	**mâshin-e khayâti**
spade	**bayl**
spanner/wrench	**rench**
string	**târ**
telescope	**teleskôp**
varnish	**wârnis**
wire	**sim**

26. THE CAR

> **Driving** — Unless you already know the country well, it is inadvisable to bring your own vehicle to Afghanistan. If you do, you will need an international driving license, car registration papers and insurance. It is unlikely you will find spare parts for any vehicle. Driving conditions used to be passable in many areas, although the conflicts have taken their predictable toll on the road system. Street lighting is sporadic, and traffic lights, if they exist, rarely work. Certain areas have parking restrictions, although it is not always obvious where they are nor what the restrictions are.

Where can I rent a car?	**Kojâ mêtawânom yak môtar kerâya konom?**
Where can I rent a car with a driver?	**Kojâ mêtawânom yak môtar wa môtarwân kerâya konom?**
How much is it per day?	**Ruzi cheqadar ast?**
How much is it per week?	**Hafta'i cheqadar ast?**
Can I park here?	**Mêtawânom injâ pârk konom?**
Are we on the right road for ... ?	**Âyâ mâ ba tarafi ... ba râhi dorost mêrawêm?**
Where is the nearest filling station?	**Nazdiktarin têlitânk kojâ-st?**
Fill the tank please.	**Lotfan tânki râ por konêd.**
Check the oil/tires/ battery, please.	**Lotfan, têl/tâyr/ bêtri râ bobenêd.**

—In case of difficulty

I have lost my car keys.	**Man kelid-e môtar râ gom kardom.**
The car has broken down.	**Môtar-e man kharâb shoda.**

There's something wrong with this car.	**In môtar kodâm moshkel dârad.**
I have a puncture/flat tire.	**Yak tâyr-e môtar am panchar ast.**
I have run out of petrol/ gas.	**Têli môtar am khalâs shodast.**
Our car is stuck.	**Môtar-e mâ gir karda.**
We need a mechanic.	**Mâ ba mestari zarorat dârêm.**
Can you tow us?	**Môtar-e mâ râ kash karda mêtawânêd?**
Where is the nearest garage?	**Nazdiktarin warak-shop kojâ-st?**
Can you jumpstart the car?	**Komak mêkonêd môtar râ roshan konêm?**
There's been an accident.	**Takar shoda.**
My car has been stolen.	**Môtar am dozdi shoda.**
Call the police!	**Polis râ khabar konêd!**

driver's license	**lâysens**
insurance policy	**qarârdâd-e bêma**
car papers	**asnâd-e môtar**
car registration	**sabt-e môtar**

—Vehicle words

accelerator	**akselarêtar**
air	**hawâ**
axle	**aksal**
battery	**bêtri**
bonnet/hood	**bânat**
boot/trunk	**bâdi**
brake	**brêk**
bumper	**bâmper**

car park	**pârking**
chains: snow chains	**chên**
clutch	**kalach**
driver	**derêwar**
engine	**enjin; mâshen**
exhaust	**ekzâst; salânsar**
fan belt	**panj-bolt**
gear	**gêr**
indicator light	**eshâra-ye alâmat**
inner tube	**tyub**
jack	**jak**
mechanic	**mestari**
neutral drive	**nôtal**
oil	**têl**
oilcan	**quti-ye têl**
passenger	**mosâfer**
petrol	**petrol**
pump	**pâmp**
radiator	**râdiyâtor**
reverse	**rêwars**
seat	**sit**
spare tyre/tire	**tâyr-e eshtapni**
speed	**sor'at**
steering wheel	**eshtireng; farmân**
tank	**tânki**
tool box	**tôl-baks**
tow rope	**kêbal-e kash**
	kardan môtar
trailer	**têlar**
tyre/tire	**tâyr**
windscreen wipers	**barf-pâk**
windscreen/windshield	**kelken**

27. SPORTS

Displays of physical strength are greatly prized in Afghan society. Wrestling and horse-racing are particularly favorite traditional sports, and great tournaments are held, together with great tests of strength — similar to the spirit of the Highland Games in Scotland. If you're lucky, you may even witness a game of **buzkashi**, a game played on horseback in rural areas. More recent sports adopted include judo and other martial arts, basketball and, of course, soccer.

athletics	**warzesh**
ball	**tup**
basketball	**bâsketbâl**
chess	**shatranj**
cricket	**kriket**
final	**fâynal**
goal	**gol**
horse racing	**asb dawâni**
horseback riding	**asb swâri**
match	**mosâbeqa**
soccer match	**mosâbeqa-ye futbâl**
pitch	**partâb kardan**
referee	**hakam; refri**
rugby	**râgbi**
score	**emteyâz; natija; nomra**
soccer/football	**futbâl**
stadium	**estâdyum**
swimming	**awbâzi**
team	**tim**
wrestling	**pahlawâni; koshti**

Who won?	**Mosâbeqa râ ki bord?**
What's the score?	**Natâyej-e mosâbeqa chi-st?**
Who scored?	**Ki emteyâz gereft?** *or* **Ki gol zad?**

28. THE BODY

ankle	**bojolak**
arm	**bâzu**
back	**posht**
beard	**rish**
blood	**khun**
body	**badan**
bone	**ostokhân**
bottom	**tâ; zêr**
breasts/bust	**pestân**
chest	**sina**
chin	**châna**
ear	**gush**
elbow	**ârenj**
eye	**chashm**
face	**ruy; ru**
finger	**kelk**
foot	**pâ; pay**
genitals	**âlât-e tanâsoli**
hair	**mo; moy**
hand	**dest**
head	**sar**
heart	**qalb**
jaw	**alâsha**
kidneys	**gorda**
knee	**zânu**
leg	**pâ; pay**
lip	**lab**
liver	**jegar**
lung	**shosh**
mustache	**borut**
mouth	**dahân; dahan**
neck	**gardan**
nose	**bini**

shoulder	**shâna**
stomach	**shekam**
throat	**golu**
thumb	**shast**
toe	**shast-e pâ**
tongue	**zabân**
tooth	**dandân**
teeth	**dandân-hâ**
vein	**rag**
womb	**rahem**
wrist	**band-e dest**

Some common expressions . . .

Here are a few expressions you'll hear in everyday conversation:

âyâ...?	well...?
bas!	enough!; well now!
chop!	sssh!
bofarmâyêd!	please do!
parwâ na dâra!	it doesn't matter!
na khayr!	no!; not at all!
yâne	I mean...; that's to say...
râsti?	really?
cherâ nê?	why not?
kho!	well!
parwâ nadârad!	no problem!

29. POLITICS

aid worker	**kârgar-e emdâdi**
ambassador	**safir**
to arrest	**dastger kardan**
to assassinate	**koshtan**
assembly	**anjoman**
autonomy	**khod mokhtâri**
cabinet	**kâbena**
charity *organization*	**mo'asesa-ye khayriya**
citizen	**tabeyi**
civil rights	**hoquq-e madani**
civil war	**jang-e dâkheli**
communism	**kamonizm**
communist	**kamonist**
concentration camp	**kamp-e ejbâri/zendân**
constitution	**qânun-e asâsi**
convoy	**kârwan**
corruption	**ekhtelâs; fesâd**
coup d'etat	**kudatâ**
crime	**jenâyat**
criminal	**jenâyat kâr**
crisis	**bohrân**
dictator	**diktâtor**
debt	**qarz**
democracy	**demokrâsi**
dictatorship	**hokômat-e diktâtori**
diplomatic ties	**rawâbet-e diplomâtik**
elder (of village etc)	**rish-safêd**
election	**entekhâbât**
embassy	**sefârat**
ethnic cleansing	**pâk sâzi-ye qawmi; koshtar-e nezhadi**
exile	**tab'id**
free	**âzâd**

freedom	**âzâdi**
government	**hokômat**
guerrilla	**partizan; cherik**
hostage	**gerawgân**
humanitarian aid	**komak-e ensâni**
human rights	**hoquq-e bashar**
imam	**emâm**
independence	**esteqlâl**
independent	**mostaqel**
independent state	**keshwar-e mostaqel**
judge	**qâzi**
killer	**qâtel**
law court	**mahkama**
law	**qânun**
lawyer	**wakil**
leader	**rahbar**
left-wing	**chapi; chapgera; shâkha-ye chap**
liberation	**âzâdi**
majority	**aksariyat**
mercenary	**sarbâz-e mozdur**
minister	**wazir**
ministry	**wezârat**
minority	**aqaliyat**
murder	**qatl**
nation	**dawlat**
opposition	**mokhâlefin**
parliament	**pârlemân**
(political) party	**hezb (-e syâsi)**
politics	**syâsat**
peace	**solh**
peace-keeping troops	**qowâ-ye hâfez-e solh**
politician	**syâsat madâr**
premier	**sadr-e a'zam**
president	**ra'is jamhur**
presidential guard	**gârd-e ra'is jamhur**
prime minister	**sadr-e a'zam**

POLITICS

prison	**zendân**
prisoner-of-war	**asir-e jangi**
POW camp	**kamp-e osarâ**
protest	**mokhâlefat kardan**
rape	**tajâwoz**
reactionary	**ertejâyi**
Red Crescent	**Sra Meyâsht**
Red Cross	**Salib-e Sorkh**
refugee	**panâhenda**
revolution	**enqelâb**
right-wing	**shâkhaye râst**
robbery	**dozdi**
seat (in assembly)	**korsi (dar shôrâ)**
secret police	**polis makhfi; khofiya polis**
socialism	**sosyâlizm**
socialist	**sosyâlist**
spy	**jâsus; râpôrchi**
state	**dawlat**
struggle	**mobâreza; kushesh kardan**
theft	**dozdi**
trade union	**etehâdiya-ye tejârati**
treasury	**khazâna**
United Nations	**Sâzmân-e Melal-e Motahed**
veto; to veto	**rad kardan; wêto kardan**
vote	**ra'y**
vote-rigging	**taqalob kâry dar entekhâbât**
voting; to vote	**ra'y dâdan**

Refugees . . .
The word **panâhenda** (plural **panâhendagân**) is used as the general word for refugee. A Displaced Person is **âwâra** (plural **âwâragân**).

30. TIME & DATES

century	**qarn**
decade	**daha**
year	**sâl**
month	**mâ; borj**
fortnight	**do hafta**
week	**hafta**
day	**ruz**
hour	**sâ'at**
minute	**daqiqa**
second	**sâniya**
dawn; sunrise	**sobh dam;**
	tolu'-e âftâb
morning	**sobh**
daytime	**waqt-e ruz**
noon	**zohr**
afternoon	**bâd az zohr; pêshen**
evening	**asr**
sunset	**shâm**
night	**shab**
midnight	**nefs-e shab**
four days before	**châr ruz pêsh**
three days before	**sê ruz pêsh**
the day before yesterday	**pari ruz**
yesterday	**dêruz**
today	**emruz**
tomorrow	**fardâ**
the day after tomorrow	**pas fardâ**
three days from now	**sê ruz ba'd**
four days from now	**châr ruz ba'd**

the year before last	**do sâl pêsh**
last year	**yak sâl pêsh**
this year	**emsâl**
next year	**sâl-e âyenda;**
	sâl-e ba'd
the year after next	**do sâl ba'd**
last week	**haftaye pêsh**
this week	**in hafta**
next week	**hafta-ye âyenda**
this morning	**emruz sobh**
now	**hâlâ**
tonight	**emshab**
yesterday morning	**dêruz sobh**
yesterday afternoon	**dêruz ba'd az zohr**
yesterday night	**dishab**
tomorrow morning	**fardâ sobh**
tomorrow afternoon	**sabâ ba'd az zohr**
tomorrow night	**fardâ shab**
in the morning	**dar sobh**
in the afternoon	**dar ba'd az zohr**
in the evening	**dar asr**
past	**gozashta**
present	**hâl-e hâzer**
future	**âyenda**
What date is it today?	**Târikh emrôz chand ast?**
What time is it?	**Sâ'at chand ast?**
It is ... o'clock.	**... bâja hast.**

—Days of the week

Monday	**Doshambê**
Tuesday	**Sêshambê**
Wednesday	**Chârshambê**

Thursday	**Panjshambê**
Friday	**Jom'a**
Saturday	**Shambê**
Sunday	**Yakshambê**

—Months

January	**Jenwari**
February	**Febriwari**
March	**Mârch**
April	**Epril**
May	**Mey**
June	**Jun**
July	**Julây**
August	**Âgest**
September	**Septâmbar**
October	**Aktobar**
November	**Nowambar**
December	**Disambar**

—Afghan months

The names of the (solar) months used in Afghanistan correspond to the signs of the zodiac (given in brackets). The Afghan year starts on March 21.

Hamal	Aries
Sawr	Taurus
Jawzâ	Gemini
Saratân	Cancer
Asad	Leo
Sonbola	Virgo
Mêzân	Libra
Aqrab	Scorpio
Qaws	Sagittarius
Jadi	Capricorn
Dalwa	Aquarius
Hut	Pisces

—Islamic months

You will also hear dates given according to the Islamic calendar, which comprises 12 lunar months. **Ramazân** ("Ramadan") is the month when Muslims fast, **Zulhajj** is the month when Muslims traditionally go on the hajj — the pilgrimage to Mecca.

Muharram *(the first month)*
Safar
Rabi' ul-Awwal
Rabi' ul-Âkher
Jamâdi ul-Awwal
Jamâdi ul-Âkher
Rajab
Sha'abân
Ramazân
Shawwâl
Zulqida
Zulhajj *(the last month)*

31. NUMBERS

0	**sefer**		
1	**yak**	31	**si-o yak**
2	**do**	32	**si-o do**
3	**sê**	33	**si-o sê**
4	**châr**	34	**si-o châr**
5	**panj**	35	**si-o panj**
6	**shesh/shash**	36	**si-o shesh**
7	**haft**	37	**si-o haft**
8	**hasht**	38	**si-o hasht**
9	**noh**	39	**si-o noh**
10	**dah**	40	**chel**
11	**yâzda**	41	**chel-o yak**
12	**dwâzda**	42	**chel-o do**
13	**sêzda**	43	**chel-o se**
14	**chârda**	44	**chel-o châr**
15	**pânzda**	45	**chel-o panj**
16	**shânzda**	46	**chel-o shesh**
17	**hafda**	47	**chel-o haft**
18	**hajda/hazhda**	48	**chel-o hasht**
19	**nuzda**	49	**chel-o noh**
20	**bist**	50	**penjâ**
21	**bist-o yak**	51	**penjâ-o yak**
22	**bist-o do**	52	**penjâ-o do**
23	**bist-o se**	53	**penjâ-o se**
24	**bist-o châr**	54	**penjâ-o châr**
25	**bist-o panj**	55	**penjâ-o panj**
26	**bist-o shesh**	56	**penjâ-o shesh**
27	**bist-o haft**	57	**penjâ-o haft**
28	**bist-o hasht**	58	**penjâ-o hasht**
29	**bist-o noh**	59	**penjâ-o noh**
30	**si**	60	**shast**

61	**shasht-o yak**	91	**bist-o yak**
62	**shasht-o do**	92	**bist-o do**
63	**shasht-o se**	93	**bist-o se**
64	**shasht-o châr**	94	**bist-o châr**
65	**shasht-o panj**	95	**bist-o panj**
66	**shasht-o shesh**	96	**bist-o shesh**
67	**shasht-o haft**	97	**bist-o haft**
68	**shasht-o hasht**	98	**bist-o hasht**
69	**shasht-o noh**	99	**bist-o noh**
70	**haftâd**	100	**sad**
71	**haftâd-o yak**	102	**sad-o do**
72	**haftâd-o do**	112	**sad-o dawâz**
73	**haftâd-o se**		**dah**
74	**haftâd-o châr**		
75	**haftâd-o panj**		
76	**haftâd-o shesh**	200	**do sad**
77	**haftâd-o haft**	300	**se sad**
78	**haftâd-o hasht**	400	**châr sad**
79	**haftâd-o noh**	500	**panj sad**
80	**hashtâd**	600	**shesh sad**
		700	**haft sad**
81	**hashtâd-o yak**	800	**hasht sad**
82	**hashtâd-o do**	900	**noh sad**
83	**hashtâd-o se**	1,000	**hazâr**
84	**hashtâd-o châr**		
85	**hashtâd-o panj**		
86	**hashtâd-o shesh**		
87	**hashtâd-o haft**	10,000	**dah hazâr**
88	**hashtâd-o hasht**	50,000	**penjâ hazâr**
89	**hashtâd-o noh**	100,000	**sad hazâr**
90	**nawad**	1,000,000	**yak milyun**

first	**awal**
second	**dôwom**
third	**sêwom**
fourth	**chârom**
fifth	**panjom**
sixth	**sheshom**
seventh	**haftom**
eighth	**hashtom**
ninth	**nôwom; nôhom**
tenth	**dahom**
twentieth	**bistom**
once	**yak bâr**
twice	**do bâr**
three times	**sê bâr**
one-half	**yak o nim**
one-third	**yak sêwom**
one-quarter	**yak chârom**
three-quarters	**sê chârom**

32. OPPOSITES

beginning—end	**ebtedâ—pâyân**
clean—dirty	**pâk—cherk**
fertile—barren land	**hâsel khêz—khoshk**
happy—unhappy	**khosh—nârâzi/khafa**
life—death	**zendagi—marg**
friend—enemy	**dôst—doshman**
modern—traditional	**asri— an'anawi**
modern—ancient	**jadid—qadimi**
open—shut	**bâz—basta**
wide—narrow	**pahn—tang**
high—low	**boland—pâyin/ kotâch**
peace—violence/war	**solh—khoshunat/ jang**
polite—rude	**mo'adab—khashan**
silence—noise	**khâmôshi— ghâlmaghâl**
cheap—expensive	**arzân—qêmat**
hot/warm— cold/cool	**dâgh/garm— sard**
health—disease	**jôri—marizi**
well—sick	**sâlem—mariz**
night—day	**shab—rôz**
top—bottom	**bâlâ—tâ**
backwards—forwards	**pas—pêsh**
back—front	**posht—pêsh**
dead—alive	**morda—zenda**
near—far	**nazdik—dûr**
left—right	**chap—râst**
inside—outside	**darûn—birûn**
up—down	**bâlâ—pâyin**
yes—no	**balê—nê**
here—there	**injâ—ânjâ/onja**

soft—hard	**narm—sakht**
easy—difficult	**âsân—dashwâr/ sakht**
quick—slow	**têz—âhesta**
big—small	**bozorg—khord**
old—young	**pir—jawân**
tall—short *people*	**boland—kutâ(h)**
tall—short *things*	**boland—pâyin**
strong—weak	**tawâna—sost**
success—failure	**pêruzi—nâkâmi**
new—old	**naw—kôhna**
question—answer	**sawâl—jawâb**
safety—danger	**amneyat—khatar**
good—bad	**khub—bad**
true—false	**dorost—nâ-drost**
light—heavy	**sobok—gerang**
light—darkness	**nur—târiki**
well—badly	**khub—kharâb**
truth—lie	**haqiqat—dorugh**

Other Titles of Regional Interest from Hippocrene Books

AFGHAN FOOD & COOKERY
292 pages • 5½ x 8½ • ISBN 0-7818-0807-3 • $12.95pb • (510)

AZERBAIJANI-ENGLISH/ ENGLISH-AZERBAIJANI CONCISE DICTIONARY
8,000 entries • 144 pages • 5½ x 7 • ISBN 0-7818-0244-X • W • $14.95pb • (96)

AZERBAIJANI-ENGLISH/ ENGLISH-AZERBAIJANI DICTIONARY & PHRASEBOOK
4,000 entries • 176 pages • 3¾ x 7 • ISBN 0-7818-0684-4 • W • $11.95pb • (753)

BEGINNER'S DARI (PERSIAN)
250 pages • 5½ x 8½ • ISBN 0-7818-1012-4 • $16.95pb • (233)

FARSI-ENGLISH/ENGLISH-FARSI CONCISE DICTIONARY
8,000 entries • 250 pages • 4 x 6 • ISBN 0-7818-0860-X • $14.95pb • (260)

KURDISH-ENGLISH/ ENGLISH-KURDISH DICTIONARY
8,000 entries • 313 pages • 4½ x 7 • ISBN 0-7818-0246-6 • W • $12.95pb • (218)

PASHTO-ENGLISH/ENGLISH-PASH-TO DICTIONARY & PHRASEBOOK

3,000 entries • 235 pages • 3¾ x 7 • ISBN 0-7818-0972-X • W Ÿ $11.95pb • (429)

INTRODUCTION TO PUSHTO

343 pages • 5½ x 8½ • ISBN 0-7818-0939-8 • $14.95pb • (369)

THE ART OF PERSIAN COOKING

292 pages • 5½ x 8½ • ISBN 0-7818-0807-3 • $12.95pb • (510)

ENGLISH-PERSIAN STANDARD DICTIONARY

40,000 entries • 700 pages • 5½ x 8½ • ISBN 0-7818-0056-0 • $24.95pb • (365)

PERSIAN-ENGLISH STANDARD DICTIONARY

22,500 entries • 700 pages • 5½ x 8½ • ISBN 0-7818-0055-2 • $24.95pb • (350)

BEGINNER'S PERSIAN

288 pages • 5½ x 8½ • ISBN 0-7818-0567-8 • $14.95pb • (696)

TAJIK-ENGLISH/ENGLISH-TAJIK DICTIONARY & PHRASEBOOK

1,400 entries • 148 pages • 3¾ x 7 • ISBN 0-7818-0662-3 • W • $11.95pb • (752)

TAJIK-ENGLISH/ENGLISH-TAJIK CONCISE DICTIONARY
8,000 entries • 360 pages • 4 x 6 • ISBN 0-7818-1118-X • $11.95pb • (246)

URDU-ENGLISH/ENGLISH-URDU DICTIONARY & PHRASEBOOK
3,000 entries • 175 pages • 3¾ x 7 • ISBN 0-7818-0970-3 • W • $11.95pb • (427)

THE ART OF UZBEK COOKING
200 pages • 5½ x 8½ • ISBN 0-7818-0669-0 • $12.95pb • (767)

UZBEK-ENGLISH/ENGLISH-UZBEK DICTIONARY & PHRASEBOOK
3,000 entries • 225 pages • 3¾ x 7 • ISBN 0-7818-0959-2 • W • $11.95 • (166)

UZBEK-ENGLISH/ENGLISH-UZBEK CONCISE DICTIONARY
7,500 entries • 400 pages • 4 x 6 • ISBN 0-7818-0165-6 • W • $11.95 • (4)

All prices are subject to change without prior notice. To check on current prices, call **(718) 454-2366** f*or a free copy of our current catalog. One can also order books through this number, as well as through your local bookstore, our website* **www.hippocrenebooks.com**, *or write to:* **Hippocrene Books, 171 Madison Avenue, New York, NY 10016**. *Please enclose check or money order adding $5.00 shipping (UPS) for the first book and $.50 for each additional title.*

etmeenan = to trust

Kerdan

notmahen = trustful

trustworthy

zad / dun = fu

ba o shun = some of them

rashang = prety

dest dere

bernomeh = like?

haman = same stay

Otanxase = bedroms

ehre momhene =

impossible

moostael = indep.

xosh migganeh = to

hu fun